The 1960s

The 1970s

List of Illustrations

Introduction

Alistair Cooke was the classic Anglo-American. He embodied the cultural and political bond that linked Britain and the United States during the long half century from the Second World War into the twenty-first century. In the great game of current affairs, he was an observer, not a player. But like the best observers, he helped define the game.

My parents were ardent Americanophiles. As a result they would sit each week listening to *Letter from America*, like wartime refugees glued to a message from a land afar. Cooke kept them in touch with Strong America in the 1950s, Rich America in the 1960s, Questioning America in the 1970s and Uncertain America in the 1980s and 1990s. He never preached. He was accused of ignoring the dark side of American life, but his bias throughout was that of an East Coast liberal conservative. It was the bias of most of his British listeners.

Alistair Cooke's writing was extraordinary. He wrote in conversation and he spoke in prose. In fifty-eight years of *Letter from America* he perfected the journalism of personal witness, adapting it brilliantly to the medium of radio. His mellifluous mid-Atlantic voice treated Britain and America as if they were two armchairs talking to each other, with 'the Pond' as coffee table. Above all, he knew his craft. He never wrote a dull sentence. He never lost touch with narrative, with the commentator as storyteller, learned from his love of theatre and movies. He understood that listeners wanted more than the old standbys of anecdote and opinion. They craved context and history. As his years lengthened into decades, Cooke's journalism acquired a depth inaccessible to younger practitioners.

Here was a man who could recall Hoover and Roosevelt. He could compare Churchill and Truman as orators, for he had heard them both. He could remember the arrival of air conditioning, the building of freeways, the exploding of the atom bomb and Bobby Jones making the green in one. His letters from America brought the New World into the drawing rooms of the Old, not as a series of sensational events but as a rounded culture. His journalism published and broadcast in the United States returned the compliment. It brought British culture to American attention. In periods when the two countries seemed at risk of tearing apart from each other, he linked hands and held them tight.

Cooke's work and outlook were rooted in his past. He was born with the name of Alfred in 1908 in Salford, Lancashire. His father was a metalworker, Methodist lay preacher and teetotaller. His early theatrical and writing talent was noticed by his teachers, who encouraged him to a Cambridge scholarship. The upwardly mobile Cooke changed his Christian name to Alistair and applied himself furiously to acting, producing and writing. He founded The Mummers and edited *Granta*. By the age of twenty-two he was suggesting himself to the *Manchester Guardian* and the BBC as a contributor on theatre, poetry and literature.

In 1932 he struck gold. He won a Harkness Fellowship to Yale and Harvard. The curtain opened on what seemed an even more glittering stage. For the drama of theatre he exchanged the drama of America.

Cooke's early ambition was to become a leading theatre director. This ambition was cursed by his success in transatlantic journalism and the people he met thereby. He was taken up by another British refugee, Charlie Chaplin, and wrote scripts for him. Cooke married an American model, Ruth Emerson (a relative of Ralph Waldo), and moved back and forth between London and America in search of work, becoming the film critic for the BBC in 1934. He wrote a *Letter from London* for NBC, allegedly clocking up 40,000 words for American outlets at the time of the Abdication in 1936. Back in America, he suggested a similar venture in reverse, for the BBC. With the outbreak of war he risked his reputation on both sides of the Atlantic by taking out American citizenship, granted in 1941.

Cooke's career in America was initially that of a normal foreign correspondent. In the 1940s he worked variously for *The Times*, the *Daily Sketch* and the *Daily Herald*. In 1940 he also began regular broadcasts for the BBC, titled *American Letter* (they became *Letter from America* in 1950). Early records show the producers remarking on 'a tendency to be allusive and glib'. Yet throughout the war Cooke built up an audience approaching six million. In 1945 he was asked to cover the opening of the United Nations for the *Manchester Guardian*. Three years later he became that paper's chief American correspondent at the then huge salary of $14,000 a year, a happy homecoming for a son of Salford. He retained this post for a quarter-century.

Working for the *Guardian* in the 1950s and 1960s allowed Cooke to cover the emergence of the new global superpower. He was never a normal news hound. Most correspondents in America were, and still are, 'Beltway fanatics'. They paced the corridors and smoke-filled rooms of Congress and the White House, and saw little else. Washington at the time was still a town with a single industry, that of politics. This was not the sort of town likely to appeal to a man with Cooke's wider interests.

He duly covered America from New York, a fact crucial to the content and style of *Letter from America*. This was controversial. The *Manchester Guardian*'s Washington correspondents at the time were Max Freedman and Richard Scott. The fact that the paper's 'Chief Correspondent' was resident in New York was the source of much bickering. It gave Cooke a reputation among journalists as problematic, indeed 'a nuisance'. He was rarely at the scene of events. His witnessing of the murdered Bobby Kennedy—'like the stone face of a child lying on a cathedral tomb'—was exceptional. He called it 'a casual chance in a thousand'.

Washington reporting, like British 'lobby journalism', was that of politics and the gossip of the political street. Such coverage is necessary, but never sufficient in depicting a country. Cooke's view of America was different. His America was rich in politics, but politics seen as ordinary Americans saw it, including from television. It was from television that he wrote his celebrated Letters after the death of JFK. To Cooke, the most important event of the week rarely happened in Washington. He travelled to every state, missing only Alaska. America was 'happening' in Little Rock or Dallas or Los Angeles or Chicago. It was Ali versus Frazier, or the death of Dorothy Parker. It was a movie or a ball game or the changing leaves of a New England fall.

*   *   *

His presence in New York was also crucial for Cooke's work beyond journalism. Most Americans knew him as a writer and television presenter. He hosted a weekly arts programme, *Omnibus*, for CBS. In 1972 he produced *Alistair Cooke's America*, a television series screened in thirty countries. Recordings are in every public library in America, and the resulting book sold two million copies. He had stopped working for the *Guardian* to produce the series. This in turn led to *Masterpiece Theatre* for the PBS network. In this role millions of Americans came to associate Cooke with the canon of English literature, mostly through the medium of BBC costume dramas. This tweedy, amiable intellectual seemed the perfect custodian of the temple of English drama, from Shakespeare to *Upstairs, Downstairs*. He was to receive four Emmys for his work.

Cooke's lifestyle was that of an East Coast aesthete. His hobbies were American and fanatical: jazz, movies and golf. His first marriage failed, leaving a son, and in 1946 he married an artist, Jane White Hawkes. She came with two children by a former husband and together they had a daughter. The couple moved between a comfortable (rent-controlled) apartment on Fifth Avenue overlooking Central Park and Jane's weekend house on Long Island. The Cookes would 'season' in San Francisco and visit Britain twice a year to see their British family—such visits usually coinciding with Wimbledon and the major golf tournaments.

Letter from America formed a most remarkable sequence of sustained commentary. Its original remit from the BBC was to record 'the passions, manners and flavour of another nation's way of life'. The mission was hardly innovative—witness Cooke's own heroes Mark Twain and H. L. Mencken—but Cooke put it on radio. The result was not a 'column'. Nor does it merit the pompous style of essay. Though the Letters make much use of the first person singular, they have none of the cloying self-regard of modern 'I-journalism'. Cooke is the observer of events, not a participant. I would apply to the Letters the honourable journalistic term of stories. They tell a tale, sometimes two or three. They are one man's take on the world 'as I saw it'.

Cooke accepted the retort that this made him seem ambivalent, a fence-sitter, 'a moral coward for refusing to take a stand'. He was criticized as pussy-footing on Vietnam, and his biographer, Nick Clarke, records the *Guardian*'s view that 'he had a blind spot about the civil rights movement'. As the years rolled by he moved progressively to the right. His early adoration of Adlai Stevenson was later settled on Ronald Reagan. At the end of his life he accepted the Pentagon line on Iraq. But to every critic he cheerfully replied that 'once every four years . . . I vote'. Beyond that was only 'the discovery that in life the range of irreconcilable points of view, characters, flaws, idiosyncrasies and virtues is astounding'.

The style of the Letters was influential and much imitated in both print and broadcasting. It has come near to parody in its BBC offspring, *From Our Own Correspondent*, anecdotal, herbivorous and mildly self-indulgent. Cooke's version was in a class of its own. Though written and rehearsed for speaking, the Letters remain 'writings', owing a debt to Cooke's tutor, Arthur Quiller-Couch, a champion of simplicity and clarity. They have the laconic touch of Cooke's hero, the Baltimore columnist H. L. Mencken, and display Mencken's hatred of cant and love of plain-speaking. But the mastery of cadence and colour which made *Letter from America* so fluent on the ear was, in my view, born of Cooke's love of theatre. There is no better training for any writer than to listen to the cry of the actor and feel the lash of the newsroom. Cooke benefited from both.

The shared Anglo-American culture is rooted not in politics but in history. *Letter from America* was never a 'home thought from abroad'. It showed no Browning nostalgia for 'the chaffinch on the orchard bough' from a land of the 'gaudy melon-flower'. Nor was Cooke a post-imperial Kipling. His Fifth Avenue apartment bore little comparison with 'an old Moulmein Pagoda looking lazy at the sea'. The surprise of Cooke's America was its familiarity. It was written for and heard by those who knew America from the cinema, music and newsreels.

Britons still look to America before they look anywhere else. They visit America, they absorb American culture, they enjoy American exports, they marry American spouses. More Britons could name the Mayor of New York City or the Governor of California than the leader of any English provincial city. The metropolises of New York and London are Siamese twins, two districts of one city, two venues of one culture. They have more in common with each other than with their respective hinterlands. Hardly an American magazine or newspaper is without a British byline. Hardly a British radio programme is without an American voice. Business, academia, music, art and architecture operate by mid-Atlantic values from mid-Atlantic institutions.

At the end of the Cold War it was asserted that Britain would now 'choose' Europe. Within a decade, in the so-called war on terror and in Iraq, it was emphatically choosing America. The burst of anti-Americanism which accompanied the war was an aberration, not a norm. Indeed, much of the protest over the Iraq war was itself Anglo-American in origin. At the time of Cooke's death the Atlantic bond seemed as tight as ever and the gulf with the rest of the world as wide.

Former Secretary of State Henry Kissinger, with his long experience of office, called the bonds between America and Britain 'matter-of-factly intimate', to a degree 'probably never practised before between sovereign states'. He was echoing de Gaulle's view that Britain 'neither thinks nor acts like a continental nation'. The most recent custodian of the special relationship, Tony Blair, would tell his staff that not to be by America's side through any crisis or travail was 'simply unthinkable'.

Cooke's lifework was to be Boswell to that relationship. *Letter from America* was his diary and his testament. There may be no one America, single and true. But Cooke's America is the truest we have.

Simon Jenkins
July 2004

Editor's Note

The last collection of Alistair Cooke's *Letter from America* was published in 1979 (*The Americans*) and, along with two earlier collections (*Letters from America*, 1951, *Talk About America*, 1968), has been long out of print. Alistair had always intended to complete a fourth collection of letters taken from the 1980s and 1990s—a collection that he liked to refer to as 'The Last Post'—but as time moved on his energies became exclusively dedicated to the writing of his weekly broadcast letter. He maintained this focus of attention right up until the last letter, number 2869, broadcast on 20 February 2004, just six weeks before he died. When he appointed me as his literary executor he also assigned me the task of preparing this volume selected from the entire period of his broadcast letters, 1946–2004. As his book editor and last British publisher of his two collections of essays (*Fun and Games*, 1994, and *Memories of the Great and the Good*, 1999), Alistair knew that I understood his requirements and fortunately he left clear guidelines for this collection.

In his first published volume Alistair wrote in the Preface: 'A good many of the letters I have had from listeners to the series were from people who can hardly put pen to paper. Their taste seemed to coincide with my own: they got pleasure from talks which I felt had managed to convey some human experience in a language most people can understand. These successes average about one in five, but they are not necessarily the ones that look best in print. But by the time the series had run to two hundred there appeared to be a good handful that would survive the translation into black and white. Accordingly, the pieces that follow were selected by this test. They were chosen on no other principle.' With this in mind, for the years 1946–1980, there was no need to go further than to select those letters that I consider to be the best taken from the earlier books. In this process I was much helped by the writer and editor George Perry, who proved, as always, a sound adviser.

The selections made from 1980 to 2004 required more detailed review. Several folders of manuscript letters marked on the outside in Alistair's handwriting as 'The Chosen' were found and then typed up 'squeaky clean', as he had requested, by Patti Yasek, his redoubtable assistant. I have been supported in making the final selection not only by Patti but also by Alistair's daughter Susan Cooke Kittredge. They have both provided huge encouragement and I was relieved that this final selection agreed with so many of Susan's own choices. In addition Stuart Proffitt, Publishing Director at Penguin, has contributed many recommendations and has provided valuable advice in relation to the overall selection. With such wealth of material it has been difficult to achieve a perfect balance for each decade and I have decided to give more emphasis to the second part of Alistair's career where none of the letters has, until now, been published in volume form.

As on his earlier collections I have tried my best

to apply Alistair's principle, in choosing those letters that work best in print. I have also provided a wide range of contents, and indeed tried to include some surprises that might correspond on the page to the experience of tuning in on a Friday evening or Sunday morning to hear the often unexpected topic that Alistair was addressing that day. As with the earlier collections the letters 'except for a little trimming and polishing, appear here as they were broadcast'.

There is no better preface that can apply to this collection than Alistair's original opening to the first collection published in 1951 which included the following passage:

Some months after the war was over the BBC asked me to go to London and discuss the sort of broadcasting I might do in what was then called the peace. I had been talking about America to Britain since 1934 and from America to Britain since three years after that. My one-man band met the same fate as everybody else's in the autumn of 1939. And through the war years I doubled in brass and learned to play the solemn trombone of a political commentator. Politics will undoubtedly bedevil us all till the day we die, but when General MacArthur stood on the deck of the *Missouri* and said in his resounding baritone, 'These proceedings are closed,' I took him at his word and, like most other people, yearned to get back to the important things in life. Even the prospect of early annihilation should not keep us from making the most of our days on this unhappy planet. In the best of times, our days are numbered, anyway. And it would be a crime against Nature for any generation to take the world crisis so solemnly that it put off enjoying those things for which we were presumably designed in the first place, and which the gravest statesmen and the hoarsest politicians hope to make available to all men in the end: I mean the opportunity to do good work, to fall in love, to enjoy friends, to sit under trees, to read, to hit a ball and bounce the baby.

The suspicion that these things are what most men and women everywhere want led me to suggest, in London in 1946, that Britons might be more honestly enticed into an interest in America and Americans by hearing about their way of life and their tastes in these fundamental things than by suffering instruction in the procedures of the American Senate and the subtleties of the corn-hog ratio. Mr Lindsay Wellington, then director of the Home Service, responded so promptly to this that he suggested I forget politics altogether and accept an assignment to talk about anything and everything in America that interested me. To do this for a large and very mixed audience, ranging from shrewd bishops to honest carpenters, was a challenge to explain in the simplest and most vivid terms the passions, the manners, the flavour of another nation's way of life. It was a formidable assignment, for though a man might make sense of his travels in his own way for his own friends, broadcasting demands of him, if he respects the medium at all, that, as the old Greek had it, he 'think like a wise man and talk in the language of the people'. I don't know whether this has ever been done, except at various times by minstrels, the greatest religious teachers and comedians of genius.

But out of this bold ambition grew a series of weekly talks to Britain which I called Letter from America. They were commissioned in March 1946 for a tentative run of thirteen weeks; and by the grace of the BBC, the receptiveness of the British listener, and the stubborn endurance of the pound sterling, they still at this writing go on. After a year or two the number of listeners asking for copies of scripts began to strain the mimeographing resources of the BBC's New York office. Some people took so kindly to them that they urged me to put them out as a book. This has the same effect on a broadcaster as a nomination for the Presidency of the United States on a first-class cement manufacturer. The thing is patently absurd except to his cronies, but the idea first flatters, then haunts him, and he ends by feeling he must accept a sacred duty to save the Republic.

Most of these pieces were written at the end of a week's work without my knowing, as I faced the typewriter, what I was going to talk about. But they were all written in freedom and in pleasure.

Alistair Cooke's *Letter from America* was an astonishing and unique achievement that reached a listening audience of some twenty-two million worldwide. It would have been his hope that these letters will be read, as he wrote them, 'in freedom and in pleasure' throughout the world.

Colin Webb
July 2004

The 1940s

The Immigrant Strain

6 May 1946

An item came over the news-tape the other day about somebody who wanted to organize a National Hobby Club. There is nothing earthshaking in this, but it opens up a field of speculation about Britons and Americans that I should like to graze around in. I saw this item and thought at once about an Englishman I know here, an old, old friend who—to be cold-blooded about it—has a value in this country over and above his value as a character and a good friend. I am, after all, a professional student of a rare species of goldfish—the goldfish being, you will guess, the American people. If you are a goldfish, or if you swim with them long enough, it is impossible to say what are the characteristics of goldfish. But if somebody drops a mackerel into the goldfish bowl, you can see at once all sorts of things that goldfish have and the other things they lack. That is why I am grateful to this English friend, just for being himself and for being around. He forms a stimulating point of comparison. He is a British government official in New York, and though I knew him for many years before he was sent here, I have lately learned many things about him I never knew and about Americans—the race he is at present moving among. For instance, when he comes into a room, one thought always strikes me, and I can say it two ways. I can say, 'Goodness, how short his coat is' or 'Goodness, how long everybody

3

else's is'.

Now, in character—never mind his politics—he is conservative. He is an able and conscientious government official. He likes people and he likes to get through the day and attack in the evening his beloved hobbies, of which he has several. This characteristic alone would make him, in England, a typical civil servant. Here it makes him an oddity. He is a lepidopterist, an expert on moths. And when he was stationed in the Middle East he threw off what I believe to be an authoritative paper on the moths of Iran. Americans meeting him see his black Homburg and his tight coat and his rumply collar, and hear his voice; and they know his type at once. They think they do. But they don't know it at all. If you feel baffled and alarmed at the prospect of differentiating one American type from another, you can take heart. You have more hope of success than Americans, who shuffle through every stereotype of every foreign culture as confidently as they handle the family's pack of cards. Americans are not particularly good at sensing the real elements of another people's culture. It helps them to approach foreigners with carefree warmth and an animated lack of misgiving. It also makes them, on the whole, poor administrators on foreign soil. They find it almost impossible to believe that poorer peoples, far from the Statue of Liberty, should not want in their heart of hearts to become Americans. If it should happen that America, in its new period of world power, comes to do what every other world power has done: if Americans should have to govern large numbers of foreigners, you must expect that Americans will be well hated before they are admired for themselves.

4

So Americans when they meet this Englishman for the first time at once file away the reflection that though he seems amiable enough, he is rigid, unimaginative, a little pompous, a regular Somerset Maugham colonial type. Then the telephone rings—as it did one night—and it turns out that someone wants to know who sang the vocal in that early Red Nichols record of 'Lazy River'. The Americans present were appalled and relieved to hear my friend give out reams of information on these matters. 'No,' he said to another query, 'I think you'll find that record is a blue label, and it's backed by "Beale Street Blues", with Goodman and Teagarden . . . What? no, no, the cornet is Jack's brother, Charlie—that's right, Charlie Teagarden. Not at all, so long.'

He is also, you gather, a jazz fan. And according to the late great Otis Ferguson he knew more about the history of recorded American jazz than most Americans alive, and wrote knowingly about it when he was in college, years before American intellectuals began to write jazz reviews in the mid-1930s. I doubt if the Foreign Office know about this. I doubt if they care, because he is an Englishman, and eccentricity is therefore the most normal thing about him. By merely being around he makes you notice how comparatively rare with Americans is an orderly set of hobbies; and how even rarer is the quality from which hobbies spring—namely, eccentricity. Active Americans do many things. And in different parts of the country they do routinely things that other parts of the country have never heard about. But by and large they do what other people, what their neighbours, do. There is a good reason for this, and you will be

5

glad to hear we don't have to go back to the Indians for it.

Hobbies, I suggest, are essentially a tribal habit and appear most in a homogeneous nation. English boys in school sit beside other boys who are called Adams and Smith and Rendall and Barnes and Gibbs. They do not have to use up much of their competitive energy showing who is more English than another. A nation which says, 'It isn't done', is much more settled as a community than one which says, 'It's un-American'. Only thirty years ago Theodore Roosevelt made a campaign of urging immigrant Americans to forget their roots, to cease being 'hyphenated Americans'. But there are still in America two generations, the sons and grandsons of immigrants, who are trying to outlive the oddity of their family's ways. For it is a stigma for an American to talk with a foreign accent rather than with an American accent. This is snobbery, of course, but the people who instantly recognize it as such are enviably free from the problem. If it is snobbery, even in this land, it is a real humiliation: it is not the urge of insecure people to be different from others; it is the more pressing urge to be the same, and it is acutely felt among people who are insecure just because they *are* different. In very many American cities where there are large populations of immigrants, this is what happens. The son is, let us say, an Italian. As a boy he is brought up with a mixture of American and Italian habits. He plays baseball, but the big meal of the week is ravioli, and he is allowed little gulps of red wine. (If he is a Pole, he is dolled up once a year and marched in the parade on Pulaski Day.) Then he goes to school. There he mixes with boys called

6

Taylor and Smith and also with other boys called Schenck and Costello and O'Dwyer and Koshuski. He begins to find in time that ravioli is a mild joke at school.

Of course, there are millions of Americans who eat ravioli who are not Italian-Americans, but they are untouched by the kind of problem I am discussing. Ravioli is an American dish by now. And that is another thing. The boy notices that just so much as his own habits and speech were instilled by his parents, by so much does he tend not to fit in. By so much he runs the risk of being a joke; which is no joke to a child. And then, at about the age of 12, an awful thing happens. It is happening all over America all the time, and produces recrimination and heartbreak to the folks still left who came originally from the old country—from Poland or Italy or Czechoslovakia or Russia or Germany or wherever—and who will never master the American language. The boy notices that they speak with an accent. He never knew this before. But now it crowds in on him. Now he starts his own rebellion. And that is serious enough to many fine parents so that in scores, perhaps hundreds, of American cities the schools run night classes for parents, in the English language, to help them keep the affection and respect of their sons and daughters, or grandsons and granddaughters. It is a great theme in American life, and it cannot be dismissed by superficial horror or irritated appeals to decent feeling. In time, of course, masses of such sons and daughters outlive the threat of seeming different. And then, but only then, can they begin to cherish some of their oddity, especially in the way of food and festivals. Their strangeness

7

becomes a grace note to the solid tune of their Americanism. But by that time they are sure of themselves and so able to look on their parents again—God help them—with affection.

So you see how sure of your standing with your companions you have to be to start, in boyhood, cooking up interests that will set you apart from your fellows. It will be no surprise now, I think, to hear from my Englishman that nearly all the members of his natural history club in New York were older men with Anglo-Saxon names—families that have been here for a hundred years or more, that have never felt anything but American. They start with the great advantage of being already something that the Poles and the Germans and the Czechs and the Italians have to get to be the hard way.

You may wonder how an Englishman, and an English accent, fit into all this. Well, Englishmen who live here, no matter how long—first-generation Englishmen—are a special case. They may hope to be mistaken for Bostonians (but not by Bostonians). Yet if they affect any more Americanism than that which has grown into their characters, they do themselves much hurt, and both the country they came from and the country they adopted. There are Irish-Americans and Czech-Americans and Polish-Americans and German-Americans and Swedish-Americans and Italian-Americans and Greek-Americans. But there are only 'Englishmen in America'. They are always apart and always at once more foreign and more familiar.

And an English accent is by now just another foreign sound. There was a time when an English

8

accent would take an Englishman into homes on the East Coast socially more elevated than the home he left behind him. Such Englishmen were secretly delighted to discover this while believing they were only being taken at their true worth. But the hosts knew better. This social observation was a favourite theme of American writers, New Englanders especially, in the early nineteenth century. Washington Irving once boiled over about a certain kind of British traveller: 'While Englishmen of philosophical spirit and cultivated minds have been sent from England to penetrate the deserts and to study the manners and customs of barbarous nations, it has been left to the broken-down tradesman, the scheming adventurer, the wandering mechanic, the Manchester and Birmingham agent, to be her oracles respecting America.' You can still run into the type. Or you could say more accurately that this attitude is one part of most Englishmen's character that is aroused by a visit to America. But the day is long past when Americans imitated English habits in order to be fashionable. There is, however, one peculiar hangover from that period. It is the convention of speaking English on the American stage. Unlike the British and the Germans, the Americans seem never to have worked out a type of stage speech true to the reality of the life around them. Except in comedies. In most historical American plays, and plays of polite life, the characters talk a form of British English. If you chide Americans about this and say, correctly, that these people in real life would not talk at all like that, they say: 'Well, of course not; they're actors, aren't they?' I always feel in London that no matter how trivial the play, the characters being played would talk more or less that way in life. In this country it is understood as a convention, having nothing to do with social honesty, that actors should adopt an unreal mid-Atlantic lingo known, with a straight face, as Stage Standard. You may have noticed that even in American movies most American historical characters and members of Congress talk a form of British, while what are called 'character parts' talk American.

Englishmen can hardly be blamed if they assume that Americans share their sneaking belief that no American can be distinguished and yet sound American at the same time. It has given some otherwise shrewd English dramatic critics the idea that really educated Americans talk like Englishmen. The fact is that educated Southerners, New Yorkers, Chicagoans or New Englanders could never be mistaken for Britons. And there is something wrong if they could be mistaken for each other. It is a fairly safe rule that if in life you meet an American who sounds English, he is either a transplanted Englishman, or one of those homeless Americans forlornly bearing up under the 'advantages' of an education in Europe. Or he is a phoney. The American dramatic critic, Mr George Jean Nathan, was not intending to be facetious, but merely expressing a perennial American puzzle, when he wrote: 'After thirty years of theatregoing, I still can't make up my mind whether actors talk and behave like Englishmen or whether Englishmen talk and behave like actors.'

Damon Runyon's America

27 December 1946

When Damon Runyon died the papers were black with columns of sentimental farewell from all the New York sports-writers who possess an expanding waistline and a yearning to break with the daily grind of football and the horses and begin to write some profitable short stories on the Runyon model. He is already becoming sweetened into a legend, and it sometimes does take the death of a man who summed up an era or a fashion to make you feel how dead and done with that era is. But Runyon has a peculiar transatlantic interest, because the people who read him in London were not the people who read and admired him here. His English reputation, among highbrows especially, was one of those puzzles that are politely accepted as insoluble by the Americans who run into them. It produced the same sort of shock to cross the Channel and hear intense French intellectuals sneering at the talents of Jean Gabin and Louis Jouvet and wishing the serious French *cinéma* could achieve the *vitalisme* of Jimmy Cagney or 'this tenderness, cynical yet profound' of Humphrey Bogart.

Maybe you are both right. But let us for once go beyond politeness and look into the life and style of a man who, by some trick of understanding or misunderstanding, seemed to a whole generation of Britons to be the most typical American writer of his day: tricky, racy, pungent, slick, amoral. I'd

11

better say at once that I never met an American, unless he was a Broadway nightclub owner, or a racing tout, who took that view of Runyon. And the only intriguing thing about him to many literate Americans was his great reputation in Britain.

Like so many other people who later become identified with the spirit of the place they write about, Runyon was not born there. In fact he was 27 before he ever hit New York. He was born, by a funny coincidence, in Manhattan, but Manhattan, Kansas, which in 1884 must have had a population of several hundreds. Runyon's father was an itinerant printer in the Midwest and West. Runyon followed his father, and it took him through a pioneer's trail of Kansas towns, from Manhattan to Clay Center to Wellington, and finally to Pueblo, Colorado, a small town, not much more than a rundown Indian village, just near what is now the Mesa Verde National Park, where you can see the towns built in the sides of cliffs by Indians whose high civilization crumbled about nine centuries ago. It seems to this day a very unlikely place to set the imagination agog with the 'dolls' and 'characters' of Runyon's imagination.

Young Runyon at 14 ran away to enlist in the Spanish–American war. He was in and out of guerrilla warfare for two years in the Philippines, and came back to Colorado full of tall stories, a tobacco breath, and a trick or two with a poker deck that qualified him at once for the profession of newspaperman. By now his interests were settling into the groove that was to pay off very profitably in later life. He started baseball clubs, ran boxing matches on the side, and rode horses on small tracks in southern Colorado. It would be tempting to add that here he obviously picked up the authentic lingo of baseball and stables, and of the petty gangster and shill and the like. Maybe he did, but again like other writers who have been acclaimed outside their own country for their accurate ways with the spoken language, Runyon was not then or ever later a particularly good writer of American idiom as she is spoke and writ. I would say, and it's not an eccentric opinion, that he could not begin to hold a candle to Westbrook Pegler, or John O'Hara, or the late Otis Ferguson, or the living Red Smith, Jimmy Cannon, John Crosby or Robert Ruark. Some of you may be waiting for the name of Ernest Hemingway. But he would come into this discussion only because he too writes an American idiom that no American has ever spoken. It is the American vernacular heard through a very personal ear-trumpet. The Americans in Hemingway talk more like Hemingway than Americans, but somehow they couldn't be anything else but Americans and Hemingway characters. He tightens their speech and their emotions, like a man over-tuning a six-string guitar, so that the low notes have a sharper twang than they ought and the high notes sound as if they were struck on an icicle.

Damon Runyon, even back in Colorado, must have had some trick of mind and hearing much as a man with terrific astigmatism sees distant objects, in a queer way that makes the vertical lines jarring, but also more exciting than they are when he puts his glasses on. I speak with feeling about this because I am a four-star veteran of the battle with astigmatism. I remember how, at my first dances as a boy, when I didn't know there was anything wrong with my eyes, I'd look across the ballroom floor and see a whole crop of misty, tender wallflowers swooning on the vine. I would slink madly round the edge of the dancers to grab one of these houris for my very own. However, when I came within three feet of the charmer I had singled out to tread on, I saw at once why she was a wallflower, instead of being, say, Ava Gardner, out there on the floor moving like a snowflake, or—to be frank—doing the charleston. When I got close she was rarely a beauty, though she looked human enough and surely had character; but that is unfortunately not what a 15-year-old is looking for in girls. I used to take a quick, mild dislike to these girls, however, because they seemed to have pulled a Jekyll-and-Hyde trick. I discovered from some patient clinical testing later that this is the characteristic deceit of astigmatism. Almost any attractive woman at thirty yards looks to me like a beauty, because the astigmatic gaze softens the hard vertical lines, irons out all the wrinkles, and turns any deep-set pair of eyes into pits of tenderness. In general, the great gift of astigmatism is to rob a face of its peculiar lapses from the ideal and leave you with the Platonic copy of the girl that is laid up in heaven.

That's the way I think it was with Damon Runyon. He first saw New York from afar, and heard about it from the lips of gamblers and soldiers and racetrack touts who had made a haul there, or gone on an immortal bust, or captured some fabulous 'doll'. He swam into New York through the romantic haze of his astigmatism, put his glasses on, liked the Colorado myth a good deal better, and kept his glasses off. He didn't care to

14

put them on again, because he did very nicely selling America and Europe a romantic commodity easy to recognize at a distance. He didn't need, either, to listen for Broadway's slang. The private circus in his mind's eye had a lingo all its own, and he made it up as he went along.

A character in a movie Runyon once wrote called somebody a 'mooley'. The censors wouldn't pass the movie till they'd checked with Runyon. 'What's a mooley?' they asked him nervously. 'A mooley?' he said. 'Why, I don't know, I made it up.' That's the way with nearly all his slang. Most American slang was never made up by writers. It derives from a long American experience of work or play—from the collision of Dutch and French and German with English, or from the Spanish days of the Southwest, or from pioneering, mule-driving, railroading, baseball, poker, the cattle kingdom, mining. A newspaperman famous for his exposures of corruption in labour politics said to me the other night that he thought he might soon turn his attention to the rackets that go on in the insurance business. Reflectively he said, 'I think I'll sink a pick in it. Might be some pay-dirt there.' That is authentic and natural. There is no such slang phrase current as 'to sink a pick'. But I guess it was a common working expression seventy years ago. It recalls at once the Western miners, who looked at a likely mountain range, spat on their hands and sank their picks in, and came up, some of them, with a fortune in silver.

On the contrary, Damon Runyon's slang is as contrived and romantic as Dickens, as synthetic as Broadway. Perhaps that's why it fits, even though Broadway doesn't talk it. If Broadway characters had a vein of crazy property, they might talk that way.

Runyon as a writer never goes as deep as Ring Lardner, and his irony was superficial enough not to sadden him with the knowledge of human meanness and vulgarity, as it did Lardner. Runyon accepted it and was fond of it, which might make him a healthier man and not so good a writer as Lardner. He saw, as a stranger, one very small and flashy section of New York life. He made it over into a puppet world of his own, where gangsters are lovable bums, and greed and vulgarity are fun and hurt nobody—for long. He was able to do this because he preserved and exploited his original innocence, like a certain kind of confidence-man. The British view of Runyon is as confident and odd as Runyon's view of New York, not so much because distance, like astigmatism, lends enchantment, but because Runyon distils and sterilizes for a foreigner the swarming colour and frightening behaviour of the animals known as New Yorkers. All the most popular comic writers deal with some recognizable place, and then flatter your foreignness by letting you in on the secret, the confidential, the positively gen-u-ine low life of the place. So Damon Runyon saves you the expense of the voyage, the very real puzzles of the real thing. He puts you in the know, and the knowledge is a cure in itself because it gets you away from the daily grind and the recognizable life of Leeds or Glasgow or London—or, I ought to add, New York.

You do not have to be a stranger to describe or enjoy this pleasurable and simplified view of the country or a town. I know a wealthy tycoon who

16

now lives in New York. But he started life out West, as a timekeeper with a railroad gang. He has acquired without pain, in later life, a romantic Eastern view of the West, thus throwing into reverse the imaginative mechanism of Damon Runyon. This man is always asking me to come and visit him at his winter home in Arizona. Great country, he says, great people, great life. I mumble something about having work to do. At my age, he too had work to do. But now he goes off before the January snows and comes back in April, when the trees are blossoming. He has taken on a stranger's view of the West that is large, enraptured and sentimental. I thought of his father, who had no view of the West, but just broke it and made it liveable.

I have meant not to answer but only to ask the big question: can anybody ever know what is typical of another country? Is Lawrence's Arabia really Arabia, or only what Lawrence's gallant and secret imagination wanted it to be? Would Byron's poems on Greece have made a Greek laugh, as the English editions of Runyon make Americans laugh, with their glossaries of what the English editor thinks is American slang? We are up against a great and humbling question. And the only consolation I can offer is that the answer is open to anybody, the field is free. I have noticed that insight into American ways has nothing much to do with intellect or education. Most people find in a foreign country what they want to find. And when it comes to handing out the laurels to another nation's writers, the native critics are only the muscle-bound trainers of the day. They have been wrong before. If you go back into the last two centuries and look over their selections of the living immortals, you will be given faith in your own fumbling hunches. And even though we on this side may shudder at the notion that you think we go around talking like Damon Runyon's characters, maybe you are right about his permanent fame. After all, you have been right before, notably about Mark Twain, when all the best people in America, and the most respected critics, considered him something as low and fleeting as a comic strip. Maybe Damon Runyon *has* created a legend more enduring and endurable than the reality, because it is neater and funnier and more exotic and sympathetic—that is to say, more artistic—than crummy, sluttish old Broadway could ever be.

Roughing It

15 October 1948

A hundred years ago the first ship sailed out of New York bound for San Francisco and the American River, where, according to the reports that had drifted East, you lowered a pan into a sluggish stream, shook it several times and sifted out a fortune in gold. By ship round the Horn was only one way, the most tedious and the safest. You could go by way of Panama and Nicaragua and run the risk of malaria or yellow fever. You could sail down to Mexico and face a shorter journey across its width through almost trackless desert and the chance of epidemics and slaughter by bandits.

Most people in the East who for one reason or

another felt the urge to Go West decided to go the overland way. Today it is impossible to experience the human ordeal of that great migration, one of the last epics of purely human function before the Industrial Revolution transformed our lives. These people, in New England, and New York and Maryland and Ohio, sat down and planned to walk nearly two thousand miles from St Joseph, Missouri, or Independence, where the locomotive and the steamboat ended and the Middle Ages began. Independence was a more thriving place a century ago than it is today, because it was the outfitting centre for the Forty-Niners. From there you were on your own. You went by mule and drove your wagons and cattle along with you for the remaining eighteen hundred miles. You used a route map drawn by somebody who had once made it and survived. You depended very much, too much, on the hearsay of these people to know where the water-holes were and where you could take a short cut through the mountains.

There was no archetype of the Forty-Niner. They were of every human kind. But early on they learned that they had better travel in packs and most of them elected what they called a captain and two lieutenants. A quartermaster was chosen to look after the provisions. They may sound very martial in a noticeably non-military nation. But they knew, the later companies at any rate, that there were certain unavoidable hazards: flash floods, the rotting of their food, Indians, disease, and the constant challenge to their discipline and courage of reducing the weight of their pack—their implements, even their food supply—when the route was too much for their animals, who set the pace. They figured correctly that no group of human beings, however individually noble, would be likely to stay noble in the desperation of thirst, or spontaneously organize themselves in the event of attack. By the time they started the long journey from Missouri, most of them had formed themselves into companies and agreed on written or unwritten laws. Many of them spent weeks in the East before they left, drawing up written constitutions. Some of these were abided by all the way to California. Others were torn up in anger, stuffed down the captain's throat, or buried with a dead cow.

Most of them through the late spring of 1849 took far too many provisions. It was said that the summer companies had the routes laid out for them by trails of abandoned stoves, pillows, beds, pots and kettles, crowbars, drills, ploughs, harness, trunks, bellows and dishpans. These, they found, were luxuries to a pioneer. And the word got across the continent that what you needed was one wagon to carry the supplies for every five persons, a mule apiece, rifles and shotguns, a rubber knapsack, an oilcloth cap, two pairs of boots, eight shirts, an overcoat, one pair of drawers, three blankets, a hundred and fifty pounds of flour, twenty-five pounds of bacon, fifteen pounds of coffee, twenty-five of sugar, some baking powder, salt and pepper.

That's as far as I want to go in describing the famous journeys across the plains. But I suspect that any American who started out today, fitted out just this way, and got to California, even if he stuck to the countless concrete highways that slam across hundreds of thousands of miles north and south and east and west—such a man would become some sort of national hero or crank. He would be paced by the newsreel boys, met at intervals by the advertising salesmen of whoever's flour and bacon he was carrying, he would be greeted by the Mayor of San Francisco, he would in the end be flown to Washington and shown in all the papers shaking the President's hand in the White House.

Nothing persists more in the fancy of Europeans, and in the superstitious pride of Americans themselves, than the conviction that Americans are tough and rough and ready, scornful of the European niceties and primmer ways of travel. The last thirty years have turned this belief into unmitigated legend.

One of the most precious books to American book collectors is a copy of Baedeker's *United States* for, I believe, 1906. In the conscientious Baedeker way, it warns the comparatively domesticated European of the coarse pleasures and inconveniences he will have to settle for if he decides to take a holiday in the United States. It is always Baedeker's consolation, however, to the intending tourist that no matter how constant the public spitting, how hard the beds, how ankle-deep the roads and primitive the hotels away from the big cities, the traveller who has any pioneering spirit in him will never regret his courageous visit to the United States because nowhere else will he see the singing colour of the New England fall, the blossom of the South in spring, the grandeur of the Yosemite, the Yellowstone, etc., etc. This guidebook is greatly sought after precisely because today it reads like such a gorgeous joke. If you changed the place-names and made them European, an American could read it with a straight face, since it would record most of his grouches about travelling in Europe today. The application of American technical genius to the mechanics of living has not merely turned the tables on Baedeker, it has turned the American, however reckless or self-reliant his individual character, into the world's most urbanized, most petted traveller.

Mr Richard Neuberger, who lives in the Far West, in Portland, Oregon, has taken up this theme in a magazine piece. He was in Alaska during the war having, as he puts it, 'the sort of experience we had read about eagerly as boys, in the tales of James Fenimore Cooper, Jack London, and Zane Grey'. And, he adds, 'we hated it . . . we talked nostalgically of percale sheets and fluffy towels, or breakfast in bed and tiled bathrooms'. They complained—in Alaska, this is—about 'draughty privies and the lack of dry-cleaning facilities'. Mr Neuberger concludes that 'with a few bold exceptions, we Americans have come to regard the steam-heated hotel and the internal combustion engine as indispensable to any foray in the open'. Nowadays, more millions than ever before (the latest published count was 29,608,318) visit the American National Parks. But according to the Department of the Interior fewer and fewer people each year attempt the two-day hikes, or even drive up the highest peaks, or, having looked at the Grand Canyon, will undertake the day-long mule journey down to the overnight camp at the bottom. It is very hard to say how Americans would compare with other peoples in this newfound lassitude. Driving around most of the National Parks is pretty strenuous in itself. If you could put

Yosemite and Yellowstone together, you would have something about the area of Wales whose geography is a combination of Switzerland, Persia and the Day of Judgement. But even so, these parks were lovingly created two generations ago by men who chopped through thousands of feet of lumber, who rode into them on a horse, who discovered the sublime with an axe, a botanist's kit, a piece of bacon, a tent and a stout heart. Now through all of them, even over the hair-raising pass into Tuolumne Meadows on top of the Yosemite, American engineers have built incomparable cement highways, blasted through prehistoric rock, encircling mountains where no other race would dream of cutting out a dirt road.

This suggests a cheerful contradiction. That even if the traveller is a sissy sitting over an internal combustion engine, the heroes who on his behalf comb cement to the smoothness of toothpaste under the desert sun, and build his highways through the Rockies and Sierras: they are Americans too. And this leads us into a famous cliché. I hope I can then lead us out of it. (I have nothing against clichés. Most of them are true, though you have to live through the denial of them to know it.) It is the assumption that the Americans have grown soft and unable to fend for themselves, that their enslaving gadgets, through which they flip their way so expertly, are crutches or props to living, essential to a people sinking contentedly into a decadence that out-Romans the Romans.

I'm sorry to report that the Americans' devotion to urban comfort, their ingenuity with gadgets, even their reliance on them, proves no such thing. In my own experience, the Americans who are most devoted to convertible automobiles and glass-enclosed showers made no complaint on this score when they ripped up Japanese jungles for airfields or waded ashore at Okinawa. The women I know who can whip up a delicious meal in ten minutes with the skilled aid of pressure cookers, bean slicers, electric beaters and deep-frozen vegetables are also the ones who can make the best meal the slow way with none of these things. And the most skilful fisherman I know is a man who can charm a trout with his fingernail, but prefers to have a compact tackle-box along, which contains exquisite scales the size of your thumb and a leader cutter which is a little circle of plastic moulds that exudes fine wire and cuts it in one motion.

Most Americans, even rich ones, were brought up in a culture that never expected somebody else to do the rough work. Most boys in college who can afford good cars can also take them apart and put them together again. This may all be changing. Still, I doubt that a devotion to gadgets is a reflection in the American character of a terrified dependence on them. They are loved for themselves, for the humorous felicity with which they dispose of elementary labour. A Texan I know, whom I would never like to meet in anger whether the choice of weapons was a jet-propelled torpedo or the back of the raw hand, put it neatly once when he said to me, 'I'll ride fifty miles on a horse for the fun of it, but out of necessity I drive.' One of the irritating troubles about Americans, in violation of the best advice of the best English divines, is that they just don't believe that whatever is uncomfortable is good for the character.

Joe Louis

18 March 1949

The day Joe Louis retired must have brought a moment's pause and a sigh from many people who don't care for sport, the sense of a promised date that would never be kept such as non-musical people felt when Caruso or Paderewski died. On 1 March 1949 it came home to some of us that we should very likely never again see him shuffle with great grace up to some wheezing hulk of a man, bait him with a long left before he brought up the shattering, awful thunderbolt of his right, and then toddle considerately away and wait for the referee to call the roll on yet another ruined reputation.

There are some idols you acquire too early, who later turn into walking parodies of themselves, like a favourite uncle who gets to be a vaudeville bore. There are others—the artists of popularity—who stay just far enough away from the hungry crowd and never glut the appetite they tease. Joe Louis was one of these. I doubt I should ever have seen him, or cared to, if he had not at one time connected with a private occasion. I went down to Baltimore the first day of summer in 1937 to stay with an old friend, a doctor at the Johns Hopkins hospital, who promised himself next day an afternoon off from his messy labours with stomach-aches and corpses. We drove out into the blossoming Worthington and Green Spring valleys. The purple twilight fell. It had been a perfect day, of the kind that makes you grateful for your friendships and stirs the memory of how they first started. I had met this man years before on such an evening when he stopped by my room in college to admire a battered record I had carried across the Atlantic. It was Fats Waller singing the 'Dallas Blues'. Driving back into Baltimore he remembered that Fats was on tap in person just then. 'How about,' he said, 'we go down to darktown and catch him?' There was a little vaudeville house deep in the coloured section of town, and that's where we went. We packed ourselves in with several hundred Negroes too many. They clapped and stomped in time and sweated like the plebs at a Roman circus. It was possibly 95 degrees outdoors and 110 inside. Nobody seemed to care. In the middle of one number, though, something happened outside that rode above the rhythm of the band and the hallelujahs of the audience. Far off from somewhere came a high roar like a tidal wave. The band looked uneasy but played on. It came on nearer, a great sighing and cheering. Suddenly there was a noise of doors splintering and cops barking and women screaming and men going down grabbing their toes and snarling obscenities. The band stopped and the lights went up. The black faces all around us bobbed and flashed. Women threw their heads back and shrieked at the roof. Some people embraced each other and a little girl in pigtails cried. Other people cuffed and swung at each other. We managed to get out whole. Outside, in the villainously lit streets—they still have gaslight in darktown Baltimore—it was like Christmas Eve in darkest Africa. This, it turned out, was the night that Joe Louis won the heavyweight championship, and for one night, in all the lurid darktowns of America, the black man was king.

The memory of that night has terrified and exhilarated me ever since. The phrase, 'Arise, you have nothing to lose but your chains', must have a terrible appeal to the Negro. Most Southerners know it, and it is why in some places they watch fearfully for every Negro flexing his muscles and wonder if he is somehow connected with the Communists. That immediate fear was not besetting America then as it is now. But the lesson was plain: one Negro had outboxed all the living contenders, no matter how white (and Braddock was whiter when he came out of the ring than when he went in), and he was a racial god.

It took several years, and a run of inevitable victories, and wide familiarity with Joe in the ring and on the newsreels, for Americans to learn a special respect for this quiet, beautiful, mannerly youth, who never thought of himself as anybody's god, who never played his colour up or down, kept his mind on his work, stepped scrupulously aside when an opponent stumbled; and who, when it was all over, said such embarrassing things over the radio that they had to whisk the mike away from him to the loser, who could usually be depended on to say the clichés that were expected of him. They pushed the microphone up to Joe in December 1947, when he had been fought into a dazed parody of his younger self by another old Joe—Jersey Joe Walcott. A sharp little announcer chattered, 'Did he ever have you worried, Joe—at any time?' This is a question expecting the answer, 'No, I felt fine all the time, never better.' Joe said, 'I was worried all the way through. Yes, sir, I ain't 23 any more.'

I know it is hard, perhaps impossible, for any white man to appraise the character of any Negro. If you have lived all your life around Negroes, you inherit certain attitudes towards them. If you are a stranger to them, there is the danger of making them out to be quite the nicest people in America. In a way, nice Negroes have to be; for though Negroes are as good and bad as anybody else, they have one thing in common: they have had, most of them, a worse deal than the white man. A variation of this condescension is to think so poorly of the Negro in general that when he does anything as well as a white man, you have to make him out to be unique. You hear a coloured band and shout that nobody can play a trumpet like a black man (it depends, of course, which black man is being compared with which white). Then you run into Louis Armstrong, who tells you of the first time he heard a white boy—a very pasty-faced boy from Davenport, Iowa—play the cornet. And Armstrong broke into tears. 'Man!' he said, 'might as well lay you down and die, nigger.'

When you come to look at the life and career of Joe Louis, there is the special dilemma that he is a black man, and that even when you have done your best to judge him as other men, there's no way of denying that if he is not the best boxer that ever lived, he is as near to it as we are ever likely to know. He was born in 1914 on a sharecropper's cotton patch in Alabama and was as country-poor as it is possible to be. In theory the farm was—it had been rented as—a cotton and vegetable farm. But the vegetables did not feed the family, not by the time Joe, the seventh child, came along. His father broke, as sharecroppers do, from the daily strain of not making enough in crops either to feed his children or put shoes on them. They had no money to send him to a hospital. So he was carried off to a state institution where he died. A widower came to help out and soon married Joe's mother. And his five children moved in with the eight Louises. Joe got a little more food and went to a one-room school. Then the family moved to Detroit, where the stepfather worked in an automobile factory. Joe went on to trade school and worked in the evenings doing the rounds with an ice-wagon. Then came the Depression, and the family went on relief. This, said Joe, made his mother feel very bad. Years later Joe wrote out a careful cheque for $269, which was the amount of the relief cheques they had had from the government. That, said Joe, made Mrs Brooks, as she now was, feel better.

Whatever a big city means to the poor, Detroit meant to Joe. But it means something else to a hefty Negro lad short of cash. It means gymnasiums and the prospect of a quick take of two or three dollars in improvised fights. When Joe was 18 he came home very late one night and found his stepfather blocking the door. 'Where you been, Joe?' he asked.

'Over to the gym,' said Joe, 'working out.'

'I thought so,' said Mr Brooks, and lectured him about the fate of no-goods getting punch-drunk in gymnasiums. 'You go on foolin' around with boxing, you're never gonna amount to nothin'.'

He says this had him really worried. He asked his mother about it. She said it was all right to be a boxer if that's what you wanted to do most. And that was, in a way, the end of Joe's wayward life. The rest was practice, and workouts, and learning, learning, being knocked to pulp, and learning some more and coming again with a new trick or two.

There is a biography of Joe Louis, there may be several, that makes him talk the way sentimental writers always think simple men talk. It is a fairly nauseating work. But just before Joe retired two first-rate newspapermen, Meyer Berger and Barney Negler, got hold of him for many long sessions and, presumably with one hand in their pockets, transcribed exactly how he talked and what he said, without paying any more attention than Joe Louis does to grammar, simplicity or morals. From a few sentences of this report, I think you can get closer to the sort of man Louis is than from reams of official biographies. Take the bit about his being born with a catlike tread. 'When I got up in fighting,' he says, 'newspaper writers put a lot of words in my mouth. They wrote I was born with movements like a panther, and how I was a born killer. I never said it was wrong before, but the real truth is I was born kind of clumsy-footed. My mother says I liked to stumble a lot when I was a baby . . . That footwork the writers say was cat-sense was something Chappie Blackburn drilled into me. That was learned, it wasn't a born thing. He saw I couldn't follow my left hook with a right cross without gettin' my right foot off the floor. It takes a lot of learnin' before you can do it without thinkin'.' Or his explanation of why he never says much. 'When I got to be champion, the writers made a lot of noise about how hard it was to get me to talk. My mother said I was no different when I was a kid. When I went to school the teacher made

30

me say words over and over and by-and-by I got stubborn, I guess, and wouldn't say them at all.'

After he lost a fight in early 1934, before his professional career was technically on the books, his manager told him to stop staying out late with the gang. 'He treated me real good,' says Joe. 'I got to wear some of his clothes made over.' The night he became champion, the night it seemed the whole population of darktown Baltimore poured into that vaudeville theatre, Joe summed up his feelings in an immortal sentence or two:

'He fell in a face-down dive. That made me heavy-weight champion. People figure that was my biggest thrill. But I don't remember no special feelin', I just felt good . . . maybe it was because I figured I wouldn't feel a real champ until I got that Schmeling. That's what I fixed on.' (Schmeling it was who rang the only jarring note on Joe's professional record. At the end, it read: 61 bouts, 15 knockouts, 9 decisions, knocked out once. That was in 1936. And exactly one year to the night after he became champion, Joe had his revenge. He did what he 'fixed on'.)

Maybe you will get from this the idea that Joe Louis is a simple soul with quiet manners, a good boy who never had a crafty thought. Of course, he doesn't talk about his respect for his opponents, or his decency and casualness with the crowd, because these are fundamental, the characteristics that a man hardly knows about, or, if he does, keeps quiet about. But there is one remark he makes about his pride in money that should round out the picture. 'People ask me,' he says, ' "Joe, what will you do when the big money from fightin' stops comin' in? Won't you have to cut down?" I tell 'em, I'm gonna live good, retired or not retired. I got investments and I got ideas. I'll keep on livin' good. It's them who lived off me who won't be livin' so good.'

Well, there he is, the Brown Bomber no more, a memory of incredible speed, a slow shuffle, a solemn face, a gentleness, a shy acceptance of his greatness. All things considered, a credit to his race. So long as you add Jimmy Cannon's necessary afterthought—the human race, that is.

Washington, DC

9 September 1949

In the Library of Congress in Washington, in the catacombs devoted to the Fine Arts, there is a wonderful piece of nonsense—a painting done by a British artist with the forthright title, *The Burning of Washington by the British in 1814*. It is a boy's re-creation of what was certainly a lurid but also a workmanlike and almost casual piece of destruction. The Americans, who were then in the downy youth of their nationalism, being only twenty-seven years old, had an itch to flex their muscles and get into a fight with the Champ—Great Britain, need I say. They had neither the army, the navy nor the money to fight anybody, and the British regulars landing in Maryland joined up with the British Marines stationed in Chesapeake Bay, who broke their snooze, yawned slightly and walked forty miles to Washington. There they calmly burned down the Capitol, the White House—then known as the President's Palace—

and the rest of the new public buildings that in those days were all that distinguished Washington from a fishing town on a marsh. It must have been a very humiliating event, for the President and his wife had to lodge in a boarding-house, and Congress was forced to meet in the Post Office, which had (in the general boredom of the undertaking) been overlooked.

Anyway, the British artist who painted this picture made of it the sort of three-colour advertisement that nations conscious of their strength insist on in their official art, the sort of thing which is now reproduced on breakfast-food containers, under some such title as American Victories, First Series. The picture shows the banks of the Potomac River ringed with cannon. Across the river come the British marines, either standing astride small sailboats, or pointing swords with one knee crooked in the approved position of my Lord Nelson, or sitting placidly rowing and admiring the view. And what a view! Nothing seems to be actually burning, because this would rob the spectator of the careful drawing of proud little buildings that are *about* to be burned. But from every bridge and tower and roof to the horizon puffs what looks like a swarm of barrage balloons, or those wavy circles that enclose the dialogue in comic strips. It is fire and flame. And even the harmless American ships on the opposite shore are writhing in great bags of smoke as impressive as medical illustrations of ulcerated intestines.

The contrast must be obvious between these valiant redcoats waving swords, and the British Treasury experts periodically sitting down in that same city showing their account books to the

Americans who can have little fear that the White House will shortly go up in flames. But the contrast I want to go into is not so much about our sadly reversed status as between Washington then and now. Washington exists in everybody's eye as a newsreel image of a dome, a huge statue of Lincoln, a parade of some sort, and Mr Truman on the White House lawn, receiving a model fire-hydrant from the fire chief of Oskawassa, Arkansas. Washington is so much a source and factory of the daily news that we rarely pause in our sleuthing to see what sort of a town it is and who are the people who live there.

Well, it is a town made in the triangular join of two rivers. When I say a town 'made', I mean made. For it is the legitimate boast of Americans that theirs is, like Canberra, one of the few national capitals which was chosen as a plot of naked land and designed as a centre of government and built up brick by brick, instead of—like most other world capitals—having the honour of 'capital' imposed at some late date on a city already mushrooming into importance.

In 1787 the Continental Congress made a nation, made its constitution, and looked around for a place to call its capital. The Southern states almost seceded in a row over the location, and for a time there never seemed to be a possible chance of the choice falling on what its enemies called 'that Indian place in the wilderness'. However, there was a certain dinner-party given by Jefferson, and a few bottles of smooth Madeira persuaded Alexander Hamilton (in exchange for the support of a bill he was sponsoring) to promise to deliver enough Northern votes to clinch the choice of this area on the Potomac, which was cut out of Maryland and Virginia; which General Washington personally inspected and approved of; and which was chosen and called 'the city of Washington in the district of Columbia'. Washington hired a man called L'Enfant to design a federal city. Now L'Enfant was a Frenchman and an eighteenth-century man. He was hipped on the subject of 'vistas' and the idea, which he lovingly copied from Versailles, of having great diagonal avenues cross a gridiron or rectangular network of long streets. The idea was that everywhere the diagonals crossed a vertical and a horizontal street you would have a three-way vista. You could see poachers in all directions. You could put cannon there as a point of tactics. What's more, you'd be able to see the great buildings, when they got built, for miles. It all sounded very elegant and modern. But the real-estate men liked it because it offered an endless series of money-making intersections. This obsessed Frenchman shocked them greatly when he showed up with his plans. For of the six thousand acres set aside for the city, over three thousand were for highways, preposterously wide avenues, anything from a hundred and sixty feet to four hundred feet wide. President Washington stuck by him, and he got his great diagonal avenues. Which is a blessed thing, because it's about all that's recognizable of L'Enfant's plan and still gives to Washington whatever it has of splendour and spaciousness.

The Congress, then, after wandering from Philadelphia to Princeton, to Annapolis, to Trenton and New York, set up shop in Washington in 1800. But the city had a hard time getting itself built, getting lighting and paving and sewers and

35

water. Nobody wanted to finance it. The Congress showed a healthy instinct in the early days, which it has since unhappily suppressed, of wondering why it should put up money to prolong anybody's stay in a mess of shacks on a plain that rises only forty feet above the noxious Potomac. For I should tell you that, from that day to this, Washington lies securely in what the guidebooks call an amphitheatre and what you and I call a swamp. And it has a damp, wheezy, Dickensian sort of winter hardly equalled by London, and a steaming tropical summer not surpassed by the basin of the Nile, or those outposts on the Persian gulf where bad vice-consuls are sent to rot.

For half the nineteenth century, L'Enfant's immense avenues were the joke of all visiting Europeans. To get on to them, you left somebody's house and then, like poor Miss Martineau, had to hoist your skirts, climb a stile or two, slush through a bog on to the highway, and cross a field and a sliver of street to get to another human habitation. Along these Versailles avenues that fell like ornamental swords across a rubbish-heap went big-bellied Congressmen in cutaway coats, hunters in coonskin caps, judges lugging their law books with them, acid New England ladies, Indian chiefs (there were the remnants of thirty tribes there when the so-called Father of His Country moved in to take possession). Dickens said in the 1840s that Washington was a place 'of spacious avenues that begin in nothing and lead nowhere; streets a mile long that only want houses, roads, and inhabitants; public buildings that need but a public to be complete'.

The 1840s were a bustling time, what with

36

railways getting to be taken for granted, and the telegraph, and canals being dug everywhere. To the good businessmen who roamed around Washington hoping for industry and finding none, the capital city was a flop. The towns south of the Potomac managed to get all their land given back to Virginia. Georgetown, to the north, wanted to go back to Maryland but never succeeded. But during the Civil War, Washington was the base of the Northern armies, and into it swarmed everybody who had a favour to sell, a bridge to mend, a new kind of gun, any sort of influence which might help or threaten the Union. It was in those years, and in the lush and corrupt days of the Reconstruction, that Washington became what it has ever since remained—the headquarters not only of the government but also of pressure groups and lobbyists, of manufacturers and pimps and fixers who conceived of a capital as a city dedicated to the manufacture of wealth by intimidating the government. The District itself was in wretched need of money. Its citizens were Americans without a vote (they still are) or a city government to call their own. It had a debt of about $4 million, which in 1874 was increased to $22 million. The federal government had to guarantee this debt and it wasn't paid off until 1922.

In the late 1870s it was decided that somebody would have to try and govern the city, and a municipal corporation was formed with three commissioners chosen by the President.

In this period there was a man called Shepherd, a builder, who gave to Washington its second blessing: a wealth of fine trees. He also got the city clean water and workable sewers, but most of all he started planting trees at a furious rate against a howl of protest from people who thought it was a shameless way to waste public money. He lined L'Enfant's great avenues with English elms, thus for ever defeating the original idea of long, uninterrupted vistas. But he made of a marsh the most shady and leafy town in the United States. Today the streets and squares tower with American elms, with sycamores, with all the glorious variety of American oaks, with lindens and willows, with trees from all over the Union and from many foreign places. The little square right opposite the White House, for instance, has a hundred varieties, with spruce, redwood, magnolia, cherry, holly, basswood, and I don't know what else. And springing up in the unlikeliest places is the Oriental gingko, the Chinese pagoda, and ringing the tidal basin those embarrassing Japanese cherry trees, which when we were at war with Japan had to be called something else, but are always the same, and always perfect.

*   *   *

The best guidebooks seem to be incapable of describing the physical look of Washington from any place but the air. That may be because the commanding avenues seen from the earth look like deserted parade-grounds. From the air, of course, they look like landing-strips, a misconception that several pilots from the hinterland acted on, until the city built a few years ago a big modern airport well outside the town. The man from Mars might well assume that Washington was, indeed, another name for Athens taken over by the American Air

Force. For arising at majestic intervals from great avenues are what to the pilot look like more Greek wedding cakes than you'd see at a French chef's golden wedding. When you get nearer to those sleek forbidding piles of white stone, cement and plaster of Paris, you might think them more Roman than Greek, and some more vaguely Italian. I doubt, however, whether you could see in Athens or in Rome such an imposing stack of porticoes and rows of Ionic columns and saucer-domes and inset-arches. They are, you would be right in guessing, government buildings—the Capitol, the Supreme Court building, the Treasury—which is almost an Acropolis in itself. Washington started to build in the 1790s in the inrushing fashion of the Greek Revival (a style in which Americans did delicate and beautiful things when they domesticated it in wood, in the South and New England, as the proper frame for houses and little churches). But whatever was good about the earliest Washington buildings is now to be seen only in the White House and the noble federal houses of Georgetown. For the Greek Revival style was soon succeeded by others, by red-brick Georgian of a humble kind, then by Romanesque, then by all the monstrous colonnades and curlicues of the mid-nineteenth century. At the end of that century there was a World's Fair in Chicago, showing the grandiose plaster-of-Paris façades of the Beaux-Arts exhibition in Paris. Ever since then Washington has lusted after these Roman monsters like a Girl Guide after Mark Antony. Washington would be about as intimate as Nuremberg used to be, if this was all. But happily it has a magnificent park, the finest scenery inside a city's environs, said

39

Lord Bryce, of any city he knew. And it crawls through this graveyard like Virginia creeper over a tombstone. The city is also nibbled at on all sides by suburbs—which city isn't? Some of them are old red-brick Georgian and some we'd better just say are suburban. Indeed, if you went to live in Washington and by some strength of character managed not to be a government employee, you might live in many parts of town and say that rows of nineteenth-century boarding-houses were more typical of Washington than rows of Greek columns. It's true; the two shapes most characteristic of Washington are the Italian palace, where the wage-slaves work, and the bow-windows, where they live.

You'll see that it's impossible to talk about Washington without getting preoccupied with the government and its buildings. But that's because there's practically nothing else. Washington is not a capital like London, which is a government capital but also a capital of banking, of music, of theatre, of eating, of writing and reading, of public sports, of shipping. All those things other than government are centred in New York, which Washingtonians contemptuously think of as Babylon-on-the-Hudson. Washington has no permanent theatres—it is wary of opening them to Negroes, and Washington is embarrassed by Negroes for exactly the same reason that Alabama is: nearly a third of its population is coloured.

Washington has little music that can begin to compare with the great orchestras of New York, Boston, Minneapolis, San Francisco or even Philadelphia. It has indifferent public food. It is as close as Baltimore to the huge Chesapeake Bay, but whereas the tables of Baltimore swill with terrapin stew and snapper-turtle soup and groan with expiring lobsters of a fatness that has to be seen to be believed, Washington for some reason makes no decent use of the gorgeous fish that come gasping up at the end of its streets. The answer may be that Washington stays home. It is not a night-owl town. The Congressmen don't like to be seen in their cups in public. And I doubt if either Sodom or Gomorrah was ever kept going by a population of respectable clerks.

This is another—in fact, the major—by-product of Washington's being nothing but a government city. It is the only town I know which has bred its own species of employee—the 126 clerks who came here in 1800 were neat and sober and have neatly and soberly reproduced their kind, to the tune of 300,000 government clerks. You do not see here the clashing variety of human shape and style and colouring that makes American cities such a challenge to the pleasant senses and some others. In other national capitals it is on the streets that you see mankind's variety. It is indoors—inside the courts and the parliament—that you see a mass of officials, who look as if they'd been run off on an assembly line. Not so in Washington. Here all the types in America, and all the accents, are drawn from the plains and mountains and deserts into the House and Senate Chambers. And on the streets—a population of quiet, slim, self-effacing people in glasses. Indoors, the human jungle, outdoors—the clerks. For it is the Congress and its hangers-on that ride the roost and set the tone of high life. You do not walk down the Strand side-stepping MPs at every turn or cluster around a church to catch Mr Aneurin Bevan at his devotions. In London the

Members of Parliament enjoy their true glory only when they are inside the House of Commons. Once outside, they dissolve into the formidable and dominant race known as the Cockneys. But in Washington the politicians, the puffing gauleiters from the provinces, are the rulers. It is this status which gives to the natives of Washington a meek, subterranean life, like that of Parisians during the occupation. They are resigned to it, as a Blackpool landlady is resigned to the profitable uproar of August Bank Holiday.

So, to continue what Mr Churchill would call 'this true account', we have a government capital obsessed and absorbed with governing, and all the feuds and deals and crises that go with it. We have a city with poor food, a nightmare of a climate, dignified by great avenues and by the cascading foliage of magnificent trees. But how, you must be saying, how about the high life, the air of great events, the intrigue?

It is usual to say that Washington is a nest of intrigue. And so it is. And undoubtedly there are more luxurious and louder parties held there than most of the ancient capitals can any longer afford. In this country you would expect the social arbiter to be a woman. And so she is. But ever since Mrs Perle Mesta got made the Minister to Luxembourg there has been a fine rivalry going on, and much well-bred miaowing in well-kept gardens, about who is to succeed Mrs Mesta as the town's leading hostess. I should add here that though not many Washington wives can aspire to toss a battalion of pressed duck at a thousand guests, Washington wives are another breed all to themselves. I never yet met a wife of a man anywhere near the government who didn't bear up splendidly under the intimate knowledge that her husband really swung the election and gave the word for the date of the invasion of Europe. This all, surely, implies a very harem of intrigue.

But intrigue in a capital city suggests the splended briberies of a Talleyrand, the sort of masked ball at which the Secretary of State forgets to dance with the wife of the Turkish ambassador and boom!—another crusade is on the march. Washington is indeed choking with intrigue and gossip. But its intrigue is less like that of the court of Louis XIV and more like that of a vast church bazaar, in which hot-eyed matrons wink and whisper in the hope that Mrs X's pickles will be rejected as too tart and Farmer Y's Poland Farceurs will come in a poor third.

You have heard the word 'pork-barrel'—the President's pork-barrel—and must have wondered what a pork-barrel was doing in so elegant a place as the White House. It is, alas, a permanent though invisible fixture. To be more accurate, it is two fixtures. For there's one pork-barrel for the President and one for the Congress. Like many another American institution, they were created by self-denial and ended by giving a licence to self-indulgence.

Jefferson and his excellent Secretary of the Treasury followed the English custom of using the national income as they thought fit, disbursing lump sums to each department and accounting for the money when the money was spent. But at the first complaint from Congress they decided to adopt the more chivalrous method of asking the Congress to specify its wants and name a price for each of them. The result is the Congressional pork-barrel, which persuades some Congressmen to postpone for ever their interest in what is best for the nation and sends them circulating through back-rooms, offices and parties, ogling an old friend here and charming a stranger there, in the hope of swiping for their constituency an army camp, or getting a new post office built or an old river drained.

The President's private pork-barrel was left him by the Constitution as a consolation prize for having to get the Senate's consent to his appointment of all the big federal jobs, like Cabinet officers and ambassadors. He was allowed to keep certain 'inferior offices', which his party has ever since been eager to help him fill. He it is who appoints a postmaster in Santa Claus, Arizona, a food inspector in New Orleans, a tax collector in Red Cent, Utah. If this seems a harmless vanity, it should be remembered that there are many thousands of these 'inferior offices' scattered across the land and that every one of them represents a Congressman appeased or a Congressman flouted. They tot up to a nice balance of favours and insults that registers with painful accuracy when some bill the President is dying to have passed comes to the vote in the Congress. On a dark day of the Civil War, Lincoln confessed he looked more ashen than usual not from any concern about his armies but because he was worried over a postmastership in Brownsville, Ohio.

Washington was accordingly long ago described as 'a huge hog-wallow where every man's snout is at the pork-barrel'. It is an uncouth image, no doubt, but it is a truer symbol of Washington intrigue than any boudoir gallivanting ever recorded in the White House. Washington tries to perfume this reality with a lot of scented legend about George Washington's eye for a pretty ankle, and how Martha Washington was a fragrant thing in her day. But even this myth doesn't hold up. In our day she has given her name to a wholesome candy. Imagine 'Josephine Buonaparte Cough Drops'!

You have seen that I have done my best to give you a vivid and unprejudiced account of this great capital city where now the ancient empires bow to the dollar. I should like to take you around some more of its glories, but, like Mr Fitzpatrick in the travelogues, we must say a reluctant farewell to the federal city on the Potomac. And so as the sun sinks into the Tidal Basin . . . excuse me, I have just time to make the fast train up to Babylon-on-the-Hudson.

The Fall of New England

21 October 1949

There are times of the year when anybody with an itch for travel must think of those parts of the earth that God favoured above all others when He handed out the seasons. There are two of these that I have enjoyed many times but I still find myself goggling and marvelling every time they come around. One is the English spring and the other is New England in the fall.

The best of English poets have celebrated the rich, sombre English autumn, but an American fall bears little resemblance to that 'season of mists and mellow fruitfulness'. Many famous Britons have put on record their astonishment at the youthful, trumpeting quality of the fall, at the hot days and the Mediterranean blue skies encircling a landscape of blinding scarlet and gold. Lord Bryce, not a reticent man about American vices, couldn't trust his English reserve to speak properly about its virtues. Lloyd George confessed after his only trip to America that no matter how inconclusive his political mission had been he would at least go home remembering the overwhelming experience of the fall. A hundred years ago, Mrs Trollope, who liked very little about these United States, broke down and wrote that at this season of the year 'the whole country goes to glory'.

The fall ranges throughout the whole hardwood or deciduous region of the country, from the north woods of Maine clear across the Midwest as far as the Dakotas and way down South to the foothills of the Rockies in Texas. Since no American can bear to believe that he or his parents chose a second-rate place to be born in, there is no agreement about where the fall is at its best. The residents of the Great Lakes say that no sumacs flame like their sumacs. And the pride of a man from Arkansas in his blazing hawthorn trees is a wild grab at plucking a virtue out of necessity. A native of another land can simply report that the fall of New England is as a four-alarm fire to a lighted match. There is no way to describe it or talk about it, except in the language of Milton and Shakespeare, who never saw it.

But it is possible to say why it's so. Everybody enthuses about the fall but nobody explains it. It is due to a happy accident of climate, a steady brilliance of October sun going to work on the great variety of American hardwoods and the fairly arid soil they stand in. The superiority of New England's fall—of that in Vermont, New Hampshire and Massachusetts especially—is due to their latitude. These states are far enough north to get an early cold spell to quicken the sap before the prolonged sunshine of October brings it out as colour in the leaves. They are far enough south to escape a continuous and withering frost, which is what nips the Canadian fall before it can come to its prime. Farther south—in Pennsylvania, Maryland, Virginia and the Carolinas—they get no cold, except at high altitudes, and by the time the sap is forced up and ready for showing off, the leaves are crumbling and falling.

In most temperate countries the strong pigments that have been hidden from view in the greens of summer never do come out, because the autumn brings in rain and mists and threatening grey skies. The whole trick of the New England fall is nothing more complicated than that of a photographic negative handled by a superior developer. In the autumn, the countrymen tell us, the sap is blocked from the leaf by a new growth of hard cells at the base of the twig. So the greens fade. Now all you need is an October of brilliant light and warmth to develop out the yellows and the reds. The only other qualification is a lack of rain. On rich and rainy soils like those of England the leaves stay green too late till the frost kills them. New England, on the contrary, has many causes to lament its rather poor soils. But it never regrets them in the fall, for their very lack of nitrogen stimulates a great range of yellows and golds. And the acid in the leaves is what burns them scarlet. The fall, then, is nothing more than the thorough burning out of what is poor in the soil and what is bitter in the leaf. 'It is,' says Donald Culcross Peattie, 'essentially death that causes all the brave show.' But it is a fierce and productive death.

I once went north from New York City at the very beginning of the fall to meet the peak of it wherever it might be between Maine and southern Connecticut. The first signal of the glory to come is a bare tree, which is never bare until the fall is ready to ripen. It is the butternut tree, and it sheds everything just as the bushes and berries are beginning to trickle out their purple. By the green edge of the parkway on which I was driving, little piles of brown leaves, already dead, lay at the foot of hickory trees. The ferns were dry. The bracken and blueberry bushes were wine-dark, the sumac a throbbing vermilion. Everywhere there was the smell of burning wood, letting off violet wisps of smoke to smear the cloudless sky—like trickles of milk on window panes.

At this point I wanted to take off my glasses, which a notation on my driving licence forbids. This is another thing about the fall. The sparkling clarity of the light gives to short-sighted people the constant sense that their eyesight has marvellously improved and that they are seeing fences, barns, steeples and billboards in the sharp outline they probably have for other people all the time.

I drove up and over the hills across from New York State into Connecticut, past roadside stands

48

piled high with jugs of cider and pyramids of pumpkins. And then I started to follow a river whose banks were black with stands of evergreen. By now a green field was just another daub on the crowded palette of the landscape. We were still far from the fall's peak. It was still the small, treeless things that were trying to be splendid. The briar and bushes and vines were sparkling. I do not know them well enough to single out their separate charms, but it is an annual joy to see brush which most of the time is a mesh of old wire suddenly disclose a jewel of a flower. Pokeweed, and pitchpine cone, and unpretentious things like partridge berry and jack-in-the-pulpit. All of them have a special shining berry, a bursting husk, a momentary bloom.

I got out of the car and wallowed in the silence and the singing colour and the balmy heat. At the rim of my tyre I noticed that the smooth white cement of the highway had cracked under the tension of a cranberry vine. And through this crack, and edging into the highway, wild cranberries grew. I looked ahead at the engineered boulevard of the highway, pouring like two ribbons of toothpaste to the horizon, quite heedless of its defeat by the concentrated violence of a tiny and delicate vine. That just about put industrial know-how in its proper place. And I climbed back and went on, warming to the excitement of what was to come.

And now the trees took over. After another twenty miles, the evergreens came in thick and fast. Even a pine looked like a new invention seen in its inkiness against a flaming maple. Now I was surrounded by two other properties that make the New England fall unique. First and above all the maple, with its bursting sugar which blazes into scarlet. And then the oaks. An Englishman is surprised to wonder about many slender trees and hear them called oaks. The fat old oak tree of England, with his legs planted solidly on lush damp ground, is a rare sight. But New England has a teeming variety of oaks, and their value as a spectacle is that in the fall they entirely revise your ideas about the infinite fine range of colour between gold and lemon. And beside this perpetual shower of scarlet and lemon and gold, the white birches slid by like slivers of mercury. And rising from the foam of every valley, slim as thermometers, were the white spires of colonial churches, keeping count of the general fever. I had hit the peak, and the state of our language being what it is, in my hands at least, there is no more point in going on about it in prose. Some great composer might convey the majesty of it. Only a child in ecstasy could hit off the youth and hilarity of it. For children are natural impressionists, taking the adjectives of music and knifing them close against the nouns of sight and touch. Every child knows that colour sings and trees walk. But puberty is the end. They acquire the logic that is death to the spirit and life to what is called maturity, and like the rest of us repress the wild energy of their instinctive knowledge. And so we can only guess at the form of art in which perhaps some hundreds of years from now the New England fall will come to be represented. I would take a bet that, by our present resources, Cézanne and Handel together might give a fair account of it. For the present I can only tell you that the fall is wonderful in life and awful in painting.

*　　　*　　　*

In this setting you can find an American life, proud but not prosperous, that also seems doomed to die in the industrial democracy that surrounds it. Don't imagine that the small village I am taking you into, in the south of Vermont, is typical of New England today. It is typical of nowhere else, but New England is many things besides small memorials to the declining eighteenth century. The New England puritan of English stock has not been the typical New Englander for two generations. Sixty per cent of the people in the six states of New England have at least one parent foreign born, against only 5 per cent in the Southern states. Today the Connecticut Yankee has only one chance in three of being, like the first settlers, a Protestant with an English name. It's two to one that he's an Italian or a Pole, and a wise newspaper editor once warned me to take for granted that any stranger I met on the streets of New England was a Catholic. To make certain that what I am going to talk about, though once radical and typical in New England, is now conservative and odd, I should also warn you that the typical Yankee is no longer a farmer. In 1790, ninety-seven New Englanders in every hundred lived on the land, and three in towns. In 1870, it was still only twenty-one townsfolk against seventy-nine countrymen. Today in the United States, 56 per cent of the people live in cities. In New England, 77 per cent of the entire population lives in cities, only 23 per cent in the country. So New England is the most industrialized of all American regions. If this shocks you, it would

51

shock most Americans more, for they stubbornly think back to New England as the source and replenisher of all their canniest and most down-to-earth virtues.

Bearing in mind, then, that we are looking at a tiny green spot in the upper-right-hand corner of the turbulent industrial landscape of the northeastern states, let's take a look at the sort of place that bred New England. It is a small valley six miles long and two miles wide. You might say that it was bound by mountains, but to a Westerner they would be low, well-wooded hills, for the hills that enclose this valley are nowhere higher than a thousand feet. Yet the valley is more fertile than most places in Vermont, with grass for summer pasture and winter hay. It grows corn and perhaps a crop of oats. And the farmer's cash in the bank comes from the one cow a year he sells. To a stranger it would look like good sheep country, and so it would be if there weren't out West the vast hills of Montana and Wyoming and Colorado to make it hardly worth while for a Vermonter to breed them. Then, there's so much rock and boulder in the hills of Vermont that by now the oldest Vermont joke tells how the sheep have their noses sharpened so they can get at the grass (God anticipated the plight of Vermont by making sheep with cleft lips).

If you were to motor along this valley, and your car had some sort of trouble, a quiet, hard-bitten Vermonter would in time—his time—appear and tinker awhile and in the end put it right. He wouldn't say a word. And you'd have to be an outlander to try and pay him in any way. For Vermonters, settled long ago on a poor soil, and used to winters that hold more snow than the Arctic, don't expect a smiling face from Nature and don't reflect it in themselves. An Englishman coming here and going straight to Vermont and expecting to meet casual, backslapping people would be in for a ghastly surprise. A man is a stranger there up to the third and fourth generation. And the only reliable way they have of placing a face or a name is to ask who his mother was. (His father simply served his mother's turn.) It's been said that Vermonters look on life as a necessary struggle against evil, a struggle you must make and expect to lose. It's also the only state in the United States where you will hear the word 'thrift' used all the time. They never throw anything away. In a little booklet about this valley I am talking about, written by a couple of natives, you will read this sentence: 'The people are friendly and always willing to help a neighbor. This means more to us who live here than material wealth, which none of us possess.' To walk into the centre of this village of Newfane, you would never believe it. It is a handsome common with a couple of shops, an inn and a quite magnificent courthouse. The town was settled in 1776, but the county courthouse didn't go up until fifty years later, and we can be thankful for that. For in the interval Americans conceived a passion for everything Greek. Believing that they had just successfully established the first genuine democracy since the Greeks and the grandest Republic since Rome, they took to naming their towns with classical names. Hence Philadelphia, Annapolis, Laconia, Athens, Sparta, Seneca, Cicero, Troy. Thomas Jefferson built a home with a columned portico.

And soon country courts, and inns, and farmhouses were doing the same. It may sound like a dubious fad, but Americans stuck to their preference for wooden houses, and today New England is glorified with hundreds of churches, houses, courthouses, the wood painted white, with pillared porticoes and graceful spires. In this small village in Vermont, the county courthouse is an exquisite symbol of what Americans did in wood with Greek forms.

Opposite the courthouse is the inn, which is also the jail. Newfane has kept up its habit of feeding its prisoners from the inn, and since the inn serves the best food around here, it's sometimes hard to get the inmates out of jail. Theodore Roosevelt said he would like to retire here, commit some 'mild crime' and eat his way through a cheerful old age.

If you went along the valley you would be walking without knowing it through another town called Brookline, for Brookline is simply the scattered houses of the valley. It has less than a hundred people, mostly farmers, and they are their own rulers. Its first town meeting was held in 1795 and the last one was held last week. The names at the first meeting are still there: Moore and Waters, and Ebenezer Wellman and Cyrus Whitecomb, and Christopher Osgood (there has always been a Christopher on the Osgood farm). Walking along the road you might run into the tractor of a Mr Hoyt. He is to all intents a farmer. And so he is. He is also the road commissioner of the valley. His wife, Minnie Hoyt, is the town clerk, a justice of the peace, and when she isn't doing the farming chores she's busy signing fishing licences, or marrying a visiting couple, or telling the comfortable city-people who have made a summer home here that by a decision made at the last town meeting their taxes will be twice as much next year. What is striking to an Englishman here is that the few fairly well-to-do people are all what they call 'summer folks', people who made a farm over as a summer retreat from New York or Boston. But the summer folks are strangers and underlings. The valley has heard many delicate sounds through the years. But it has never heard the advice of a squire or the accent of *noblesse oblige*. The farmers are ruled and rulers. The wealthy stranger goes cap in hand and pays his rates according to Minnie Hoyt and does what Mr Hoyt says to keep his part of the highway safe and sound.

Our pilgrimage ends with an odd little building, a round schoolhouse. It was put up in the 1820s and is shaped like a silo, just one room with five windows equally spaced in a circle around it. It was so built, they say, because at that time the valley lived in fear of a highwayman called 'Thunderbolt', whom no one had ever seen. The schoolmaster, a Scot from Muirkirk, one Dr Wilson, had his desk facing the door and could see through all the windows the first approach of any robber, or of the dreaded Thunderbolt. Thunderbolt's presence seemed to have haunted the valley for a couple of decades, but one gets a reassuring picture of Yankee vigilance in the dour figure of Dr Wilson, spelling out his lessons to the valley children and in the twilight letting his fingers play on the barrel of his shotgun as his protective eye rolled around the five windows.

I leave you with this comforting image of the rude forefathers of today's New Englanders.

Having led you so far into a mystery, though, it occurs to me you may wonder if they ever caught Thunderbolt. Yes, they did.

When the good Dr Wilson died they took off the high scarf he always wore and on his neck they saw scars and the marks of chains. Sure enough, *he* was Thunderbolt.

Letter to an Intending Immigrant

16 December 1949

I was going downtown in the subway and was flattened up against the door reading the morning paper of a man breathing into my ear. If anybody in this train had had room to ram his elbow into my lungs, chances are I wouldn't have noticed it. That would have been just an occupational hazard of travelling in New York during the Christmas shopping season. But what I became aware of after a mile or so was a gentle nudge somewhere down there in the direction of my floating rib. This was such a friendly gesture that I tried to swivel my eyeballs in the direction it was coming from. I saw the upturned face of a man who might have been about five feet three or, then again, might have been a six-footer simply frozen at that altitude. He grinned and asked me if my name was Cooke. I said it was and he said his name was Schofield and he'd been in school with me in England twenty . . . well, several years ago. Before we lurched to a stop, his stop, he had time to tell me that he was working in a big department store downtown and had been

56

over here for just about two years. I asked him if he was here for good. He gave a little laugh and said he certainly was. 'I just upped and left,' he said, and the train stopped and he vanished into the gasping school of New Yorkers peering at us through the aquarium windows.

This whole episode didn't last longer than thirty seconds, but it made me glad for him and set me contrasting his obvious good spirits with the fate and the faces of other English people I've run into in the past few years who also 'upped and left'. There was, for instance, an English girl who decided when the war was over that instead of having her children come back home to her from Canada, she would join them over here and start a new life in a new land. Her boy, it turned out, developed one of those boy soprano voices of remarkable purity. She began to fret—in the little Canadian town she'd settled in—and think back longingly to the church schools in England where this voice might be trained. Of course, she was homesick for more things than an English boys' choir. It was a useful and sensible excuse to give to friends on this side. She is back in London now, very contented in austerity, and her boy is proudly singing his head off.

I think also of a young man in his middle twenties who came here, hit on a good job and quickly acquired the usual admirations: the bright tension of New York, the vigour and irony of its people, the autumn weather, the food, the women, the motor parkways, the theatre. For a time he didn't seem to notice that this was costing him twice or more what these good things would have cost him at home if he'd been able to get them. He didn't need to notice, because he was a bachelor and such things as insurance and social security seemed like an old man's babble. This young and strapping Englishman was undoubtedly by now uprooted. His enthusiasm for many American customs was really a surprised contempt for his own previous ignorance of them. This is not a good basis for permanent admiration and he began to lose some of them, as he came to take them for granted. His job didn't pan out, and he found in the short and ruthless space of one month that New York is a bad town, and America a bad country maybe, to be poor in. With what he had left he went to Jamaica. Restlessness of course is a personal thing, but there was a conflict in it that I've noticed in other Britons who've sailed in here with shining eyes and left after a time in a mixed mood that is not pleasant to admit, for it is a mixture of disappointment and defeat. There is surely nothing to be ashamed of in disappointment. But many of these intending settlers can hardly fail to feel that American life is a far more severe challenge than they had figured on, and it has beaten them.

A century ago the whole adventure was, I think, materially harder on the people who made it, but psychologically not so tough. They knew before they ever left home that they were coming to a land with many less material comforts than Europe had to offer. They knew that the essential qualifications were physical hardihood, self-reliance, cheerfulness in the face of the adversity that was bound to come sometime, an indifference to social niceties, and a shrugging acceptance of dirt, bad luck, violence and bankruptcy. The visitors who didn't prepare themselves for these hazards had nowhere to turn for sympathy. Their criticisms sounded niggling and effeminate. Thus in 1820, Washington Irving described such Englishmen: 'They miss some of the snug conveniences and petty comforts which belong to an old, highly-finished and over-populous state of society; where the ranks of useful labour are crowded, and many earn a painful and servile subsistence by studying the very caprices of appetite and self-indulgence. These minor comforts, however, are all-important in the estimation of narrow minds.'

It sounds just like a British criticism of the travelling American today. Only the other day a young American film star (who was born on a small farm) caused a commotion in an 'old, highly-finished' hotel in Paris by demanding an air-conditioned room.

Nowadays an Englishman's complaints would not be likely to turn on such things. Now the material scales are weighted in America's favour. Today you can cross the three thousand miles of the American continent and never want for a private bathroom, a cement highway, a night baseball game, an airplane connection, a pair of nylon stockings or a gallon of ice cream in six different flavours.

But the catch is that America is no more willing than it has ever been to give these things away for free. They are not in this country the luxuries that a secure upper class once exacted from a swarming and servile lower class. They are the minimum demands of comfort made by a population as fertile as its resources, in a country where comfort has accordingly turned into big business. A share of that comfort, a bigger share of satisfying and ingenious comfort than any nation has ever known, can be bought by any worker with a steady wage. But the measure of that steady wage is the energy he can maintain. Visiting teams of British factory managers have remarked on the tenacity with which American workers compete through incentive schemes. You have only to lean out of any midtown window in New York, or in a score of other cities, to notice the furious concentration and energy of construction workers while they are on the job. At 5 o'clock they will quit like an exploding light bulb, but up to that moment they haul and hammer and drill and bulldoze with fearful zest.

A little time ago I left my office, as I usually do, about seven in the evening (not having the instinctive zest of the natives) and saw that the whole lobby of the skyscraper office building—which spans something like the floor-space of Piccadilly Circus—was covered with tarpaulin from which arose a network of ladders and scaffolding, a whole series of wooden platforms running about seven or eight feet from the ceiling. This scaffolding alone looked as if it might take a day or two to put up. But none of it was there at 5 o'clock when the offices of this building disgorged their three or four thousand employees. However, this was only the preparation for the job in hand. The job in hand was the painting of the whole of this great ceiling, which is about thirty feet from the ground. Sixteen men at various intervals were already up on the platforms and beginning to wave a kind of big flat brush, which from my angle looked about as wide as the tail of a whale. I had to come back that night to my office to catch the midnight news. There was not a man in sight, nor a paintbrush, nor any tarpaulin or scaffolding. The night cleaners were already busy with their monster vacuum cleaners. And the ceiling was gleaming with its new paint.

This kind of shock greets the stranger wherever he goes. You have your house painted, or a wall knocked down, or new lighting sockets put in. And I should warn any incurable English perfectionist that half the time you will get a finished job something less than what would satisfy a first-rate craftsman. But this is neither their aim nor their interest. They do what they contract to do with remarkable speed and skill. Then they clean up your disordered home in a final cheerful burst and are on their way back to their wives, their shower-bath, their steak and television sets. These men get paid better than any working-men have ever been paid, allowing for the exchange, the higher cost of living, and all that. The painters I just told you about were earning a $130 a week—£46 10s.— which will take care of quite a lot of high cost of living. (I ought to add, though, that they pay just about the same, £46 10s., one week's wages, for the monthly rent of a small house.) If they work this way, they will keep their job. If they don't, they won't: that is the simple, brutal rule of life in America in prosperous times.

You can see how hard it is to start from scratch in this country, which already has a labour force of over sixty millions, and the fiercest kind of competition at all levels, from the labourer to the managing director. It sounds like a nightmare, and it may well be so to gentle, sensitive people who have no sympathy with the fight for life and merely want to earn enough money to give them leisure in their evenings, some fields to walk across, a little light and air. In the big cities of America these things too come at a high price. I sometimes feel that the house agents and real-estate men in all the big cities have measured every building and gauged exactly how many cubic inches of every little room are touched by sunlight for a few hours of the day. That room, once the estate agents discover its secret, will have its rent doubled. Several million middle-class families in the cities of England have a little back garden which they could reproduce in New York for a mere £5,000.

It is hard for the romantic Englishman or woman to talk to Americans about these anxieties. Apart from seeming a chronic complainer, you will also tend to sound to Americans like a kind of immigrant they were long ago warned about. Washington Irving was on to this type too and wrote of them: 'they may have pictured America to themselves an El Dorado, where gold and silver abounded, and the natives were lacking in sagacity; and where they were to become strangely and suddenly rich in some unforeseen, but easy manner'.

Well, that sort of character will be around for quite a time yet, but he grows increasingly peevish. It may be that present-day America, or rather the movie and magazine myths about it, attracts a semi-playboy type that is too soft to take the known risks of a hundred years ago. Unfortunately, the austerity and anxiety of Europe produce, too, many unassuming and honest people who are looking for nothing more than a competence and a little peace and quiet. To the newcomer there is no easy guarantee of it. Sons of wealth can have it without any effort, for this country now has the biggest class of hereditary rich of any nation on earth. But for the newcomer there will be little concern about how he lived or what he was used to, or the kind of people he moved among. If he wants the same society in America, he must buy his way into it. Not what you seem to be, but what you prove you can do: that is still, for the stranger, the persistent pioneer requirement. You have been warned.

The 1950s

The Summer Bachelor

16 June 1950

An American telephoned me the other day to ask me what was meant by 'flannelled fools'. I had to explain to him that in Britain the summer game is played in flannels. He jumped, wrongly, to the conclusion that boxing was the British summer pastime and that everybody got fitted out for it in long skiing underwear. I introduced him gently to some of the mysteries of cricket, not the least of which is why grown men stand around for most of the day doing nothing at all in temperatures of 50 degrees. I tried to keep my exposition to simple words, but when you are talking about transatlantic weather the simplest words are the most deceiving. I remember once picking up the Paris edition of the New York *Herald Tribune* and looking up to the left-hand corner of the front page to see how the people were faring in the Manhattan midsummer. It prints the weather report of London, Paris and New York, and the newspaper naturally has to take on trust the language of the weather bureau of origin. It said, 'London, fair, 71 degrees, continued hot; Paris, 78, warm; New York, clear, high 83, seasonably cool.'

This could serve as a text for the British export drive, which falters always on the presumption that an American means the same thing as an Englishman when he talks of a 'light suit'. In Britain, it appears to mean light in colour. Here it means light-weight. If this is understood, the golden rule for the textile exporter will then be clear: it is to coax the American buyer into purchasing large quantities of the raw material in Britain—as sheep, if you like—and then let him use it and cut it according to his habits and his needs. For British clothes in America will make a man feel uncomfortable outdoors in summer and indoors in winter. It is possible for a North European to feel at home here any time up to Christmas. He could keep his old habits and his regular suits and feel he was still in a temperate climate. The New Year transports him to the pole, and in a temperature of one above (above zero, that is) the word 'cold' will take on a sharper meaning for a Londoner, say, who has never in his or his forebears' lifetime known anything colder than 9 degrees. Summer here is, however, the bigger problem for the Briton. He is rightly aware that New York is named after old York but he goes on to the fatal assumption that the trip from one to the other involves a direct east-to-west passage of three thousand miles. What he rarely knows is that he has also gone eight hundred miles south, that old York is located on a level with the tundra of Labrador, whereas New York is at the precise latitude of Corfu.

This clash between the romantic legend of our sameness and the facts of life is what sparks the Englishman's shock. He discovers that the changeover from winter to summer life is brutally abrupt, and that to adjust to the violent swing of the thermometer he has to acquire habits more suited to a fieldhand in a banana republic than to the gentle vagaries of a London heatwave. (I recall another London headline: '75 Again Today! No Relief in Sight.') He will discover that New York is more of a summer furnace than a summer festival. He will learn that it has created unfamiliar local institutions. He will soon hear about the summer bachelor, the forgotten man of American folklore.

To appreciate the pathos and charm of the summer bachelor, you have to learn the stages by which a normally jogging and contented husband becomes one. Last week, then, the family took off for our summer house at the end of Long Island. (This is a custom not restricted to what used to be called the upper-middle class. The continental mainland of the United States sweats abominably from May to October and any humane husband who is not fettered to the marriage bed will rent a shack anywhere in the mountains, by a lake or a seashore, as far as possible from Chicago, St Louis, Pittsburgh or a score of other infernos.) The induction into summer bachelorhood is almost as violent as the season that causes it. One day you are living in a normal house or apartment, with carpets, grocery deliveries, timed meals, friends and everything; and the next you'd think the Russians were coming. Your wife is out of bed like a rocket. She beats around the house like a beaver. 'Excuse me,' she says, as I am in the middle of a shrewd sentence on the typewriter, and up comes the carpet. Up come all the carpets. At 10 a.m. the kitchen doorbell buzzes and a huge man in an apron clomps in and, with the aid of three helpers, lugs the carpets away to be stored.

There is a clatter of china in the kitchen. All the civilized eating utensils are going into boxes and cocoons of tissue paper. My wife breaks in again and lifts a warning finger. She indicates one shelf and one drawer. 'There you are,' she says. For the

69

next three months or more I am to use two cracked kitchen plates, a chipped saucer, drink my coffee out of a premature Coronation mug (Edward VIII) and stir it with a spoon bought fifty years ago by her mother, a relentless Southerner. It looks like a petrified alligator, and that is what it's meant to look like. It says on it, 'A present from Jacksonville, Florida'.

Now there is a noise not unlike the furious exhaust that sets in at the tenser moments of science-horror movies ('The radio-isotope, Fleming, throw the safety rod, man!'). It is a team of vacuum cleaners. I stumble into the living room, for it is in darkness. The curtains have come down and four shades have gone up, two white ones on the outside, two green ones inside. The nifty satin upholstery on the sofa is obscured by a dingy slipcover. So are all the upholstered chairs. The lamps are swathed in bedsheets, giving them the appearance of Arab sentinels. A screen is being pulled across the open entrance to the living room, and my wife gives the annual order: 'Stay out of here, remember!' (I have no theories about American wives. They are, so far as I'm concerned, wives.) A mountain of laundry is piling up in the hall. There is a tearing sound coming from the clothes closets—the winter clothes are being entombed in plastic hangers and all the clothes give off a characteristic smell. It used to be mothballs. You used to hear them rattle around in the night. Now they tinkle, for they roll up and down small perforated tins with hooks on them that hang on the racks. The closets are squirted with some noxious chemical, and the ones that contain the winter suits are dynamited with bombs of DDT.

This may all sound very drastic. Alas, our insidious summer enemy is a beast unknown to a true temperate climate—the buffalo moth—and if you ignore him, you are apt to confront an interesting wardrobe in the fall, of garments that might have served as targets on a rifle range.

So now, the blankets are entombed, the sheets changed, rooms closed off, refrigerator defrosted and denuded of food (it looks neater that way, to my wife at least, when she returns in October). I am permitted to run the refrigerator sometime later and it will soon contain tins of beer, a mouldy tomato, a box of crackers, and some limes and lemons. Just before the family leaves, she issues the battle orders for the summer campaign: 'Always put the garbage out before you go to bed, never start on a new bottle of milk before you've finished the old one. Never go out and leave the windows open. Keep the shades drawn in the living room. Right?' Very good, General, and goodbye.

The winter cycle is completed the summers that the children go to camp. There is a special fuss to be made with duffel bags and blankets and swimming shorts and two blankets and name tapes. And you all go off to Grand Central Station and align your brood with one of the many regiments of children lined up and waiting for the call to their track and their train. And again you hear one of the most powerful folk songs of America. A stationmaster stands by a large board and he looks at a card in his hand that lists all the names of the camps and the platforms of their outgoing trains. Nine-thirty strikes. And he warms up his baritone and chants: 'Indian Summer—track nineteen. Shining Mountain—seventeen. Pine Grove—

71

twenty-one. Camp Wawokeewe—nine. High Wind—fifteen. Meadow Lark—eighteen. Thunderbolt—twenty-nine.'

It is over. They are gone. You leap to a telephone and locate another displaced person. You bathe and shave and hear yourself singing forgotten songs of liberation. This first evening is unusually high-spirited. The drinks flow free and so does the coarse interchange of remarks about family life. You decide that your companion is a fine man you have tended to underestimate. Then you go home and recall with a start that you are on your own again. You hear your shoes crackle on the dust of the desert that is the long, dark hall. You peek into the living room and switch on a light. The standing lamp by the switch is a dim figure indeed. Its shade has been wrapped around with a fez of crinkly white paper, and it stands there like Lawrence of Arabia in ambush. You duck out and into the bedroom. The silence is chilling. You get a beer and read a little, or stay up and watch the late show, and then the late late show. At three you turn in, and at eight you feel terrible. Each weekend, you suffer the troop trains of the New Haven or Long Island Railroad and limp raggedly into the bosom of your family. On Monday it starts again.

At this point a suspicion will have crossed your mind that has certainly crossed the mind of the summer bachelor. Indeed, George Axelrod made a play about it and called it *The Seven Year Itch*. The title itself suggests a clinical thesis and we will leave it with its author. For most men it does not take seven years to recall that New York contains, among its martyred and lonely millions, an old girlfriend, or some agreeable but impeccable social worker, or some other honest female whose devotion to her work denies her the blissful exile your wife is now embarked on. Peter Arno captured and immortalized this suspicion—of yours—in a cartoon that showed a portly gent, one of those waggish Blimps with the spotted bow tie, marching smartly down Park Avenue with a very trim young woman on his arm. Coming up the avenue, and just level with him, is a majestic matron of about his age. 'Why, George Fitzgerald,' she cries, 'what*ever* keeps you in town?'

I will not blemish a family programme with any other comment than the thought that one of the most profound of all American idioms is that priceless old catchphrase: 'I love my wife but oh you kid.' I bring up this touchy subject because an accident of technology is, I think, about to produce a sociological revolution in the United States. And I know that you expect me to keep you up with sociological revolutions. The cause of this one is the air conditioner. In the old summer days, the summer bachelor went at weekends from the oven of his apartment to undressed days and what he thought of as cool nights. Now he leaves the ice-cool paradise of his apartment for the hot days and the dank nights and the midges and bugs of the country.

Two days ago, a Wednesday, I pressed the elevator button of my apartment house and as the door slid back it revealed the capacious frame of a neighbour of mine from the twelfth floor. He is a retired old gentleman, a notable fisherman and a solid but saucy character. I asked him what kept *him* in town in mid-week. 'Are you kidding?' he said. 'It's like the basin of the Ganges out there. I retreated to this wonderful apartment. And you know what? My wife showed up this morning. God damn!'

'If this goes on,' I said, 'it's going to play the devil with fishing.'

'Fishing nothing,' he said. 'It's going to play hell with marriage.'

It's a Democracy, Isn't It?

15 June 1951

I was standing on the corner of Lexington Avenue on a Sunday in May waiting for a bus. It was a gorgeous day, hot and golden, and there were not many people around. Sunday is more than a bearable day in New York because for one thing there are about a million less cars than usual. No trucks. Suburbanites in for the day pointing up and down and walking with their feet out. A couple of cabs parked outside a lunch-room, the drivers gone for a beer. A family or two hand in hand, taking the children off to the park. A well-dressed upper-crust couple coming across from Park Avenue also hand in hand—a very common sight in New York, for Americans are not much concerned in such matters with what looks proper or what the neighbours will think. A good day—the sort of day when, for all the panicky newspaper headlines, your faith in people, and their needs and inclinations, is restored.

Suddenly, I heard a ghost. It was a familiar ghost, an invisible man somewhere in mid-air saying in a brisk monotone—'Strike. The count is two and two. Runners on first and third.' This lingo, or the language of which this is a snatch, is something you would hear in a hundred places—homes, cafés, saloons, cars—from then till the end of the first week in October. It is a radio sports announcer covering a ball game—a ball game being, as you probably know, a baseball game.

The voice was coming from nowhere. A young Negro couple, arm in arm, was ambling towards me. But the man's free arm carried a little box. Of course, it was a portable radio. They went down the subway steps, and as they pattered down into the darkness the voice went on floating up, more excited now: 'A base hit to left field. Fuselli's in, Rodgers coming into third.' Nobody else on the street seemed to notice or to care. But if you had cared, and wanted for one day to get away from radio, I don't know where you could have gone. Out at Coney Island, thousands of bodies would be lying in close proximity not only to thousands of other bodies but to hundreds of other little boxes, tuned high. And the air would be so full of 'He's out' and 'The bases are loaded' and 'Full count', that you'd have had quite a time knowing what the wild waves were saying.

This little picture is meant to produce a shudder in you. If it doesn't, then Britons are not what they used to be, and their passion for privacy, and what's more for respecting the next man's privacy, is dead and gone. Don't misunderstand me. I approve myself very strongly of this feeling. I share it. But it makes me all the less of an American. Only a week ago, I heard a plonking sound, allied to music, quite faint, coming up through the living room

75

floor. It was a neighbour in our apartment house who is either 6 years of age and a promising pianist or 40 years of age and a dope . . . because she—why do I say 'she', I wonder?—has been stuck on that same piece for a month or two now. I grumbled about the sameness of her repertory, and my 12-year-old daughter, idling over a book, said, 'Relax, Pop, you don't have to hear it if you don't want to.'

By this simple remark my daughter didn't mean that I could get up and go downstairs and start a riot, or that I could call the police or take out an injunction. She simply meant I should shut my mind to the sound. I made sure this is what she meant, because when I played aloud with the idea of strangling our tinkling neighbour, she said, 'I don't think that's very nice. She paid *her* rent too, you know.'

Now, I should like to say that I am proud of my daughter and usually turn to her for a response that is commonsensical and unshocked (by, so far as I can make out, anything in life). But I wasn't aware she had acquired so young a fundamental mood or attitude of what Americans call democracy. In Britain, one of the minor duties of good citizenship is not to disturb the private life of other citizens. In this country, it's the other way around—not to disturb other citizens who are enjoying their private life in public. That, as you see, is a heavily loaded interpretation of an attitude that is universal among Americans. And there are limits. Just the same, the decision of a Washington court of appeal not to let advertisers broadcast in public buses only shows how far you can go in America without being stopped.

Americans regard most of us born in Britain as

dull, decent, amiable people but given to being rather testy about our rights. So 'Relax, Pop,' says my daughter and goes back to reading her book with one third of her mind, listening to the pianist downstairs with another lobe, and at the same time dreaming on all cylinders about some absent male of the species. Quite aside from the principle involved, this attitude entails a considerable physical feat. It is the ability not to hear what you don't want to hear, what the most famous radio critic in America calls 'selective deafness'. He says it is a faculty essential to an enjoyment of American radio, and it is a faculty that most visiting Britons would rather not develop. Because they soon learn, as Mr Crosby—John, not Bing— remarks, that the advertising people are aware of this conditioned reflex and so from year to year, like drug addicts, they increase the dose of the sales talk they cut into the programmes. Still, nobody hearing his favourite comedian or forum discussion or symphony concert bothers to turn off the 'plug'. He lets it chatter on about some soap that 'atomizes dirt' or a toothpaste that is 'kind to gums but murder on film'. And then, the ecstatic announcer stops, and so back to Bob Hope or 'Whither Europe?' or the Second Symphony of Beethoven.

To watch an American on a beach, or crowding into a subway, or buying a theatre ticket, or sitting at home with his radio on, tells you something about one aspect of the American character: the capacity to withstand a great deal of outside interference, so to speak; a willing acceptance of frenzy which, though it's never self-conscious, amounts to a willingness to let other people have and assert their own lively, and even offensive, character. They are a tough race in this. You are expected—far beyond what other peoples would say were the restraints of manners—to assume that one man's opinion is as good as another's. The expert is an American idol, but only in certain understood fields. He is safe from contradiction if his expertness is in a science—in medicine, technology, industrial research, or in making something with his hands (better, if he uses somebody else's hands, because that shows he has mastered a process which can be left to drones): such things as an automobile, a waterproof watch or a non-riding girdle. But when it comes to ideas about life and love and religion and education and architecture and painting and music, indeed all forms of pleasure, there is a national conviction that an expert is a phoney, or 'wants to be different', and that what matters is you should know what you like and—this is a democracy, isn't it?—speak up and say your piece. It may well be born from generations of living close to many races and many prejudices and temperaments and having to strike a liveable compromise that may not be as smooth as some other societies; but at least it is a society, a going concern, which had to be built not out of a theory but out of the urgent practical need to get along at all.

At any rate, if you want to live here in any spiritual comfort you have to allow for a wide variety of temperament in your friends and neighbours and approve a sharp clash of tastes. An insistence on privacy in such a society looks, as it would not look in Britain, like a form of conceit or neurosis, a refusal to admit the status quo by which you all live. So if the issue ever came up in argument, I think most Americans would say that it is merely elementary good manners and good citizenship to look on yourself as only one member of the community, whether that community is a town, a party, or a family.

It may be what makes Americans so easygoing about their children. I don't know if anyone has ever taken a statistical count, and there may be just as many nagging parents here as anywhere else, but my impression is that if you are what they used to call a severe disciplinarian with children, you get known to the neighbours as a crank. There is a sort of cheerful, unstated assumption that children will grow up and be polite soon enough and that there's no sense for the first fifteen years or so in pretending they are anything but inhabitants of the jungle. (There is a certain family pride in seeing your child become king or queen of the jungle.) The children themselves are of course not aware of being particularly bad or violent or ill-mannered. They have no other system to compare themselves with, and like all children don't even know that any other system exists. Remembering this, you can appreciate that if a 6- or a 10- or a 15-year-old passes you on the street, looks up and says, 'Hi!' he is paying you far more the respect of genuine liking than if he said, 'Good morning, sir'—which would be a very alien, not to say sarcastic, sound in these parts.

The same sort of tolerance explains too, I think, such a seemingly irrelevant thing as the variety of men's clothes in a big city. There is not among Americans anything remotely resembling the uniform of the English city businessman. They dress for themselves, with their own tastes in ties, shirts, shoes; and this gives to an American street a colour, often a garishness, and it makes it pretty impossible for a foreigner to guess at the occupation of the other men around. With women, it is even more difficult. A flock of girls comes into a restaurant and you can't tell the debutante from the shop girl. I remember a Swedish girl on a skiing party watching the swirl of people in the snow and saying, 'Which are the nice people? Who are my kind? Give me a sign.' There are signs. But they are small and subtle and would take her years to learn. And if she stayed here long, she would insensibly shed the signs she sought.

I was taking an Englishman the other night up to my apartment, and as we approached the entrance of the apartment house, I saw a man who lives in the building polishing the radiator of his car. I hissed to call my friend's attention to him as we came close. 'Tell me quick,' I said, 'what sort of an American is this—I mean is he a banker, a real-estate agent, a baseball player or what?—look him over.' My friend leered politely at him sideways. He was a middle-aged dark man, with a black moustache and big eyes. He was hatless. He had on a blue sports coat, slacks of a different colour, a button-down collar and a bright tie. He was polishing away and coughing smoke all over the radiator. Then he bent down to start on the wheels. Standing genially over him was the janitor, saying the utterly meaningless sentence, as we came on it: 'No, sir, not for my money . . . but some guys are that crazy, I reckon.' When we got inside I looked at my friend.

'Oh, I don't know,' he said, 'I should say an

advertising man or perhaps the owner of a chain of drugstores.'

'That,' I said, as we went into the lift, 'is a dethroned Archduke.'

He was dethroned by the bullet that shot his great-uncle and started the First World War.

The European's America

23 October 1952

It is the fall. The fall of the year, an American institution now so well known, and even respected, in Europe that you no doubt expect me to take off, as I annually do, about the scarlet maples pouring like a fire through New England, the brilliant light everywhere, the thin milky trails of woodsmoke that rise into a bottomless blue sky. Well, once you've created a stereotype it is time to demolish it. The fall has refinements, even perils, that the autumn in other countries does not share. Once you've learned the big clichés of a country, which are true and which are not, it is the off-beat clichés that really fix the place in your mind, and make it like no other, and may even endear it to you, years later in another country far away. Let me illustrate.

The other morning, just after breakfast, a lady by the name of Miss Frieda Sims was going her rounds on the twenty-seventh floor of a New York hotel. Miss Sims is a floor supervisor and she was looking to see which rooms were vacant, which ones the maids could get into to clean up, which rooms needed to have the breakfast tables removed. She unlocked room number 2752, peeked in and saw the happy disorder of breakfast dishes. She went in to wheel the table out, but she came out in a hurry with no table, and she was screaming.

This sounds like the beginning of one of those classic American crimes, like Miss Lizzie Borden going into the kitchen on a very hot morning to get a cup of coffee. And it goes on promisingly enough, because the next incident involves the hotel's security force, which came running and verified Miss Sims's report. She had stopped screaming by now and she was able to stammer out that there was somebody in there. It wasn't a guest, not like any guest she had ever seen. It was an owl, just a common or garden American barn owl (*Strix flammea* to the initiated), which looks rather like an African wood carving or the top of a totem pole. It seems the owl was just cruising by the hotel at a twenty-seven-storey altitude (there's the New York touch), saw the open window, glanced in at the breakfast dishes and decided to make a landing on the remains of a melon and a couple of shirred eggs. The commissars of the security force (what, before the iron curtain, we just used to call house dicks) evidently made the bird secure. They threw a blanket over it. Then they telephoned the SPCA, which seems a contradictory thing to do, since they were busy smothering the owl. However, a Mr Norton soon came up from the Society with his equipment, a pair of thick gloves; for you should know that the American barn owl has a four-foot wingspread, a curved beak, and what the New York *Herald Tribune* (which gets its reporters into the damnedest places) described with relish as 'razor-

82

sharp talons'.

Mr Norton put his gloves on, embraced the owl with professional tenderness, took it off into the park and set it free. This fugitive from the world of freedom got tangled up in twentieth-century civilization, but within half an hour a man put his hand in the air and the bird flew away in one swoop back to the primitive world from which we all originally came. There is a technical snag to this fable. An eye surgeon tells me that no owl, however wise, could look into a hotel room after breakfast. The owl, it seems, is a kind of hotel dick in its own right and can look into hotel rooms only at night. I see that Audubon noted this over a hundred years ago. 'Owls', he wrote, 'seem to us a dull and stupid race, principally because we only notice them during the day, which nature requires them to spend in sleep, the structure of their eyes compelling them to avoid the light and seek concealment in hollow trees, in caves and obscure retreats.'

What started out as a children's story, then, full of sweetness and light, is in fact a near-tragedy. This bird was lost and plunging through a blinding world of light and saw a barn, an obscure retreat, which turned out—pitifully—to be Room 2752 of a New York skyscraper.

This is the kind of story that could only happen in the fall. There is, indeed, a special anxiety that overtakes bird-lovers then, when the great migrations to the South begin. Many fine species have not yet heard about the invention of the skyscraper, and some ordinary birds are even wildly attracted to it. The starlings, for instance. It is a happy fall during which flocks of starlings don't smash into the Empire State Building, which is four times the height of the tallest California redwood and higher than any building anywhere, even—I'm afraid—in the Soviet Union. (When the jet aeroplane came in, there was a more perilous hazard from the starlings. In several crashes, it came out that they had been sucked into the engines.) These accidents have a poignant appeal to anyone who, in the fall, has to work in a city and who knows that beyond the city limits lies a world crammed with colour and beauty and old habits that unfortunately play no part in the European picture of that detested 'American way of life'.

The day before the barn owl flew into the hotel, I was reading a piece in an American magazine by Mr Cyril Connolly, a writer with whom I feel a strong sympathy and never more than in this piece, which was about the widespread Americanizing of Europe. What are those influences which many Europeans think of as all America has to offer, and which they wish had stayed on this side of the Atlantic? Connolly lists them: 'jazz, gangster stories, bad films, tales of violence, science fiction'. I could add some others, especially the compulsion to break up the relics of London as an eighteenth-century country town and riddle them with chromium-plated fronts and dingy 'American' snack bars and amusement arcades and the tattiest attempts at modern 'American' architecture. Not to mention the Cockney's surrender to what he imagines is American slang, the frantic imitation bebop, the transatlantic zoot-suiter. The point is that these influences, picked up I suppose from the movies, are almost always bad imitations of crummy originals. What is alarming, and what the

European seems unaware of, is that they are often planted firmly in a solid English background, in the sort of place they would not be found in the American background. They do not have chrome cocktail bars along the noble stretch of North Street, in Litchfield, Connecticut, or snack bars at the bottom of Zion Canyon. Along the new motor parkways of New York and New England they do not even allow the petrol companies to build their own pumps. The stations, like the overpasses, must conform to a design sanctioned by the commissioner of parks or highways and be made of the local stone. And the fences that bind the parkways are the same for a hundred miles or more and are made from a pine that fits the landscape. It is an unexpected and admirable thing about the development of the automobile age in America that Americans have developed a sense of style as watchful as that of the men who gave us the urban style of eighteenth-century London and the country style of eighteenth-century New England. (The billboard lobby and the freeways are now doing their damnedest to date this compliment.)

I sometimes think that a European deploring the horror of Pittsburgh and Detroit and St Louis and 'your Midwest cities' is not really criticizing the Midwest or American cities but the nineteenth-century city anywhere. But it is also a fact that though American towns may, and do, seethe with the random horrors that are now so faithfully transplanted to British towns, it is almost easier over here to get away from them. My European visitors are always surprised to discover how much virgin forest there appears to be on the edge of town. Theoretically, there are only two big stands of the forest primeval in this country, one in the Cascade Mountains and the other in the Bitterroots, both far out on the northwest Pacific Coast. But I'm thinking of long-settled country. I have taken Englishmen in a car fifteen minutes from where I am talking to you and once beyond the George Washington Bridge they are weaving around great rocks and little woods as dense as the New Forest. A half-hour from Times Square (all right, then, two hours in the rush hour) they can be in something that looks like Fenimore Cooper country, and it is not hard to imagine on dark nights an Indian slipping through the trees, slinking across the six-lane divided highway and standing as aghast at the lights of Manhattan as I am when I see what the 'developers' have done to Regency Mayfair.

For nearly two centuries now, there has been a continuous argument, sometimes amiable sometimes bloodthirsty, about which country was influencing the other the most. Until about fifty years ago, the example was all one way, and the way was east to west. But it has been changing very fast. Every world power leaves indelible imprints even on countries that pretend to hate it. And as Europe comes to admit, which it soon will have to, that the United States is now the ranking world power, its customs and gadgets and manners and literature and ways of doing business will powerfully influence the young. They may reject it later on, as Europe pulls itself around and asserts again, as I don't doubt it will want to, its own pride and independence.

But in the meantime, Britain still retains an advantage which will not pass over to America, I think, for a long time to come. It is this: Americans who have not been in Europe tend to imagine what is best about her, Europeans who have not been in America tend to imagine what is worst. Ask a few simple Americans what Britain means—ask a schoolgirl, a farmer, a shopkeeper, an elevator man (I have just tried it) what comes to mind when you say 'Britain'—and they will say something like: 'Oh, old buildings, more easygoing than us, I guess, beautiful countryside, tea in the afternoon, Shakespeare'; and, as my elevator man added, 'And I understand they are very dignified, very strict, they tell me, in their law courts.'

This may sound very naive to you. But it picks up a flattering myth and not, like the other way around, a libellous one. My own daughter, 14 years old, swings violently between wanting to go to England and being afraid to. Why does she want to go? Because she imagines the place peopled with Mr Pickwick and Romeo and Juliet and Robin Hood, not to mention Laurence Olivier; and because she is crazy about the tables that Sheraton designed and the chairs and desks of Hepplewhite and imagines that every little house in England would throw out anything less graceful. She has, indeed, heard rude things about the cooking. But I tell her that this is steadily improving. I tell her also that it is true about the parklike countryside and the fat cattle, and the sheep as big as buffaloes in Scotland, and it is due as much as anything to the fact that the grass pack of English dairyland is five times as dense as the proud grass pack of Iowa. She thinks the English countryside must be heaven. (By the way, she takes entirely for granted the stupendous beauty of the Tetons and the desert and Yosemite, which leave Englishmen feeling that they have come face to face with their Maker.)

And why *doesn't* she want to go to England? Well, she explains, wriggling nervously, 'Everyone would expect me to be on my best behaviour, they are so polite and—everything.'

This is quite a reputation the British have built up. And the other tourist countries of Europe are not far behind. We read here about the exquisite care the French take over their food, and the dedicated way they tread on their grapes, and the devotion they bring to their public buildings. We do not hear about the really garish modern housing that begins to sprout in the Parisian suburbs, or about the alarming incapacity of the French for self-government. We read about the ruthlessness of the Mafia as it goes about its business in New York or New Orleans but not about its stranglehold on the enslaved slum of Sicily. From Italy we read rather about the preciousness of a new Roman 'find' in Tuscany or about the charm of the Appian Way, not about the clutter of billboards that disfigures it.

It will surely be a great day when you ask an Englishman what comes to mind at the mention of the word 'America' and he replies: 'The white villages of New England and the eighteenth-century houses, the neighbourly warmth of the Midwesterners, the contributions of American scholarship, the buffet meals that young American housewives whip up, the style and colour of so many American homes, the outdoor life of California, the god-given glory of Bryce Canyon and the man-made marvel of Hoover Dam.'

Getting Away from It All

11 September 1953

The real end of the American year is not 31 December, but the old festival of Labor Day. It is the day when the summer is put away, the swimming trunks squeezed for the last time, the ashtrays in country cottages filled with mouse-seed and rat-paste, the storm-doors hammered into place, the lock turned for the last time on your private world of sun and sand and picnics and the pride of growing children. Labor Day brings you back to the world of schools and offices, to sniffling colds and insurance policies, to taxes and radio commentators, to dark nights and the dark horizon of politics.

We sat around for the last time in our cottage at the end of Long Island. We had brought in the furniture from off the porch and the rusty barbecue grill we haven't used in four years but always put out in the sun at the beginning of summer as a symbol of our pioneer instincts. We had phoned the electric company to turn off the current. Called the phone company to disconnect same. Left a note for the garbage-man, same for the milkman. What else has to be done? Defrost and clean the refrigerator. Draw the curtains across the windows on the east and west sides. Sprinkle moth-flakes on the rugs. Try to hide a smelly fishing rod in a dark closet, and fail—your wife coming at you saying, 'Could this be bait?' It is. It is a poor, dried-up piece of squid that was chewed on by a whole school of porgies and sucked dry.

We sit around finishing a last bite. The baby is snoring placidly in a house reeking of camphor and good old mouse-paste. We bury and burn the last load of garbage. We pack the car while we wait for the baby to wake. Some of the grasses on the dunes have started to turn the fall colours. So children who normally treat them as considerately as bulldozers now develop a collector's passion for bayberry and pine branches and feather-grass. Somebody sees a gramophone record worn so grey you'd think it had been played with a poker. It is 'Good Night, Irene', and it too is suddenly an object of tenderness. We finally leave, with the rear end of the borrowed station wagon looking like an army camouflage squad, bushes and plants and a bedstead growing out of each side of 'Good Night, Irene'. We are on our way.

We stop and say goodbye to Mrs Horton, who sells eggs and collects antiques and whose family has farmed the same plot since 1649—not so hot, perhaps, to a European, but impressive to us. We wish a good winter to the Ryskos, who sell groceries; to Grathwohl, the builder and sometime carpenter; to the Doroski brothers, who run a gas and service station; to Josie Wanowski, the little bent old toothless Polish woman who has taken in washing these many years and for many of them kept a crippled husband, and who raised four astonishingly handsome children, two straight beautiful girls with shining teeth, who might be movie starlets but are in fact a nurse and a schoolteacher; two boys, one in college, one ex-army air forces.

It is much the same as any other leave-taking in

the fall. But there is an ominous note or two. The bank manager is off to Riverhead: there is a meeting of the new civil defence evacuation committee—a committee, that is, to plan the evacuation of doomed New Yorkers to the potato-fields of Long Island. A young man who came out of the Navy four years ago, who chose to be a potato-farmer the year of the big drought and went into debt for $2,000, is not around any more. His troubles were all scattered by a letter one morning from the President of the United States, beginning—'Greetings!'—a cordial invitation to come back into the service, or else. Eddie, the boy who drives the grocer's delivery truck, says 'Well, I'd better say goodbye', in a strange, shy way. He too has had his call.

These little things give you a shock, and you wonder about them on the way up to the city. Everything looks like the familiar fall, the maples turning, a milky stream of smoke from burning leaves curling up into a blue, bottomless sky. But as the swift twilight comes on we are at the end of the parkway, past La Guardia Field, over the Triboro Bridge, and there are the vertical city and the plunging spires: New York again, splendid as ever in the autumn light. Not quite the same, though. We curve round and down off the bridge and pass a billboard advertising a new de luxe apartment building somewhere. The big sign has stars against the features it is specially proud of: thermostat heat control in each flat; all-electric kitchen, with deep freeze, laundry and dish-washing machines, and garbage-disposal unit; air-conditioned units available in summer; two bathrooms for every four rooms. The last item, the last star, says: 'Adequate sub-basement atomic bomb-shelter'. One of the children reads it aloud, and it makes a pompous sound, so that the baby claps her hands and chortles like a wise old man. And we all laugh.

*   *   *

Back in the city, people with copper tans who ought to be congratulating themselves on being able in the first place to get away from the New York summer, began in recent years to find themselves fingering the real-estate sections of the Sunday papers and peering through advertisements for 'desirable country houses'. Why should lucky and comfortable people be so fretful and restless for more idleness? It was not idleness such people sought but a more dreadful thing: safety. Lately the phrase 'getting away from it all' has taken on a sadder and more furtive meaning in the minds of parents who live in industrial cities. It needs no winks or meaningful glances to arouse a fear that everybody feels and a few talk openly about. It is the padding fear of the atom bomb.

I heard of a man who lives in Washington who had quit his job, fallen back on his savings, bought a little place deep in the hills of Arkansas and gone off there to farm with his wife and five children. Far off in the Black Hills of South Dakota, some pessimist as thoughtful as Noah has bought a mountain cave and invited prudent couples—one male, one female—to abandon their regular lives and batten down underground at an annual cost of $2,500 per person, all found. This may appear to be the furthest pole of lunacy. But during the San Francisco organizing conference of the United

Nations, the citizens of the Black Hills, bidding for a lasting fame as the chosen headquarters of the United Nations, challenged the delegations with maps (Dakotas projection) to find a spot anywhere in the United States more swiftly accessible by air to Moscow, Cairo, Tokyo or London. Maybe this pessimist was acting from the same melancholy discovery.

Then in the late 1940s businessmen caught the epidemic. Businessmen, I should say, who have factories in the East, in the ring of cities round the southern rim of the Great Lakes, or out on the Coast. An aircraft company in Bridgeport, Connecticut, announced it had decided to move bag and baggage to Dallas, Texas. Now, this is quite an undertaking. The company worked on 1.5 million square feet. Its factory cost $10 million. It employed about ten thousand people. The company invited its skilled workers to go with it. As an American migration, this one would not be without its epic and humorous side. Bridgeport is a typical New England industrial city, except for the untypical fact that it has a socialist government. Its workers are mostly of Italian and Czech, Hungarian and Polish stock. They are used to cold winters and New England ways. It would be quite a sight to see them in West Texas, mimicking the Texas accent, being baffled by the Mexican foods, wondering when the hot dry winds of spring and the steaming misery of summer would ever end in—as the song says—'that Texas town that never seen ice or snow'. For a few excitable weeks, the unskilled men had a happy time joshing their superior brothers who had signed up to go. They bandied around the nicknames Sagebrush, and

Tex, and 'Hi, there, Dallas!' Jokers appeared in ten-gallon hats and called a work-gang 'you-all'. But however gay the workers felt, the company's announcement caused a nasty jolt to other defence industries along the East Coast. Any company that would make a move as dramatic and costly as that must, they figured, have 'heard something'. The Defense Department was rattled by telephone enquiries verging between anxiety and hysteria. The callers were told in as non-committal a way as possible that there was no 'immediate' plan to go underground, to move industrial cities, to decentralize the basic industries that surround the Great Lakes. It was made officially plain that the Bridgeport company had made up its own mind and the National Security Resources Board had given its nod. The company's work had to do with testing jet-planes, and the directors had decided that the congested seaboard was a poor place to accommodate, without an expensive new airport, the special and alarming habits of jets. The Texas central plain is—if Texans will pardon the expression—flatter than Kansas. It seemed just right. But many industries, big and little, leaped to the conclusion which they dread and which—by the peculiar chemistry of deep fear—they half-hope to have fulfilled.

The telling point about the Bridgeport story is, I think, the current emotional disposition to believe the worst. The atomic age offers us the raw material of a civilization larger, more efficient and more humane than any that has gone before. But this promise and this challenge are lost sight of in the energy that goes and must go into making weapons of war. This energy has the real excuse

94

that never before in history have free men faced the threat of a tyranny so large, so merciless and so painstaking as that with which the Soviet Union confronts us. Dangling between these two unique worlds—a world of unequalled slavery and a world of incomparable riches—we build the storm-cellars and hope for the best.

Most men find the problems of political power insoluble and tend to despair before a world that has shrunk in scale and enlarged in complexity, so that the knowledge of how it behaves seems more and more to be open only to the specialist. There never was a time, except perhaps in the fearful pestilences of the Middle Ages, when men hungered more for a decent private life, and when they are tempted to match in their joys the intensity of the sorrows all around them. I believe that this impulse, far from being an escape, is the only right way of asserting that human dignity which gives sense to the phrase 'an appetite for life'. What reasonable hope can an ordinary man have for himself and his family? Must we oscillate like crocodiles between panic and apathy? What more adult way is there of coming to terms with the alternatives of the atomic age?

I should like to have the wisdom and the knowledge to suggest something at once practical and noble. But all I can think of is an incident from the American past that comes nearer to home every day and seems to me as sensible as anything written since Hiroshima.

The time was 19 May 1780. The place was Hartford, Connecticut. The day has gone down in New England history as a terrible foretaste of Judgement Day. For at noon the skies turned from

95

blue to grey and by mid-afternoon had blackened over so densely that, in that religious age, men fell on their knees and begged a final blessing before the end came. The Connecticut House of Representatives was in session. And as some men fell down and others clamoured for an immediate adjournment, the Speaker of the House, one Colonel Davenport, came to his feet. He silenced them and said these words: 'The Day of Judgement is either approaching or it is not. If it is not, there is no cause for adjournment. If it is, I choose to be found doing my duty. I wish, therefore, that candles may be brought.'

Ladies and gentlemen, let candles be brought.

The Court and the Negro

20 August 1954

When I first went South, I was in the South but didn't know it. I was on my first visit to the home, and the home country, of my first American college friend, who is now a doctor in Maryland and was brought up on the edge of a beautiful valley outside Baltimore. (Today only a couple of golf courses hold the landscape against the encircling post-war suburbia and a maze of freeways.)

This man holds a special place in the history of my friendships because in the early 1930s he was a tolerant and amiable teacher about all things American. He instructed me in the wry, and often barefaced, realities of city and state government. We had a common interest in jazz and maintained it against the prevailing conviction of ninety-nine college boys in a hundred that Ellington, Louis Armstrong, and other combinations were 'dinge stuff', that is to say a minority fad indulged in by Negroes. He had an affectionate knowledge of the local trees and flowers and first showed me something of the variety of American oaks, and introduced me to the pink and white dogwood and the Maryland golden aster. He was also responsible for my first taste of crab cakes and terrapin stew and for easing me into the pleasing custom, on hot summer nights, of spreading a newspaper on a table on the back porch at midnight, slicing a watermelon into quarters, and lolling back and burying your face in a quadrant till you came up for air with a drooling sound and paused to spit seeds at the moths.

Many of these pleasures came our way through the stealthy solicitude of Miss Minn. Miss Minn was the cook, first maid, second maid, laundress, nurse, cleaning woman, mother confessor and hub of the household. She was the first Negro I ever knew and to this day is a great mystery. Even twenty years ago she admitted to no age. She was rumoured to be a grandmother, though she never seemed to know how many times. She was not so much an employee in the house as a presence, like a clock that never tells you it's there until it strikes the hour. And hours would go by without any thought of Miss Minn, for she made no noise at all until you began to search for a newspaper or felt hungry or thought aloud that a glass of beer would be just the thing. At such times she would amble through the room or the garden like a forgotten ghost, accidentally bearing the newspaper or a tray with two beers. She was never called and was never out of reach, giving the impression—whether you were upstairs or downstairs, in the garden or the kitchen—that the house was loaded with Miss Minns.

She had no politics, no grievances and—I almost said—no life of her own. But much of the raillery and lazy banter that went back and forth between the family and Miss Minn was about another existence, the echoes of which drifted to us from the edge of our world and the beginning of hers. It was—to us—a very vague, timeless world that sounded, from the hints she dropped, like the libretto of a low-life opera; in which husbands came and went, forgotten sons turned up from distant places, stayed over a carefree weekend and consumed festival meals of snapper turtle, whole crabs dunked in beer, steaks as big as doormats, and then left and showed up again a month or a year later as buck privates, or on crutches from a car crash, or with a new wife and two children. Miss Minn never went into this side of her life for more than a couple of sentences and I honestly don't know when she managed to live it except on certain weekends, when she was off and the family was reduced to camping out of the icebox. Her own style of talk conveyed that these sons and lovers and erupting relations were creatures of the imagination who flitted like elves or stray animals through a shadowy forest.

Miss Minn had been with my friend's family for thirty years and expected to die with them. She is the last of an ancient breed. I don't believe that if you put the question to her she would have had any notion what you meant by 'the Negro problem'.

She might have asked, 'Which Negro?' For all her vaguely suggested problems were about a particular person in the here and now. To me, a new arrival in the country, Negroes were at once a rooted part of the landscape and a fascinating novelty. The 'white' and 'coloured' signs on the doors of waiting rooms, toilets, and the automatic retreat of coloured people to the back of buses and theatres were a shock, but this was the Americans' country and maybe they knew best.

If this sounds callous now, let me say that the mass of people at any given time are rarely better than their lights. And I picked up the attitude of my friends, which in the North was one of lumping the Negroes with poor people everywhere and overcoming the unconscious discomfort of this attitude by praising with particular warmth any Negro who had pulled himself out of the morass of his race with a special talent: a Negro pianist, dancer, poet.

My friends in the South had a quite different feeling. The Negroes were close to their lives, the essential servant, handyman, labour pool, but also confidant, childhood friend, licensed clown, grumbler. The great mass of Negroes who grew the cotton and tobacco and ploughed their squalid little farms were off there somewhere over the horizon. Their lot was wretched but we didn't think about it too much; the legend was passed down from generation to generation that they could put up with squalor much better than us (they had to) and that they mostly maintained a happy-sad temperament with bouts of fine singing.

The experience of the South was to come later, but Maryland is of the South if not in it, and just now I might have been talking about the Miss Minns of Louisiana or Alabama. I wasn't aware of this at the time, and the distinction between the North and South didn't come up until one night we were cruising around the countryside in the north of the state and I happened to remark to my friend that there were no Negroes around, in any of the small towns where I had seen them by day. My friend said, 'No? Let me show you something.' He turned down a side road and circled back to town, and just where the open country was planted with the first outposts of the suburbs he stopped the car, and where four roads met he beckoned me to a tree. Nailed to a fence was a wooden board and on it had been crudely painted: 'Nigger, don't let the sun set on you here.'

We were very close to the northern boundary of Maryland; we were, in fact, standing at the Mason and Dixon line, which divided the slave states from the so-called free soil to the North before the Civil War. This imaginary line is named after two English surveyors, Charles Mason and Jeremiah Dixon, who in 1767 settled an old colonial boundary dispute by defining once for all the southern border of Pennsylvania. This is a precise explanation, but to any American you might stop on a street today, the Mason and Dixon line is the division between two Americas, two worlds, two social systems.

Maryland was neutral in the Civil War. It is a border state. Many industries and customs are Northern, but once you get south of Pennsylvania, the vowels are slurred, the voices are less strident, the coats come off in the summertime, the Negroes are everywhere, and the white man is boss. He is, with shuddering exceptions among the poor whites, a more indulgent and considerate boss than the more vocal Northern liberals could ever be. They like to storm about the smugness and insensitivity of the Southerners, but they do not often get within hailing distance of a Negro they might help to take for a friend. Perhaps one Negro is the wrong unit, because self-conscious liberals and literary bohemians have regularly made a point of cultivating any pet Negro who is foolish enough to stand in as a sop to their conscience.

Now of the many Southern words that reflect the separate life of the South, none has been more taken for granted than the word 'segregation'. I know Southerners who have been brought up to give time and money and pride to the legal protection or the neighbourly defence of the Negroes who work for them. Their children and the local coloured children are close playmates (in a way that Northerners rarely are) up to the age of puberty. But if you ever suggested that their children should go to the same school as the Negroes, they would throw a fit. Well, they're going to throw a fit.

For, as everyone has heard by now, the Supreme Court of the United States has just (17 May 1954) handed down a judgement that I should think is going to cause the most revolutionary change in American social life since, eighty-six years ago, the Court decided that Negroes were American citizens like any other and were entitled to the equal protection of the laws of the United States. The Country was saved from the thunderbolt that has just descended on it by a reservation that the Court made: the status of the Negro was to be equal 'but separate'.

But today the Court recalled the famous phrase of an old judge who defended that earlier ruling. 'The Constitution', he said, 'is colour-blind.' So it is, but the people who hope to live by it are not. And in the Southland, whose sad and profound culture antedates the Constitution by nearly a hundred and fifty years, many generations of Americans have been brought up not necessarily to believe that the Negro is an inferior human being (no Southern Catholic, I hope, would be brought up to believe any such thing) but to believe with Abraham Lincoln that 'the physical differences between the white and black races (I believe) will for ever forbid the two races living together on terms of social and political equality, and inasmuch as they cannot so live, while they do remain together there must be the position of superior and inferior . . . I am not, nor ever have been, in favour of making voters or jurors of Negroes, nor of qualifying them to hold office, nor to intermarry with white people . . . I, as much as any other man, am in favour of having the superior position assigned to the white race.'

That was spoken nearly a hundred years ago and it is, no doubt, unfair to Lincoln to imply that he would feel the same way today. But it is not ridiculous to think so. Millions of decent—should we now say 'otherwise decent'?—Americans think and feel so, in the South and far from it.

It is hard in a few minutes to take up this challenge to the instincts and traditions of a whole region without doing its people a clumsy injustice. From much travel—and stopping—around the United States, I have to say that I respect more the considerate relations that many Southerners have with the Negroes around them than the glib 'social consciousness' of Northerners and Westerners whose daily life has a guaranteed immunity from Negro problems, either because there are few of them around or because they exist conveniently in some tight, slummy corner of the big city. It is one thing to talk about equality in New York or Oregon and live it in Alabama, where one person in three is coloured, or in Mississippi, where there are one million whites and one million Negroes.

So, in the South, and in the Deep South most of all, the mere force of numbers is a threat, if only in the minds of men, to the political and social dominance of the white man. When people, even the gentlest people, fear that they might be terrified or intimidated, they tend to take terrifying precautions. I am not thinking of the understandable misgivings of those Southerners who remember, through the books or through a grandfather, the Negro soldiers who patrolled the beaten South or the state legislatures run in the main by Negroes. I am thinking of something simpler and more universal. In the places where there are many Negroes the black man is invested with the force—the threatening force—of a myth. The daily experience of white people may deny this myth but in their secret heart it has great vitality. It is an image of a black man who is a little slow in his wits, terrible in anger, and above all potent (there's the rub). The scientists have proved this to be nonsense, but, even after a Supreme Court decision, human beings trust their intuition more than the demonstrable truth that their intuition is moonshine. Some of this fear of the Negro may be only the cover-up for the guilt the white man feels for the way he has treated the Negro. But I think the central fear is something else, a fear so embarrassing that white mothers whisper it to each other and intellectuals fretting over 'the Negro problem' will not deign to consider it. It is summed up in the old folk question, muttered behind the palm of the hand: 'Would you want your daughter to marry a *N-E-G-R-O*?'

The revered Lincoln saw only one solution to the problem of the Negroes' suffering: colonization somewhere in an unsettled land. The late, detested Senator Bilbo of Mississippi saw two possible solutions: 'Separation or Mongrelization'. At the moment, it would be difficult to advocate or argue these solutions and be taken seriously. But it seems to me, at least, frivolous and superficial not to face the fact that after a generation or so of mixed schooling, social barriers will tumble, young people will pick their friends for themselves, they will fall in love, as they do everywhere, with the girls and boys around them.

This is a consummation which is at present being devoutly ignored. The traditions of American life are strong enough, *so far*, to make intermarriage prohibitive in the thirty-one states where white and coloured do go to the same schools. Oddly, it is in the South, where the races are separated in school and church and in theatres, that the Negro is woven deep into the texture of society. And it is in the South that the test will come of whether the white man can live and work with the black man as a social and political equal and create a new kind of American society which has at last relaxed the powerful tensions of three hundred years. In the exhilaration of the Supreme Court's trumpet call, we should not, I think, expect too much of whites, now or later. We can only say that to proclaim the attempt at a new American society should give tremendous pause to the racial propaganda that rages over Asia. If it works, 1954 will come to be a date in history as momentous as the year of Magna Carta.

The Colonel of the Plains

21 April 1955

When Colonel Robert McCormick, the publisher of the Chicago *Tribune*, died in Chicago even his enemies among the Midwestern papers couldn't suppress a sigh over the passing of their feudal baron. Right or wrong, he was their man, the son and champion of that part of the country that is variously known as the Midwest, the Heartland, the Farm Belt, the Isolationist Belt, and the Cow Country. Local pride in America is a complicated emotion, which permits—at different times—the separation and the overlapping of different loyalties: to the town, the county, the state, and the allegiance that embraces and swallows them all— regional pride. For, if I may say so, this is a big country; more, it is a continent and its natural regions span four time zones and a range of terrain from true desert in the Southwest and semitropical swamps in the Southeast, up through semi-desert and high plateau country to wheatlands and lush pasture country and, in the West, to the forest primeval, until the whole northern verge of the country shears away to Canada and on to tundra. A man from the state of Maine, who lives on the rocky edge of a glacial coastline, can be as much of a stranger to a man from southern California as a Laplander is to a Hawaiian Islander.

Nowhere is regional pride so jealously upheld as in the mid-continent, whose capital is Chicago. Colonel McCormick was born there and he liked to think of himself as the chosen monarch of all he surveyed. He was, in fact, not chosen at all. He was the self-appointed defender of the Midwest against its perpetual legendary rival and persecutor, the financial East. He saw himself fondly as the original pioneer, the valiant son of New England who had the get-up-and-go to desert the effete comforts of New York and Philadelphia and hack through the forest and emerge at last to build a plain, brave, wholesome life on the vast Central Plain. So he thundered through a long life against the New York bankers who supposedly held the Midwestern farmer in thrall. He half-believed that industry was born in the Midwest. He was quite sure that self-reliance and honest-to-God Americanism were. Till the day he died he never ceased to lament that New York and Washington and Boston were little better than British outposts drugged by the decadence of Europe and periodically perverted by a loyalty to Britain which he considered little short of treason.

I have deliberately painted no picture of Colonel McCormick himself but rather let off a volley of his favourite gunfire in the hope that through the clearing smoke you could picture for yourselves the honest, granity outline of him: a rugged, downright rough diamond, unaffected, unlettered, but unbowed, the very archetype of the Irish and Germans and Poles and Swedes and Czechs who built the railroads and ran the factories and sowed the prairie soil and intermarried to produce a new man in the world whom we know as the Midwesterner. Well, let me now give you a closer look and unveil the details of this splendid statue of a man. It is true that his grandfather was the same McCormick who developed the McCormick reaper, which reaped the grain and raked the cuttings off the platform and bound the sheaves in a mechanical operation. This great invention guaranteed an historic development of wheat farming on the endless high plains, where the climate had always been ideal but where there were never enough human beings to harvest it by hand. It also guaranteed that the next generation of McCormicks would be very nicely taken care of.

So the first thing is that young Robert Rutherford McCormick was born in the lap of luxury that he came to despise. His father was a diplomat who was sent, when the boy was only 9 years old, to serve in the American Embassy in the hated colonial capital of London, England. Consequently, the boy had a rather lonely childhood, and his humiliation as a native Midwesterner began very early in life. For he was first sent to school, and to a fashionable prep school, in England. From there he went to Groton, in Massachusetts, which in those days was considered, and still might claim to be, the American Eton. There, by the way, he met another little boy, not at all a solitary type, a genial, sunny, slightly dude-ish Easterner. This boy was to become his lifetime enemy, a symbol of everything he disliked about the eastern United States: the effortless assumption of breeding, the rather prim, la-de-dah manners, the mawkish concern for old Europe and the tendency to run to her aid in time of trouble. This other boy's name was Franklin Delano Roosevelt. At Groton, McCormick was one form ahead of Roosevelt, so by the stern code of schoolboys he was able to regard young Roosevelt as a junior and a whippersnapper. In later years, it was something to be grateful for.

From school, McCormick passed on to Yale, which was then hardly a plebeian retreat. By this time, his family was in what used to be called Petrograd and is known to us as Leningrad. The boy had the best reasons to feel neglected and put-upon. His family lived abroad and the apple of its eye was his eldest brother, who was being trained to succeed his grandfather as the publisher of the Chicago *Tribune*.

Suddenly, in 1910, the brother died and Robert Rutherford inherited the paper. In the next ten years, he transformed it into a technically brilliant production. He bought up huge forests in Canada. He always regretted having to secure his pulp from the country which, he calculated, would be the jumping-off ground, or staging area, of the next British invasion of the United States. But, on the Salvation Army principle that the devil's money is as good as any, he imported the forests and downed his pride. He took the incoming immigrants under his wing, much as William Randolph Hearst did in New York; and it must be said that he shared a forgotten virtue of Hearst in his early days: which was that he understood profoundly the social plight of the shoals of newcomers, from central Europe especially, who poured into a new land with a new language and strange habits, different in different places, and who were already too old to go to school and learn the language or the elementary facts of American history and American customs. Hearst deliberately set out to teach them and to make his newspapers family newspapers in the novel sense that they helped to make the immigrant feel like a member of the American family. Of course, this entailed a good deal of flag-waving and bombast; but Hearst, and McCormick after him, took to heart the remark of the other Roosevelt (the 'manly one', as he was sometimes known in the family to distinguish him from Franklin the dude). America, said Theodore Roosevelt, was too far-flung already to be able to afford millions of what he called 'hyphenated Americans'. If all these strangers were to be melted into the pot of a single powerful brew, the sooner the better for people to stop identifying German-Americans, Polish-Americans, Italian-Americans, and so on. What Hearst tried to do for the workers of the cities of the East, Colonel McCormick did for the new Chicagoans and the Midwest. They rewarded him by buying his paper. And the Colonel—he earned the title in the First World War and never afterwards dropped it— quadrupled the circulation of the *Tribune* and chose, about twenty-five years ago, to call it flatly 'the world's greatest newspaper'. In case there was any doubt about it, he printed the slogan as a subtitle at the top of the front page.

The Colonel lived in what was called 'quiet luxury' in a thirty-five-room house. He had a bony long rectangle of a face, a guardee's moustache, the quizzical gaze and the slightly bloodshot eyeballs of a retired Indian officer or a master of foxhounds. He wore two wristwatches, one on each hand, for he was always afraid of anyone getting the jump on him; and in his crusade of saving America for the Americans and setting it free from all foreign entanglements, it was always later than you think. He took tea at precisely 4.30 in the afternoon, a custom indulged in in this country only by the most rabid Anglophiles. His voice could hardly boast a single Midwestern vowel, uvular *r* or cadence. In horrid fact, he had more than a trace of a British accent. So that if you went to Chicago looking for that archetypal Midwesterner you would never have found him. He looked indeed like a Tory clubman, a Bond Street polo player, of the vintage of 1912. Freud, thou shouldst be living at this hour!

How is one to explain this remarkable contradiction between the spirit and the flesh? Well, I have talked about him because, although he was rare enough to be that rare thing, an American eccentric, he yet embodied a conflict in the Midwestern character which usually throws up no signals on the surface. It lies in the sort of dislike that involves a strain of envy. Colonel McCormick, I think it fair to guess, was secretly angry with cultivated Easterners and Europeans of his own type because they were so obviously and irritatingly more self-assured than the Midwestern natives and immigrants with whom he had thrown in his lot. But make no mistake, his feeling for the Midwest and its destiny was very genuine. I got the impression from him that he wished American history might jump a hundred years so he could demonstrate that the Midwest had just as many good clubs and representative museums and fine universities and civilized people as the detested East. His criteria of civilization were the same as the Easterners, in spite of his prodigal's embrace of the farm and the factory and the honest uproar of the streets. If he had only known it, he was Colonel Don Quixote tilting at windmills that had collapsed long before he died. For the first thing a foreigner has to learn when he arrives in this country is that it has no unchallenged capital city. Washington is the capital of government, New York of publishing and show business and fashion. But the vast, and vastly separated, regions, like the old Greek states, have their own capitals. And in the hundred years of its growth, Chicago need hardly bow to any other American city for the quality of its medical schools, its art collections, its social amenities. It is actually a national leader in advanced engineering, agriculture, and Oriental languages. It was the cradle of modern American architecture. It was to Chicago that Sir William Craigie came to edit, on the model of the great Oxford dictionary, the dictionary of American English. Chicagoans know all this but they still fear that they are best known for Al Capone and the railroads and the endless troop of livestock, who come into Chicago as cattle and go out as steaks or tennis racquets.

As you push west from the eastern seaboard, it is impossible not to notice the Midwestern chip on the shoulder, which Colonel McCormick elevated to the dignity of an epaulette. Old de Tocqueville, over a century and a quarter ago, spotted and pinned it in two marvellous sentences. Writing about the bleak New England coast where this nation was born, he says, 'This tongue of arid land was the cradle of those English colonies which were destined one day to become the United States of America. The centre of power still remains here; while in the far backwoods the true elements of the great people to whom the future control of the continent belongs are gathering almost in secrecy together.' Secrecy is the word. In Midwesterners, of whom Colonel McCormick was an ideological caricature, there is always the secret fear that perhaps the Midwest has not in fact achieved 'the control of the continent' or the grandeur it imagined for itself in its youth.

HLM: RIP

3 February 1956

The other night, the most famous man who has ever come out of the city of Baltimore (pronounced by all natives Bawlamer) showed to the door an old friend from the Peabody Conservatory of Music, came in to say good night to his brother, who had lived with him through the twenty years since his wife died, and went upstairs to bed. It was just after 9 o'clock. And for a man over 75 who had had a stroke seven years ago, and a heart attack two years later, 9 o'clock was the witching hour when the good things of day—and at that age, alas, of life itself—begin to droop and drowse.

A little man, a stocky man with a bull neck, eyes as blue as gas jets, white hair parted exactly down the middle in the fashion of the early years of the century, and tiny hands and feet that added four surprising grace notes to the solid theme of his body, which was that of an undersized German pork butcher. The Sage of Baltimore, they called him, after they had forgotten the furious years in which they had called him every scurrilous name they could coin for a rebel against respectability, gentility and the social order he chose to call 'the church, nobility and commons': a chuckler at all bankers, bishops, politicians, Methodists, feminists, city fathers, labour leaders, and 'every other sort of faith healer'—a lifelong unbeliever. This little man was in the flesh a genial and even kindly sceptic, and he was very much at home in the society of which he pretended to be the scourge. He was, to those who knew him, Mickey Mouse playing Tamburlaine the Great.

He yawned and doused the stogie of his last cigar and he ambled slowly up the two storeys to his bedroom. He turned on the radio to hear some music. There was a programme that night of Beethoven, whom he had worshipped all his life and who combined, he wrote, 'The glory that was Greece, the grandeur that was Rome'; and Bach, whom he summed up in the single metaphor, 'Genesis 1: 1'; and Mozart. Since the two-hundredth anniversary of Mozart had let loose on the night air a silver flood of his music, let us hope that it was mainly Mozart. If so, no more angelic sounds could have been arranged for the end of an old man who seven years before had roused himself in an oxygen tent long enough to say, 'Bring on the angels.'

Around 11 o'clock, his brother passed along the

113

corridor and heard him snoring, with the music still on. Next morning, a coloured houseman, one Rancho Brown, having prepared the coffee and laid the breakfast table, went upstairs and knocked on the old man's door. 'Eight o'clock,' he said. 'Eight o'clock, Mr Mencken, sir.' But Henry Louis Mencken did not answer and never would again. He had departed what he called 'the cosmos we all infest' sometime in the night and embraced without any struggle the end he had groaned for these many years. When all your life is bounded by books and ideas, and you yourself have a magic way with them, it is a bitter judgement on a man to find for his last seven years that he can neither read nor write and is reduced—by an affliction they call a semantic aphasia—to a vegetable, contemplating other vegetables in his small back garden, laying a brick or two, shambling off in the evening to the one entertainment he had always despised: the movies. The fact was, or came to be, that they provided the most animated and passionate contact he had with human beings (about twenty years after everybody else he fell violently in love with Myrna Loy), but he could not bear to renounce the anathema of a lifetime, and he explained his fondness for the old movies they showed around the corner on the muttered grounds that 'their imbecilities amuse me'. In the fall of 1948 he had come down with a cerebral thrombosis, which left him paralysed and babbling for a time, but, to everyone's surprise, the paralysis left him and one morning he woke up and demanded a boiled egg and a stein of beer.

His old enemies lamented that he might have been stricken but he was not yet cowed. He went home to the row house on the edge of Baltimore where he had lived since he was 3, where his brother, August, a retired engineer, nursed and did for him. And H. L. Mencken, the American Bernard Shaw, the cheerful juvenile delinquent of genteel American culture, the three-volume-classic authority on the American language, the man who could read at a glance a page of anything— theology, criticism, medicine, law, the news—the man to whom the English language was green pasture to romp in, a three-ring circus to perform in to the delight and terror of the onlooking 'boobs': this man got home and extended his index finger and, at the prompting of a patient nurse, learned to identify it like a 3-year-old. He learned all over again the simple physical nouns and the things they stood for. 'Fin-ger, finger,' he repeated, and 'plate', 'spoon', elbow', 'chair', 'floor' and, worst of all, 'book'. For it turned out that the damage had settled in the part of the brain that synchronizes sight and meaning, the ability to see and the ability to make sense of what you see. This disability never left him. He could focus the written page but what he saw was an orderly array of meaningless symbols. So he never read again. He could see and he could talk, pretty much as he had always talked, with sass and pungency and scornful humour. The last time I saw him he made little of the then general fear of the Russians. He had been out on the streets looking at the billboards and store signs. 'Why do they fuss about the Russians? It appears to me,' he said, 'that the Chinese have already taken over.' But sitting in his library with several thousand books buried on the walls, he was like a crippled castaway surrounded by the mocking ocean, the one element he had loved and mastered.

Henry Louis Mencken was the grandson of a German who had deserted the troubles of 1848, settled in Baltimore, and left to his son a prosperous cigar business. Young Henry was meant to take it over but he was temperamentally unfitted to following in anybody's footsteps. As a boy in the 1880s he lay on his back on the kitchen table and shot lemon rind from a catapult at the flies which, in the days before fine-mesh door and window screens, camped on the ceiling. 'The hired girl,' he wrote, 'when she was in an amiable mood prepared us enough of these missiles for an hour's brisk shooting, and in the morning she had the Red Cross job of sweeping the dead flies off the ceiling.' Having tasted what he called 'the red mammalian blood that leaked from the biggest horseflies', he looked around in adolescence for fatter fry. For a time he masked these bloodthirsty instincts in a bookish stoop, which alarmed his father so much that he sent his son off to a gymnasium hoping—said Mencken—'to make a kind of grenadier of me. If so, he was in error, for I remain more or less Bible-backed to this day and am often mistaken for a Talmudist.'

When he was 9, young Mencken read *Huckleberry Finn* and it opened up to him astonishing vistas of life in the world outside. He decided a little later on that to be a newspaperman would offer the priceless opportunity, as he put it later, 'to lay in all the worldly wisdom of a police lieutenant, a bartender, a shyster lawyer, and a midwife'. At 19 he descended on journalism with a whoop. He was extremely spry and industrious and

116

he very soon went from a reporter to a city editor and rollicked in the absurdities, the pomp, the small scandals and big bores with which any self-respecting big city abounds. 'The days chased one another,' he wrote, 'like kittens chasing their tails.'

Now, he looked around for the horseflies. He found them in public life and in the late-Victorian beliefs which, before the First World War, gave life its earnest meaning and society its complacency. He had developed a stinging prose style and an essentially humorous view of human idealism. Like Voltaire in one country and Shaw in another, he let fly at his own. And for about ten years, through the prime of his forties, he skinned every respected institution in the land which he thought had grown fat and uncritical. He regretted the arid theology of the puritan fathers and debunked the heroes of the Revolution. George Washington himself he thought would be today 'ineligible for any office of profit or honour' in the Republic, and he begged the American fiction of the 1920s to cure itself of its 'marshmallow gentility'. The new young realists swarmed to Mencken like Polish underground refugees to London during the Blitz, and he started a magazine and printed their first, and then considered pretty revolutionary, work. O'Neill, James Farrell, Dreiser, Sherwood Anderson, Ring Lardner, and more. They were the rude natives he defended at the gates of the Governor's garden party. Through the 1920s and until the Depression gave people simpler and more urgent troubles to think about, Mencken was the rebel god of American letters. Soon after that his influence wilted, for he was suddenly a gadfly in a charnel house, and he turned to his work on *The American*

Language and to the writing of his enchanting memoirs. Every four years he would enjoy a ribald excursion into his old never-never land by way of reporting the Presidential nominating conventions.

This outrageous, cocky, gallant, cynical, sentimental, greatly gifted man went out suddenly last Sunday without even a coughing fit, snoozing in his bed as the dawn came in over the city he had loved and terrorized. If he could have seen the way he went, you may be sure he would have fired off a final impenitent chuckle. For it contradicted something he had noticed long ago: 'The human tendency to make death dramatic and heroic has little excuse in the facts . . . A man does not die quickly and brilliantly like a lightning stroke; he passes out by inches, hesitatingly and, one may almost add, gingerly . . . the abominable acidosis sneaks upon us, gradually paralysing the adrenals, flabbergasting the thyroid, crippling the poor old liver, and throwing its fog upon the brain. We pass into the blank unconsciousness of infancy and then into the blank unconsciousness of the prenatal state and finally into the condition of undifferentiated protoplasm . . . the dying man doesn't struggle much and he isn't afraid. As his alkalis give out he succumbs to a blest stupidity. His mind fogs. His will power vanishes. He submits decently. He scarcely gives a damn.'

Living or dying, it was Mencken's special glory that he didn't give a damn. He was all of a piece, from the boy on the kitchen table firing slingshots at horseflies to the old man whose last political comment to me was that the old soldier, General MacArthur, 'is a dreadful old fraud but he appears to be fading satisfactorily'. 'All of a piece' is a phrase we seldom hear any more; we prefer the solemn word 'integrity'. It may be the word I am looking for, though it is taken as a Christian concession to allow the word these days to men who are wholly dull or wholly predictable because they give no rein to the warring impulses in all of us, to men who would better be called conventional, or prudent, or obstinate, or plodding, or enslaved by the codes they never made. Mencken was an original with the courage to live by his sometimes outrageous convictions. Like all writers of surpassing talent he was offered huge sums to do some other man's bidding. But he early on turned down the big money and never wrote a piece he didn't want to write. In a persuasive plutocracy, he was impervious to the seductions of the rich because he liked his life and was devoid of envy. 'In the face of another man's good fortune,' he once wrote, 'I am as inert as a curb broker before Johann Sebastian Bach.'

Of the advice he gave me as a starting newspaperman in the late 1930s, I have always been grateful for one rule, or rather three, which a reasonably honest man might get to respect but only after a long convalescence from painful bruises: 'Never accept a free ticket from a theatre manager, a free ride from the chamber of commerce, or a favour from a politician.' He lived absolutely by this rule. He wanted to have his say, and he knew that a very gifted man who isn't interested in money is very hard to tame.

With his father's admiring help he became an agnostic as a boy and stayed one for the rest of the seventy-five years, four months and eight days of his life. There was no weakening at the end, no yielding at last to lifelong temptations to throw in his lot with this sect or that, religious or secular, no sloppy concession that there are no atheists in foxholes. As old age came on he was noticeably more tolerant, even of types he abominated, like evangelists, city politicians and golfers. He was challenged towards the end by an old opponent to confess what he would do if he discovered there was an afterlife by the simple fact of finding himself in one. He replied that if he did indeed 'fetch up beside the Twelve Apostles, I should simply say to them: Gentlemen, I was wrong'.

He prepared for his end with singular sprightliness and care, appealing in his will for no parsonic 'whooping and heaving' at the grave, a little poetry perhaps but nothing that would offend his irreligious scruples. In an astonishingly well-ordered life, his secretary was asked to appear at the same split second every morning. He answered every letter by return of mail. He took a daily nap at the selfsame hour. He locked away his files at six precisely, and they were as elaborately card-indexed as the personnel records of the Pentagon. As the sun faded from the front parlour he mixed the martinis, for he was ready to observe the second half of another lifelong rule: 'Never accept a drink by day or refuse one by night.'

In such a life it would have been an odd oversight if he had not prescribed the proper sentiment to go on his tombstone. Since he ordered that there should be no fuss or ceremony at the end, he was cremated, and the only service was a reminiscent get-together of a few friends. But he had not overlooked his epitaph. He wrote it over forty years ago. It is chiselled on a brass plaque that greets you today in the lobby of the Baltimore Sunpapers building. This is it: 'If, after I depart this vale, you ever remember me and have thought to please my ghost, forgive some sinner, and wink your eye at some homely girl.'

The Road to Churchill Downs

8 May 1956

I was recently invited to go down to Kentucky as a house guest for a few days and wind up with a front seat at the Derby. In the early days of May this is about as sure a guarantee of heaven as a city dweller, or even a countryman, could ask for on this earth.

Kentucky is technically a border state, lying poised between the North and the South, but it deserves far more than its neighbour, Ohio, the description, 'a Northern state with a Southern exposure'. Being not quite in the South it has striven to be very much *of* it. There are no Southerners quite so Southern as the professional Southerners of Kentucky, and by practice as well as by blood they have taken on the legendary pace of Southern life, its customs and cookery, the slow twist of vowels into diphthongs, and that attractive Southern irony which is prepared to believe the best of human beings and expect the worst.

It was a little warmer than usual the day I tumbled down into Kentucky, but the Ulstermen, or as they say here the Scots-Irish, who settled here a century and a half ago soon accustomed

121

themselves to a semitropical drowse that would have choked their cousins in Aberdeen. It was at Aberdeen, by the way, that I crossed the Ohio River, and along its banks the Judas trees were in full flame. The town is terraced high on the steep slopes of the hills as they crowd down to the river, as if rushing to make a last stand before they give way to the rolling meadows of the Bluegrass country.

I tossed in the word 'Bluegrass' there in a casual way, but have no fear that it is going to go unexplained. This whole talk, if it takes the turn I hope, is going to be about the Bluegrass region, which for a hundred and seventy years has bred the fastest, proudest, most gleaming of America's racehorses. On top of the Fayette County courthouse is a weathervane in the shape of a golden stallion. It is no more possible to go through the Bluegrass country and ignore the horses than it would be to go through Nevada and ignore the slot machines. From Maysville, the first town across the Kentucky line, down to Lexington, the capital of the Bluegrass, is sixty-three miles, and there are some interesting oddities. There are handsome houses overlooking the river that were built in the spacious times when the steamboat minted fortunes as fast as the railroads that superseded them. But this was, and is, trapper country. The first white men who really roamed this hinterland were the French, the fur trappers and traders who made the most of a huge continental landscape where, unlike Europe, the mountain ranges ran from north to south, and the rivers also. There is hardly a river in the main river systems of the American mainland that has not left the relics of the French fur trappers, for they extended Napoleon's empire up the Mississippi and the Missouri and the Ohio to places far in the north. Even Chicago, it may strike you, is pronounced 'Shick-ago' and not 'Chick-ago' because the first people to come on it were French rivermen. Chicago is an Indian name, but the French had trouble with the 'chi' sound, as they still do (they can't even say, 'Goodnight, chairee'), and they had to say it 'Shick-ago'. The incoming Yankees picked up the pronunciation and it has stayed that way ever since, except, of course, out of the mouths of Englishmen, who live eighteen miles from the French but have had little truck with them.

But in this first valley that I went through, the French had been quietly obliterated by the Scots-Irish, who have a habit of taking over any place they settle in; and if they don't absorb it, they preserve the gift of not being absorbed either. Until I arrived on the edge of the Bluegrass all the names were such as Cochran, McConnell, Marshall, and Keith and Duncan. In a charming small town called Washington one of the houses that is a required stop for tourists is a two-storeyed Georgian brick house. It was built at the turn of the eighteenth century by a man who had loaded a large family on a flatboat, sailed down the Ohio, and made a home here. The point of visiting the place today is that in the grounds many of the Marshall family are buried. And there stands still the modest tombstone of a certain Mary Keith, who turned out to be the mother of John Marshall, an early and great Chief Justice of the United States Supreme Court. The epitaphs on Scottish tombstones are not, as I recall, very flowery, not even when they

123

were written in the eighteenth century, which both in old England and in New England consigned its beloved to the care of Providence with grand flourishes of the language. But some of these Kentucky leave-takings are as chilly as the Highlands. That of the mother of Chief Justice Marshall is no exception. It reads, 'Mary Randolph Keith, born 1737, she was good, not brilliant, useful not ornamental, and the mother of fifteen children.' The mind reels at the size of her progeny if she had been ornamental.

Well, by the middle of the afternoon I had come to the end of the winding river-bottom roads and was on a long, undulating upland and the true Bluegrass country. You will want to know, as everybody who has never seen it does, if the grass is really blue. It is not. Even the natives admit that it is merely green in summer. But no matter how much the Kentucky guide insists that 'only in May do the blue anthers of its blossoms give the grass a distinctly steel-blue tint', a stranger needs to wear special tinted glasses to make it appear so. The way not to disappoint your friends is to photograph it in colour in the very late afternoon, when the slanting light of the entire Western hemisphere spreads a film of milky blue on anything, even the complexion of your favourite girl. It is only fair to say that you do notice the greenness of the grass, but it would not startle an Englishman or an Irishman and it would not be much of a surprise to a native of Oregon. However, let's not be hoity-toity about this local product. It is as indigenous to this region as the Monterey cypress is to that small coastal stretch of central California. It is not matched as turf, and as pastureland is surpassed, I should guess, only by the two famous sections of eastern Pennsylvania and southwestern Belgium, which a League of Nations survey chose as the finest in the world.

The Bluegrass is a small central plain, less than eight thousand square miles, which lies on a bed of limestone and is richly veined with underground water. And this is the perfect—they say essential—recipe for the two glories of Kentucky: fine horses and bourbon whiskey. It is the limestone which endows the waters that pass through it with phosphorus and calcium. Which, as every stable boy knows (and I just learned), are two ingredients of bone and rippling muscle. This is why the Kentucky thoroughbreds are strong and fast and beautiful to look upon. This is why, as you drop south from the eroded hills of southern Ohio and up on to the downs of the Bluegrass country, the road signs change from advertisements for familiar gasolines and cigarettes to elegant signs by elegant stud farms that say: 'Brood mares, boarding and training'; 'Track entrance, 100 feet'; and 'Blue Grass Seed'.

In deference to people who were brought up in my own self-denying faith, I will quickly explain the essential ingredients of Kentucky's second famous product and then pass on. It may be regrettable but it is also true that the water that courses through the limestone has a distinctive flavour. There are simple, strong people who slake their thirst with the natural product alone and go on, I'm told, to live blameless lives. But there are others, the first of whom was one Jacob Spears, as long ago as 1790, who looked on the Kentucky water as the merest raw material for a confection that has done the state some service. The United States abounds, as you may have heard, in maize, so much so that like the English with their wheat, the Scots with their barley, and the Australians with their oats, they have adopted for it the usual counter-word for the staple crop: corn. Mr Spears earned the gratitude of uncounted generations by having the wit to take the maize and grind it and mash it and add the magic limestone water, and then distil the compound and age it. And that's how bourbon was born, so called after the name of the county that gave birth to this splendid firewater. Not surprisingly, Mr Spears' first distillery was in Paris. And the heart of the Bluegrass country is between Paris and Versailles.

These towns were so named, as were many others near by, in grateful remembrance of a stripling boy, a 19-year-old Frenchman, the Marquis de Lafayette, who offered himself in the service of the American Revolution to General Washington and beat you know who, and has ever after symbolized the special one-upmanship that the French enjoy in America. This is nothing to dwell on, but you surely can't expect me to toss off the remark that I have just driven from Paris to Versailles without explaining that we are still in Kentucky.

It has a wide, undulating, green horizon, strikingly devoid of evergreens but spotted here and there with those jetting, fanlike American elms, which, alas, have been blighted by the Dutch bug all the way from Ohio to the New England coast. The Bluegrass is rich country in more senses than one, for it must cost a modest fortune to maintain even the five-barred white wooden fences that ring the paddocks and enclose the fields and swing like switchbacks between you and the horizon. Inside these pastures is practised that strange and compelling ritual of breeding racehorses which so obsesses the insider and leaves the outsider feeling that he has been mistaken all his life about what a horse *is*. In sickness and in health, in affluence and depression, no babies anywhere in Kentucky are so jealously and delicately cared for. After the weaning comes the precisely regulated diet—a mixture of oats and corn, bran and flax seed and vitamin extracts—then the trimming of the feet, the breaking to the halter, the gentling into the paddock routine, then the exploratory trotting and cantering, and then the speed trials; all this going on for two years or more before the magic truth is revealed or exploded: whether or not the blood of the horse's ancestors and the skill of his training will merge to produce a true racehorse, perhaps a great one.

In the late winter and early spring, you could have seen on the doors of some stalls record charts—for temperature, diet and other clinical peculiarities of the tender patient inside—which are as anxiously consulted as those in a surgical ward; because no discipline is too fussy, no care too excessive to the men who match their knowledge of bloodlines and skill in training methods in the gaudy hope that one day the people may flock to see their ward run on the first Saturday of May in the Derby at Churchill Downs. And there can be few Kentucky owners and breeders who do not nurse a faint hope that later on the people may troop to a second shrine comparable with Kentucky's first.

And what is that? It is Faraway Farm, outside Lexington, and to some knowing people it is as much of a pilgrimage as Lenin's Tomb to an obedient Russian. Up against the sky and standing on a small hillock is a handsome statue of the greatest racehorse of his time, who won nineteen times in twenty-one starts, collected a quarter of a million dollars in only two seasons, sired two hundred and thirty-six horses, one hundred and seventy-six of whom were winners: the fastest, the most beautiful, the proudest son of Kentucky— Man o' War. You amble up to the statue with your hands in your pockets and a few other visitors come up, and the men take their hats off. You are surprised to find that you have done the same.

*   *   *

All this, you will have assumed, is an easy build-up to the climax of a holiday in Kentucky: the breathtaking spectacle itself, the Derby. Well, to be quite honest, I can think offhand of a dozen other spectacles that catch my breath quicker. A hooked bluefish, for instance, a glass of lager, the dimple in the chin of Ava Gardner. For I was shaken to discover that if while the race is on, you lose your programme or have a coughing fit you can miss it altogether. If anybody had asked me, I should have guessed that the Kentucky Derby was something like the bicycle race around France, and that we were going to sit through the last day of it. It turned out it takes two minutes, and for this the whole population of Louisville, and several hundred train and plane loads of gamblers from the East and West, and breeders from Ireland and

Argentina, and 'kinfolk' from the South, make plans for a year, dicker for tickets, pay regal prices for a bed, and line up for food—for a hundred and twenty seconds on the first Saturday in May. Other people's enthusiasms are always a riddle, but I shouldn't take kindly to a sneer at mine. So I will say that the reason for my being in this strange place was a promise I had given, in a wild moment a year before, to my 10-year-old daughter. By the peculiar grace of God, she has not yet become aware of one half the human race—I mean boys. That being so, what else is there on earth to rave about but horses? Her weekends are spent bouncing round the park, the only dress catalogues she handles feverishly are ones for riding gear, her room is plastered with more ribbons and horse prints than a Presidential Convention with campaign buttons. She flew in on a flawless day over the velvety pastures and the rolling farms and the gleam of horseflesh, and she said at once, 'Why can't we live in Kentucky?' I said, 'I'll tell you why. Because a little later on you'll discover that they breed boys in other places than the Bluegrass.'

The object of this trip, then, was up at dawn and out with Ned, a slim young man in blue jeans and a high-buttoned shirt, with tendons as bowed as the horse he couldn't sell. There was a choice of colts, fillies, ponies, for this was a working farm, and a working farm for other less favoured beasts. Cows sloshed their tails around in the heat of the day, and at night sheep complained to the moon and the air was dense with birds that trilled, barked, whistled, shrieked and glucked. The sun came up like a yellow rose and fell like a sweating orange. It was 94 degrees the first day, 92 the second, 96 on

129

the great day itself. But the tempo was easy and nobody was going anyplace but Churchill Downs. We lay on the grass and had lunch of Kentucky chicken hash and potato pancakes and the best succotash (corn and lima beans) I'd ever eaten. We had a box overlooking the finishing post, and for the first time since 1880 there was a challenge from the losing jockey, and a very tense pause before the stewards decided that in the stretch Tommy Lee and Sword Dancer were bumping each other in a rhythmical and entirely legal way.

Some people, I don't doubt, will be sensing with suspicion or disfavour the sort of society I seem to be sketching: a horsey, arrogant, vowel-chopping— or vowel-smearing—upper crust. Not your cup of tea perhaps? Not mine either, I assure you. While I feel like a vaudeville clown in the presence of dignitaries of the Church and State, I am practically T. S. Eliot in the presence of horsey people. I know less about a horse than—certainly—a horsefly. An Argentinian, in a mad attack of mistaken identity, asked me if I'd brought any promising fillies along. I said I had brought a ten-year-old filly with me. My daughter hopped to my side and growled in a whisper, 'You can't be a filly if you're older than four.' How about colts? I asked. 'Same thing,' she said and blushed for her city-slicker father. The Argentinian thought he was in the wrong town and wandered off.

But the great surprise, and the delight, of this interlude in the Bluegrass was to mix with a lot of people who were expert and hospitable and easygoing with their knowledge, and impossible to grade socially. You never knew whether the young tow-haired man in the corner was a Yale sophomore or a groom. For three great days, Jefferson's original image of America was restored—that of a pastoral Republic where the rich, the poor, and the in-between mingle, eat, drink, joke together, have the same manners, the same idioms, and an overriding gentleness and naturalness. A small, uncorrupted society united in a lovely landscape by a genuine love of the same thing—a horse. I discovered, much too late in life, that the same sense of an innocent community can be guaranteed by the pursuit of a ball with a liquid centre.

On the plane coming home, my daughter rattled on in ecstasy till she had to catch her breath. I jumped in with the damping reminder that it was wonderful but it was not at all like life. 'What d'you mean?' she said. 'Well,' I said as we looked down on the approaching industrial landscape of the Jersey flats, 'we might have had bad seats, or stayed in a crummy motel, or keeled over from the heat, or been bedded down in Louisville, or there might have been no horses to ride. Everything was perfect,' I said, 'but it isn't always so.'

'I don't get it,' she said, and fell asleep.

Politics and the Human Animal

7 December 1956

As sometimes happens, I was chided the other morning, in a letter from an indignant correspondent in England, for having given a talk about the complexities of American football when I

131

might better have given a sermon about the complications of the Middle East. Men were dying, he reminded me. Empires were tottering. A tyrant was squeezing the lifeblood from Britain's lifeline in the Suez Canal. In a word, I was fiddling while London, Cairo and Washington burned.

If I believed this, I should be embarrassed to talk at all about one country to another. But in all these talks I have gone along on the original theory that people are permanently curious about how other people live, and that all the politicians and propagandists in the world working on three shifts a day cannot for ever impose their line on two people sitting alone in a room. They are the only proper audience for a letter. I grant my correspondent that there are vast heavings and resettlings of power around the world; that there is a ferment in Asia and Africa; that there is a periodic flow of bad blood across the Atlantic; that the rich grow richer and the poor poorer with consequences that could end in world famine and revolution. I can only reply that I still feel no embarrassment in maintaining, in a warlike time, a civil tongue.

If this sounds impertinent in our present troubles, let me repeat a few sentences I wrote as the preface to a collection of these talks that was put out some years ago: 'Politics will undoubtedly bedevil us all till the day we die, but . . . even the prospect of early annihilation should not keep us from making the most of our days on this unhappy planet. In the best of times, our days are numbered, anyway. And it would be a crime against Nature for any generation to take the world crisis so solemnly that it put off enjoying those things for which we were presumably designed in the first place, and which the gravest statesmen and the hoarsest politicians hope to make available to all men in the end: I mean the opportunity to do good work, to fall in love, to enjoy friends, to sit under trees, to read, to hit a ball and bounce the baby.'

Am I saying that the world is too much with us, and is incurable anyway, and that we should gather roses while we may? I am saying no such thing. I *am* saying that when the nations rage furiously together we should not be misled by their hullabaloo into thinking that the world's anxieties, however grave, are the fundamental things in life and that all else is a bauble. It happens, merely, to be my daily chore to sit and watch and listen to the chief actors on the political stage, domestic and foreign, and I am struck by many things. By the ease with which a nation does something from instinct and justifies it by reason. By the careerism and vanity that dog the ambition of most politicians and statesmen. But I am struck most of all by the absence of humour, which as much as any other solvent could relax the protagonists in any quarrel, however international, and halt them in their race to murder each other from the highest motives. Most of the chief delegates to the United Nations are hard-working men but because they are trying to handle the world's conflicts they are not thereby or necessarily the most serious men around. Some of them are certainly the solemnest men around.

And however splendid the United Nations Charter may be, there is nothing inherently noble about the United Nations delegations. I suggest that my critic is making this sort of mistake. He is mistaking the label on the tin for the contents.

Most first-rate comedians are in private life more serious than most politicians and all of them are melancholy men. And what may be essential to one's self-respect may not be essential to a friendship, whether at the other end of a loudspeaker or at the other end of a room.

I have, for instance, a close friend, a merry, kindly and simple man, very able in his special field of finance. I feel agreeable in his presence and I admire his human qualities. At the shabbiest period in recent American history, when the fear of domestic Communists was most paranoid, this friend was a strong, even a devout, McCarthyite. He used to load my morning mail with the transcripts of all the testimony before the Senate Subcommittee on Government Operations, over which the late Senator Joseph McCarthy presided with—by my lights—such indignity and malevolence. Of course, McCarthyism was a fundamental issue of the time, not only an American political issue but fundamental to any man's notions of justice and decency. You might guess, therefore, that my friend's admiration for McCarthy marked the parting of the ways for us. Well, it was an embarrassment, but not to our affection or continuing association. Of course, if by some convulsion of history (a sudden depression, say, and twenty million unemployed) McCarthy had become an American dictator, my friend and I would probably have said goodbye and retreated to opposite sides of the barricades. Nobody has sharpened this point better, in my view, than the late Justice Holmes when he said that the purpose of civilized argument between friends is to arrive at the point where you agree that some day it might be necessary to shoot each other. Until that day is unavoidable, 'the democratic process', both in public and in private, is no more but no less than an acceptance of the notion that in important issues you may be wrong.

My first mentor in journalism in this country was a man who had no use for democracy at all, except in this crucial belief. 'Democracy', he once wrote, 'is the theory that the common people know what they want, and deserve to get it good and hard.' But he also wrote, 'What I admire most in any man is a serene spirit . . . when he fights he fights in the manner of a gentleman fighting a duel, not in that of a longshoreman cleaning out a waterfront saloon.' We had a tacit understanding that while I allowed him to shoot off his face about the fraudulence and guile of Franklin Roosevelt, I should then be allowed to go off and vote for him. This division never interfered with a friendship that was amiable at all times.

I believe this to be not only a sane approach to politics but essential to all the things that lie outside politics.

I hope that the blood pressure of my critic is still holding. Politics, I grant, is of great importance to us all, since it affects our survival and the future we plan for ourselves and for all the countries that lie outside our own. It is admirable, though not, I believe, compulsory, for people to take an interest in politics. But first things first. How much politics is there in the greatest novels? In Flaubert, Dickens or Dostoyevsky? How much in the greatest poetry? In Shakespeare, Yeats, John Donne or whoever? Surely nobody will deny that poets and novelists, poets especially, deal with human

135

experience at its most intense and most profound. Was Thomas Hardy indifferent to the great issues of his time because he chose to look steadily and long at the life of a few Dorset villages? Is the poetry of Robert Frost trivial because it deals with a bit of pasture or the death of a hired man? Frost, by the way, had his own recipe for the end of the world. It would not come, he thought, in the shock of avenging armies but either by lust or by hate.

> Some say the world will end in fire,
> Some say in ice.
> From what I've tasted of desire
> I hold with those who favour fire.
>
> But if it had to perish twice,
> I think I know enough of hate
> To say that for destruction ice
> Is also great
> And would suffice.

You may say that a first-rate poet, because he is a rare bird, rarer than a first-rate politician, has earned a special exemption from the obligations of politics. Not because of his special gift, he hasn't. That would be like saying that all wars should be fought by the poor and the ungifted. And although a mere journalist cannot achieve the intensity or profundity of a good poet, he still has the obligation to see things as he sees them and not as he would like to, or as somebody else says he should. If paying tribute to Caesar is not his main business in life, he must pay his citizen's due and get on with what really interests him.

What do you suppose the Secretary General of

the United Nations turns to when he goes home at night? Mr Hammarskjöld is, he likes to say, 'the curator of the secrets and prejudices of seventy-nine nations'. That should be enough to fill the waking hours of any conscientious man. But it evidently is not. When he steps off the high wire of his diplomatic circus and comes down to earth, does he agonize all over again about Suez or the Congo or the seizure of Hungary? He settles to the permanent things. He reads Eliot and Robert Lowell and André Gide and his favourite novelists —Mark Twain, Hemingway, Stephen Crane—and most of all the man whose high seriousness and perfect accommodation of his style to the thing he wants to say makes him, in Hammarskjöld's opinion, the modern master of serious English prose. James Thurber.

So let us take our stand on the Middle East, or Vietnam, or whatever, and in the process perhaps lose a friend or shoot a friend, or agree to differ and do neither. Then let us get down to life and living.

General Marshall

16 October 1959

It has been a habit of these letters to honour, as W. H. Auden put it, 'the vertical man', the Americans in all their variety who are up and doing. But Americans themselves are great celebrators of their eminent dead. And when the calendar reminds us of a great one who was born or died fifty or a hundred years ago, he is obediently honoured in the tomb by people who would have feared or hated him in the flesh. For Americans, an impetuous but ceremonial people, are soon ready to pay tribute to a man once the wind is out of him.

Lately we observed as a holiday the date kept aside as Columbus Day, which celebrates the discovery of this country by a man who neither discovered it nor ever saw it. And a few days later we nodded respectfully in the direction of Harpers Ferry, West Virginia, where—a hundred years ago—John Brown, a near-lunatic with a hot eye and a single purpose, started on his wild and brief campaign to set up a free state in the Appalachians as a sanctuary for escaped Negro slaves. Next day, a man died who had been born just across the Pennsylvania border from Harpers Ferry who had an equally single purpose but who was so prosaic, so deeply disdainful of drama and public exposure, that not one American in a million would have recognized him on the streets, and not even his close friends knew a pungent or delightful story about him. He was almost impossible for a newspaperman to know, for he winced at the word 'newspaper' and he therefore acquired no public personality, not even a couple of identifying adjectives in *Time*. In the last few years of his life he used to drive downtown most days from his small house in Pinehurst, North Carolina, buy his groceries in the supermarket, tote them to his car to the accompaniment of a nod from the townspeople, a bit of gossip with the drugstore clerk, and then get into his car again, receive the flourish of a salute from the traffic cop, and drive home again. Yet on a bright day, wherever in the world the American flag flies, it was lowered and flown for him.

I hope I won't be misunderstood if I say that he was a most un-American figure because he was so remarkably self-effacing. The United States has as many people as anybody afflicted with self-effacement, but it usually springs from social discomfort, or genuine shyness, or that other form of shyness which, as somebody wisely said, is a sure sign of conceit. This man was not shy, but the subordination of self to teamwork was almost an instinct with him, and I suppose few men who take to soldiering took to it for a better reason. Most Americans were willing to credit the reports of his eminence but it was something they had to take on trust; for General George Catlett Marshall, of all the great figures of our time, was the least 'colourful', the least impressive in a casual meeting and the least rewarding to the collector of anecdotes. He was a man whose inner strength and secret humour only slowly dripped through the surfaces of life, as a stalactite hangs stiff and granity for centuries before one sees beneath it a pool of still water of marvellous purity.

He was always uncomfortable when anyone mentioned the great Plan that bears his name, the plan to repair the fabric of European life after the devastation of the Second World War. He took no credit for it, and he was nearly right. For it was first conceived by underlings in the State Department and seized on by Under-Secretary Dean Acheson when he realized that all the largesse of UNRRA and Bretton Woods, and the loan to Britain, and other loans to Greece and Turkey, were far from enough. It was time to jettison Europe or to throw

139

out a lifeline. Acheson developed the Plan, and it was worked on in the White House, and he floated it as a trial balloon in a speech at Cleveland, Mississippi. No one in the country took particular notice of it. Marshall had been in Europe and when he came back, Acheson told him about it, not without misgiving, for Americans had not marvelled at his trial balloon, and a sudden Communist stab at Hungary might puncture it once and for all. Marshall, it must be said, now saw the necessity of speed and a public forum and contrived within two days to speak at the Harvard commencement. He was no orator, and the dramatic novelty of the Plan went unnoticed by everybody except a trio of British correspondents and the British Foreign Secretary, Ernest Bevin, who sat by his bedside in England and heard a transatlantic broadcast and responded to it at once as 'a lifeline to sinking men . . . the generosity of it was beyond our belief . . . we grabbed it with both hands'. So it is not for the Marshall Plan that we honour the General.

Imagine now a sturdy, well-knit man, stiff-necked it would be fair to say, certainly in the physical sense, with sandy hair and mild blue eyes and a homely, underslung mouth from which issued unspectacular remarks in a throaty voice. A student of war, from the books and the maps but also from the arms contracts and the quartermaster records, and from a personal knowledge of the battlefields picked up on private walks when the bones of the dead were long overgrown.

It is possible—we shall never know—that in his private imagination he was another Robert E. Lee who dreamed dreams of high deeds in the cannon's mouth. But for almost fifty years he was fated by his superiors and, in the crisis of his career, by his own conscience to return as always to the drawing board, to revise the training methods of a tank corps, to compute the comparative tactical efficiency of a 55-millimetre machine gun in close combat and in desert warfare, to gauge the competing need for anti-aircraft of the slums of Chungking or the docks and ports of Iceland. A high subordinate who worked with him assures me that in the history of warfare Marshall could not have had his equal as a master of supply: the first master, as this West Point colonel put it, of global warfare. I suppose we must defer to this expert judgement. It was enthusiastically seconded by the three or four senior British generals during the Second World War. But to most of us, unifying the command of an army outpost or totting up the number of landing barges that could be spared from Malaya for the Normandy landings is hardly so flashing as Montgomery's long dash through the desert, or MacArthur's vigil on Bataan, or even the single syllable by which General McAuliffe earned his immortality: 'Nuts!'

A layman is not going to break out a flag for a man who looks like a stolid golf-club secretary, a desk general who refused an aide-de-camp or a chauffeur and worked out of an office with six telephones. Even though 1984 comes closer every day, this is not yet an acceptable recipe for a hero. Though no doubt when Hollywood comes to embalm him on celluloid, he will grow a British basso, which is practically a compulsory grafting process for American historical characters in the movies. He will open letters with a toy replica of the sword of Stonewall Jackson (who was, to be truthful, a lifetime's idol).

But in life no such colour brightened the grey picture of a man devoted to the daily study of warfare on several continents with all the ardour of a certified public accountant. In a word, he was a soldier's soldier. Nor, I fear, is there any point in looking for some deep and guilty secret to explain his reputation for justice and chivalry. There is, however, one voice that has been silent. No syllable of praise or criticism has come from a soldier who can coin resounding epitaphs when he so chooses. General MacArthur has said nothing, and I dare to wonder about his silence only because it reflects a conflict of character and temperament that was conducted on both sides with shattering dignity. It will by now be no surprise to learn that on Marshall's side it was a most undramatic quality: the gift of making at fateful times sensible decisions that elevate another man and swing the spotlight away from you.

We have to go back to February 1956 for the last public word about Marshall by General MacArthur. 'General Marshall's enmity towards me', he wrote, 'was an old one.' Discounting the word 'enmity', let us say that the original row—the sort of thing that elephants and politicians never forget—goes back to the First World War, when Marshall, a colonel on the Operations Planning Section of the American Expeditionary Force, was planning the recapture of Sedan, the historic town which three German armies in the last century have broken through to lay waste the lands of France. Marshall's plans did not allow for the impetuous ambition of a young brigadier general to summon his own division and take Sedan at a bound. The brigadier general was, need I say, MacArthur. He leaped through a loophole in the Marshall plan and took Sedan in his dashing stride. From then on he vaulted ahead of Marshall in everything but prudence. By 1930, when he became chief of staff, you would have had to scan the army lists with binoculars to see what happened to Marshall.

After the First World War, you might have thought that his appearance at the side of General Pershing as a personal aide would have assured a flashier or more enterprising type some quick preferment, but it was downhill again for another fifteen years. As late as 1933, for instance, he was appointed senior instructor to the Illinois National Guard, an appointment that would have thrilled a scoutmaster. But for an able soldier, 52 years of age, it was the pit of his career. Once MacArthur retired, in 1935—and it may be no more than coincidence—Marshall had his feet on the ladder again. Two days before the Germans swept into Poland he was made chief of staff.

I said that in the supreme crisis of his career it was his own conscience that sent him back to the commanding obscurity that was his habitat. Nobody has told this incident better than the late Henry Stimson, Roosevelt's Secretary of War. In a letter to the President in August 1943, Stimson wrote, 'I believe the time has come when we must put our most commanding soldier in charge of this critical operation [that was to be the invasion of Europe]. You are far more fortunate than was Mr Lincoln or Mr Wilson in the ease with which that selection can be made . . . General Marshall

143

already has a towering eminence of reputation as a tried soldier and as a broad-minded and skilful administrator.' The British had, in fact, suggested him. Churchill assumed he was already picked and Stalin had vouchsafed a wily nod of approval. There came a day in Cairo when President Roosevelt and Marshall lunched alone. It seems to be accepted among Marshall's close friends that he had all his life yearned for a combat command. The most majestic command in history was his for the asking. Roosevelt had already made up his mind but, as usual, allowed himself room to manoeuvre (and lament) if things didn't turn out his way. He asked Marshall whether he would prefer to stay in Washington as chief of staff or take the supreme command. Stimson kept some notes, made from Roosevelt's account of the lunch, and in them he says that Marshall declined the gambit. It was, he said, entirely for the President to decide. He warned the President that if he was chosen to go to Europe, there was only one man he could think of to replace him in Washington. It was the new general, Dwight D. Eisenhower, who had commanded the North African landings. The President decided that Eisenhower had neither Marshall's grasp of worldwide strategy nor his familiarity with Congress. So he picked Eisenhower, and Marshall congratulated him, and the lunch was over. At the end of it, Roosevelt said, 'I couldn't sleep nights, George, if you were out of Washington.' (Roosevelt is the only known man who ever called General Marshall 'George'.) When Stimson heard of this he was, he said, 'staggered'. He gave to his diary the note that 'at the bottom of his heart it was Marshall's secret desire above all things to command the invasion of Europe'. But Marshall himself had advanced the deciding argument. Who else would oversee the war of supply, who would review the war in both oceans, from the necessary desk in Washington? He never by any sign showed that the President's decision was not the perfect one. The British too were staggered and apprehensive, and it was a British official who put down in his journal: 'In Marshall's presence ambition folds its tent.' Stimson put down an order sentence he had once quoted about Marshall: 'He that ruleth his spirit is better than he that taketh a city.'

When the dust and the glory came blowing up over the battlefields, Marshall was the father confessor and guru to Eisenhower. To MacArthur he was still a sullen office figure, smarting at long range over the humiliation at Sedan, but it was Marshall who urged on Congress the award to MacArthur of the Medal of Honor. Twelve years later, when Eisenhower was campaigning for the Presidency in Wisconsin, he deleted—at the personal urging of the late Senator Joseph McCarthy—a passage in praise of Marshall from a speech that he was about to give. Not a word ever passed the lips of Marshall about this dismal episode, and when McCarthy called him a traitor for the failure of his post-war mission to China, all Marshall said to a personal friend was: 'The hardest thing I ever did was to keep my temper at that time.'

There is a final story about him which I happen to have from the only other man of three present. I think it will serve as a proper epitaph. In the early 1950s, a distinguished, a very lordly, American

145

magazine publisher badgered Marshall to see him on what he described as a serious professional mission. He was invited to the General's summer home in Virginia. After a polite lunch, the General, the publisher and the third man retired to the study. The publisher had come to ask the general to write his war memoirs. They would be serialized in the magazine and a national newspaper and the settlement for the book publication would be handsome indeed. The General instantly refused on the grounds that his own true opinion of several wartime decisions had differed from the President's. To advertise the difference now would leave Roosevelt's defence unspoken and would imply that many lives might have been saved. Moreover, any honest account might offend the living men involved and hurt the widow and family of the late President. The publisher pleaded for two hours. 'We have had', he said, 'the personal testaments of Eisenhower, Bradley, Churchill, Stimson, James Byrnes. Montgomery is coming up and Alanbrooke, and yet there is one yawning gap.' The General was adamant. At last, the publisher said, 'General, I will put it on the line. I will tell you how essential we feel it to have you fill that gap, whether with two hundred thousand words or ten thousand. I am prepared to offer you $1 million after taxes for that manuscript.' General Marshall was faintly embarrassed, but quite composed. 'But, sir,' he said, 'you don't seem to understand. I am not interested in $1 million.'

The 1960s

Beizbol

13 October 1961

One of the most reliable clichés of American newspaper writing is the opening phrase: 'The eyes of the nation were focused today on. . .' There is one day of the year when this is true. It is the first Wednesday in October, the opening of what is majestically called the World Series. On that day the champions of the two major leagues play each other to decide which team, by winning the best of seven games, shall be declared to be the world champions at the old Russian game of beizbol.

We never, by the way, seem able to make up our minds whether Russian propaganda is too subtle or too crude. But it was a shrewd move of theirs in 1952 to look into the origins of the American national game and, after a severely scientific survey, conclude that it started in the Ukraine sometime in the Middle Ages. Of course, the best way to meet these objective Russian surveys is to make one of our own. And that is what we're going to do. In fact, it has been done for us—twice. Once by a commission set up in 1908, and again by a learned and curious librarian who had strong reasons to doubt the commission's findings.

In the country south of the Mohawk Valley, in the setting for several of the stories of James Fenimore Cooper, there is a town called—not unnaturally—Cooperstown. It is now a regular port of call on the tourist route because of a museum, sacred to the memory of one Abner Doubleday.

He, it says here, was the only true inventor of the national game. The museum has a lot of early relics. It has a homemade baseball supposedly used by the great man himself. It preserves prints of Union soldiers playing baseball in North Carolina during the Civil War. It has bronze plaques bearing the names of retired heroes of the game who have been voted into the so-called 'hall of fame' by 75 per cent of the members of the Baseball Writers Association. Tap an American anywhere between the Canadian and Mexican borders and ask him who invented baseball and he will reverently pronounce the name—Abner Doubleday.

Let me begin by quoting the official account as it is quite briskly told in the federal guide to New York State: 'Baseball grew quite informally from Old Cat, a favourite boys' game in Colonial days, played by a thrower, a catcher and a batter. In 1839, Colonel Abner Doubleday, a student in a local military academy, later a major general in the Civil War, limited the number of players to eleven, outlined the first diamond-shaped field and drew up a memorandum of rules for the game which he named "baseball".' That is the version confirmed by the investigating commission I referred to after its researches in 1908. It was not, by the way, a government commission, as most baseball fans like to assume. It consisted of a sporting-goods manufacturer, a bunch of baseball managers and one United States Senator who was mad about the game. Even the *Encyclopaedia Britannica* (a Chicago publication) says about this commission: 'It was appointed ostensibly to investigate the origins of the game but really to "prove" its exclusively American origin.'

Well, by 1908, any other inventor of the game who could challenge the Doubleday legend was dead and gone. Cooperstown, New York, was naturally delighted to be singled out for glory. And the commission's findings passed into the record books and the tablets of sacred Americana. However, there is another name rarely mentioned by baseball scholars, and it is not surprising, because he is a dissenter and a sceptic; once you have picked and immortalized a public hero it is an awful nuisance to discover that he is a fraud. The name of the Doubting Thomas is Robert W. Henderson, a quiet fellow who, true to the requirements of his job as a staff member of the New York Public Library, doesn't like to take things for granted. Down the years he had poked around into the baseball story and by 1939 he was ready to launch a shattering offensive against the legend of Doubleday and Cooperstown. He confirmed, for instance, that Abner Doubleday went up to West Point in 1838, the year before he invented and named baseball at Cooperstown while he was presumably on leave from his military education. But at that time, cadets never got any leave in their second year. Mr Henderson also doubted that Cadet Doubleday managed to grow into a colonel in one year as a student. Luckily for the legend, the records of that investigating commission were lost in a fire. All that's left is a small file of papers quoting the main witness. He was a resident of Cooperstown bearing the suspicious name of Abner Graves. He laid it down that his namesake invented the game and that the runner was put out by the fielder hitting him with the ball. Since this doesn't happen in baseball, and

151

granting that the man was telling the truth as he had observed it in many a stretcher case, Mr Henderson began to cast around for a game in which it did happen. He found that it had been the normal practice of an English game for a couple of centuries. He then started to go through the English records.

He found out—what even the Oxford dictionary had overlooked—that the word supposedly coined by Doubleday is first mentioned in 1744 in a letter of Lady Hervey in which she writes about the habits and pastimes of the then Prince of Wales: 'The Prince's family divert themselves at baseball, a play all who are, or have been, schoolboys are well acquainted with.' Jane Austen in one of her novels writes about a heroine who 'had nothing by nature heroic about her . . . she preferred cricket, baseball, riding on horseback . . . to books'. Mr Henderson began to pile up a mountain of documentary evidence from English literature, mainly from notebooks and journals and the like, to show that baseball—and so called—was a very popular children's game in England in the early eighteenth century. In the same year as Lady Hervey's letter there appeared a children's book of games, one letter of the alphabet for one game. B stood for baseball, and it has a picture of the player at the plate, a pitcher, a catcher and two posts for bases. The book was a best-seller and was reprinted twice in America. And in 1828, when Abner Doubleday (if he ever existed) was 9 years old, the *Boy's Own Book*, published in London, had a whole chapter about the game and illustrated it with a picture of a diamond, with bases at each corner. Many a rearguard Doubleday man will concede that

152

perhaps Abner did not invent the game but certainly invented the diamond. Not old Abner. Colonel Jane Austen, maybe, but not General Abner.

What came out of Mr Henderson's subversive labours was that a game called baseball, which looks very much like a rudimentary version of today's American game, was played everywhere in England in the eighteenth century; and that it was called 'baseball' in the southern counties, 'rounders' in the West Country, and 'feeder' in metropolitan London.

From all this there emerges the solid, objective and bitter truth that baseball was invented not in the Ukraine, and not in Cooperstown, New York, but in England; was at first an amusement of the landed and leisured gentry of the southern counties; and that they called it baseball. Now since such people, when they emigrated to America at all, shunned the rude and pious New England shore and joined the more congenial Virginia colony, they brought over the game and the name. It developed several varieties here; and six years before Abner Doubleday, that charlatan, invented it, it was being played throughout the tidewater South and later in New England. In Philadelphia there was a full-fledged club.

All right, say the desperate Doubleday partisans, forced back now into the Catskills like guerrillas, so Abner may not have invented the game or the name but he surely drew up the rules of the modern game. Well, they too must have been lost in the fire. Because the only documentary record of a complete set of rules, on which the contemporary game is based, is one printed in 1845 by the

153

Knickerbocker Baseball Club of New York. And this version of the game grew into modern baseball through the accident, if we may so call it, of the Civil War. There were over fifty clubs enrolled and competing in a national association as early as 1850. The invincible champions of that year, who never seem to have lost a game, were the renowned Excelsiors of Brooklyn. All these clubs were composed of amateurs. It is not too much to deduce that baseball followed the precedent of other sports, blood sports especially, that now belong to the honest working man, whether in the Ukraine or elsewhere. They start out as the amusement of the rich and leisured until one day the squire finds himself in a tough spot and there is an onlooking groom, stable boy or gillie with a mean left-handed curve ball.

Well, the club games stopped with the Civil War. But the Union armies spread the Knickerbocker game through the border states and the South and played everywhere behind the lines. By the time the war was over, and the survivors went home in all directions, the only possible competitor to the New York game, played with a hard ball, was a softball game, played by small boys and Bostonians, who invented it (and let's not go into that).

The New York game was, then, the core of modern professional baseball. Amateur baseball may be the glory of the high schools but in the colleges it is rapidly on the wane. Baseball has suffered from the usual afflictions of an easygoing amateur diversion that turns into a high-pressure professional business. It has a very complicated system of buying and selling, of contracts and franchises. Twice in its modern history tremendous financial scandals have almost destroyed its reputation. But let us confess that in its present form it would alarm and astonish Jane Austen and the Prince of Wales, as well as the rude outfielders of the Ukraine. It is *the* characteristic American athletic spectacle and combines in its marvellous standard of fielding and the cunning flight of the ball through the air all the invisible (I mean subtle) skill of cricket and all the very visible competitive frenzy of the English national game, which I take to be association football.

A baseball stadium is a far cry from the fields and the lowly vacant lots of its origins. And baseball bears almost no resemblance to the game which Americans make a point of deriding and ignoring: cricket. If the Atlantic alliance is to hold on the playing fields, we shall have to act on the suggestion of the late Robert Benchley, who bravely suggested that it would be better to abolish cricket and baseball and 'start all over again with a game that both countries can play—preferably baseball'.

Robert Frost

1 February 1963

It was a splendid day in Vermont when they buried Robert Frost, the sky without a cloud, the light from the white landscape making every elm and barn as sharp as a blade, and the people crunching quietly through the deep snow and squinting in the enormous sun.

155

It is a harmless sentimental custom to bury men who have been supreme in some craft with a visible symbol of their mastery: one thinks of composers whose tombstones are inscribed with a lyre, and cricketers who were laid to rest with a floral wreath of a bat and a ball. Few men must have gone to their graves amid such an exhibition of the tools of their trade as Robert Frost did the other day. From the smallest object on the horizon, a clump of evergreens or a mountain top, to the most domestic scenery that was close at hand—a maple tree, a country store, a spade—everything the mourners saw or passed among had been the subjects of his poems and the objects of his lifelong meditation. He was once called 'an original ordinary man', but whether we ordinary men are ready or able to understand an original among us is another question. And I wonder how many Americans could have honestly agreed with President Kennedy that Frost had 'bequeathed this nation a body of imperishable verse from which Americans will forever gain joy and understanding'. Because if his poetry was as plain as its surface, it was very ordinary indeed. And if it was as deep and difficult as his best admirers said, the understanding audience for it must have been as small as it always is for great poetry.

However, President Kennedy had taken him up, and in the last year or two he became a sort of unofficial Poet Laureate, more honoured, I suspect, for his connection with the White House than for any spontaneous response of the American people to the body of his work. At any rate, when he died, either 87 or 88 years of age (no one is quite sure), his last days were full of honour, love, obedience, troops of friends, as his early days had been full of menial farm chores, odd jobs that never paid off, and easygoing obscurity.

He was born in San Francisco of a New Hampshire farmer and a Scottish mother. His father died when he was 10, and his mother took him back East to settle in Lawrence, Massachusetts, and he became and remained a New Englander. From his nineteenth year to his thirty-eighth he managed to get only fourteen poems into print. In the meantime, he had tried and failed to be a student at Dartmouth College, but he did later stick out two years at Harvard. In the five years between these two grim efforts to be formally educated he was a bobbin boy in the mills, a cobbler, a smalltown editor, a schoolteacher, and at last a farmer. But the soil of New England, as he came to reflect later, is a glacial relic, for most of the year the victim of alternating fire and ice. For this reason, or possibly because he was too obsessed with the natural objects of the countryside to be a good farmer, he had to eke out a living; which he did by going from his chores to teach English at one country school and to try teaching 'psychology' (a new fetish discovered by William James) at another.

So in his thirty-seventh year he was neither a prosperous farmer nor an accepted poet. From his long meditations on the country life and landscape of New England he had shored up two small books of poems: *A Boy's Life* and *North of Boston*. Neither of them found a publisher until he moved to England in 1912 with the set intention 'to write and be poor without further scandal in the family'. There he lived and walked in the West Country and was befriended and admired by Wilfrid Gibson and Edward Thomas, two early Georgians with whom he seemed at the time to have a lot in common. He had left America with a family reputation as a dilettante, but when he came back he was greeted, by a small audience, as a pro. He had no more trouble making a modest living, and for nearly thirty years, on and off, he lived on another farm, was the so-called 'poet in residence' at Amherst, and did other agreeable stretches as a teacher at the University of Michigan, Harvard, but mostly at Middlebury College in Vermont, and then again at Dartmouth. He put out his books of poetry at about five-year intervals until the 1940s saw him at the peak of his productivity and his authority, bustling around 'collecting sticks'—as he used to put it—for what he would ignite as annual 'poetic bonfires'.

From 1924 on he took the Pulitzer Prize for poetry at regular—about six-year—intervals. This habit, because it set him up as a solid establishment poet, made his more intellectual admirers begin to think that there must be less in his work than met the eye. Indeed, Frost suffered for a long time from the incapacity of the critics to overcome certain stock responses to the various schools of poetry that were then in fashion. Because he had been a friend of the English Georgians, he was for too long taken by some people to be an over-simple rebel against the developing technology of modern life, an expatriate cricket-and-ale rustic. And because, when he got back to America, he met the high tide of the 'new' poetry of the Chicago school, he had to be looked on as a New England Sandburg. And because, in the 1930s, he

158

maintained his lifelong lack of interest in politics, the socially conscious writers of the New Deal dismissed him as a cranky escapist. We never seem to learn—though the evidence is stacked high in any library—that contemporary prejudices about a writer very rarely seem relevant in the long view. Frost was, in fact, as absorbed, and in some ways as difficult, a poet as Emily Dickinson, whose entire meditations on life were conducted inside the house in Amherst, Massachusetts, from which she barred all visitors and rarely stirred in more than twenty years. Frost was, let us say, an outdoor Emily Dickinson, which is a curiosity almost too bizarre to bear thinking about. Even when he was writing what later was admitted to be his finest poetry, his admirers were again of the wrong sort to satisfy the literary lawmakers. The people who called him 'our classic New England poet' also tended to see Will Rogers as the Mark Twain of the 1920s, and Pearl Buck as the travelling George Eliot of the 1930s. This is a kind of reverse sentimentality and a usual reflex of highbrows, who are often more concerned to validate a man's reputation than to enjoy him. It never troubled Frost much, and it would be a mistake to think of him at any time as a martyr. But for many years it made good men back away from him.

Other people, who were willing to be impressed, were put off for more honest reasons. They turned with pleasurable anticipation to his work, and what did they find? They found verses as flat and bare, and frequently as limp with bathos, as the verses on a country calendar. But if you persisted with him, you found that he had persisted ahead of you. Sometimes he reads like a man with no poetical gift

159

whatsoever who is determined to slog his way through some simple fact of nature and discover, at all costs, some universal truth. But what ought to give pause to the unwary is that there *is* always a mind at work, a wriggling, probing and in the end, a tragic mind. The very titles of his poems are deceptively ordinary. 'The Cow in Apple Time', about a cow drooling cider, sounds like a humdrum cheerful thing. But it is not. Listen.

> Having tasted fruit,
> She scorns a pasture withering to the root.
> She runs from tree to tree where lie and sweeten
> The windfalls spiked with stubble and worm-
>   eaten.
> She leaves them bitten when she has to fly.
> She bellows on a knoll against the sky.
> Her udder shrivels and the milk goes dry.

It was not until after the Second World War, when the flame of the Harriet Monroe revolution had died down, and left so many of its fiery figures mere cinders along the way, that another generation of critics noticed Frost still there, still writing his knotty monosyllables. They began to be excited by the suspicion that here possibly was an American Donne, or a Yankee Theocritus, or—a harder thing to grapple with—Robert Frost, an original. The idea that a huckleberry or a birch tree, or the games a boy played with that birch tree who was 'too far from town to learn baseball'; the idea that these things could bear the most unsentimental and profound contemplation was at first frightening, until the reader inched his way through the roughness of the underbush and, like

'The Soldier'—in Frost's poem—discovered that

> the obstacle that checked
> And tripped the body, shot spirit on
> Further than target ever showed or shone.

By the time that he was being accepted as a pure and gritty-minded pastoral poet, about as far removed from the Georgians as Thomas Hardy from Brer Rabbit, he himself was rejecting the physical world as a treacherous harbinger of winter and sickness. You could say more simply that he was a genuine poet and the oncoming of old age stirred him:

> Petals I have once pursued
> Leaves are all my darker mood.

At the age of 70 he was ready to upbraid God for the fate of Job and for His general cruelty to the human race. This challenge, in 'The Masque of Reason', was too much for him, but by now the critics were ready to grant that unlike any poet before or since, Frost had used the ordinary vernacular of a New England farmer to probe a few fundamental doubts. In poetry that is subtler in structure even than most vernacular, he transmuted rocks and flowers, wind and berries and hired men, and striking mill-workers, and boys swinging on trees, into the purest symbols of what is most hardy but most perishable in the human condition.

To the great mass of Americans, I suppose, he was simply a noble old man, said to be a great poet, who had come to be a colourful human adjunct to the refurbishing of the White House, rather like one of those plain hooked rugs, woven by a grandmother, with which wealthy New Englanders or Virginians living in exquisite colonial houses will sometimes pay a small tribute to their origins. He must have learned to live with the knowledge that to most of his countrymen he was known only by a couple of lines from one poem, 'Stopping by Woods on a Snowy Evening', just as John Donne must groan in his grave at all the twentieth-century people who know him only by the thought that 'No man is an island'. In our time, which is the age of mass marketing, we have to package our great men as quickly and simply as possible to make them acceptable to the family trade.

At the end, though, there was a lucky occasion on which his true readers and his uncomprehending large public could see him alike for what he was. In the icicle brilliance of Kennedy's inauguration he stood in 12 degrees of frost and tried to read aloud a poem specially written for the great occasion. The sun stabbed at his failing eyes, the wind slapped at him, the white light from the snow was too much for him, and he finally gave up and spoke out, stumblingly, what he knew, his fingers kneading his palms in a secret fury and his white hair blowing in sloppy waves against his forehead. It was an embarrassing moment for the President and the officials who had brought him, and for the huge crowd. But it was as good an end as any he might have imagined: an old farmer stripped down at last to a blinded oak of a man, tangled in his own branches, made foolish by the sun and the cold and the wind, by the simple elements he had once rejoiced in but which now he had come to mistrust as the mockers of humankind from Eden to Washington, DC.

The Father

22 February 1963

A simple way to turn an honest dime in a small company of Americans is to ask them on a bet how many national holidays are observed throughout the United States. They will usually count to no less than five: the birthdays of Washington and Lincoln, Independence Day, Thanksgiving Day and Labor Day. There are in fact only three. Labor Day, invented in New York as a trade union celebration, is not among them. Nor is the birthday of Lincoln. Only thirty-two states of the Union pause on 12 February to commemorate the most impressive life in the American experience. It was natural, however, that the defeated South should have taken a sour view of Lincoln for many decades after his death; and to this day, from Virginia round the whole bend of the South, through Louisiana and Texas, his birthday is officially disregarded. Once you cross the Texas line and enter New Mexico, you can begin to honour Lincoln again.

This leaves, therefore, only one American in history whom the entire country delights to honour. On every 22 February the offices and factories close down. The hundred and seventy elevators that serve the sixty thousand wage-slaves who work every day in the little plot of Manhattan ground

163

known as Radio City—they run not at all, and the wind whistles through the shafts. Over the Post Office building, looking out on a tropical sea in San Juan, Puerto Rico, an American flag is run up and languishes in the hot air. And five thousand miles to the north and west, in a forest lookout tower in the snow-capped Cascade Mountains, another flag goes up and slaps against a frozen pole. Over every public building in this country and its territories and possessions the flags are raised, and the schools are closed.

There is a Fifth Avenue dress house that always, on this day, takes away its early spring models and loops its windows with purple draperies, beneath which, in a pool of light thrown by a single high spot, stands a lump of cool white marble: the bust of a big-faced man with a big aquiline nose, a considerable chin, an eighteenth-century wig, and the drooping eyelid that novelists prescribe for what they call a patrician gaze. It is of course an effigy of George Washington, to whom once a year all sorts of men pay all kinds of tribute. Even the *Wall Street Journal* is not published on the sacred birthday, though the day before I see there was inserted a chaste two-column advertisement for a jewel firm. Its copy consisted of a single sentence: 'If, to please the people, we offer what we ourselves disapprove, how can we afterward defend our work?' An oddly moral remark, you might think, for a jeweller. But the quotation was from none other than the father of his country.

Washington towers over the generations of notable Americans as Shakespeare towers over the literature of England. He is acceptable to everybody for at least one of the same reasons: we

164

don't know too much about him, or what we have learned we have idealized, so every man can construct a Washington in the image he likes best. From time to time, most recently in the 1920s, snide authors come along to try and show that Washington was a promoter of stock companies, an exploiter of mines and timber, a man 'who knew more profanity than Scripture . . . had no belief in the wisdom of the common people but regarded them as inflammatory dolts'. But these scandals never seem to take. They get the same reception that they had from Calvin Coolidge when he was asked in the White House what effect a particularly scurrilous biography of the first President would have on his reputation. Coolidge swivelled round in his desk chair and biliously looked out the window at the soaring Washington monument, which is raised over the capital like the sword of the Archangel Gabriel. 'He's still there,' said Coolidge.

At this late date, it would be almost tasteless to compose a picture of Washington as a great if frail human being. Every nation has to have one or two blameless legends, and Americans feel as uncomfortable today to hear that Washington was a land grabber as an Englishman would be to hear that King Alfred was a cannibal or the late Queen Mary a secret drinker. Washington's birthday is as close to a secular Christmas as any Christian country dare come this side of blasphemy. I hasten to throw in quickly that the United States, though founded in the main by Christian men, was not set up as a Christian nation, since its creators had had their fill of the established Church that hounded their forebears. It may explain why, when Americans are sorely troubled, they turn for

165

official inspiration not to the Koran or the Bible but to the the colonial scriptures, to the sayings of the Founding Fathers, most of all to the speeches of Washington.

There is today a pronouncement of his that they linger over with a great yearning. It is regularly reprinted and blazoned in newspaper editorials on any 22 February that Americans feel about to be tricked into a European war or seduced into an alliance. It is a passage from Washington's so-called Farewell Address, which he gave as he took leave of the Presidency. It reads today rather like a commentary of General de Gaulle on the 'special relationship' between Britain and the United States. This is it: 'A passionate attachment of one nation for another produces a variety of evils. Sympathy for the favourite nation, facilitating the illusion of an imaginary common interest in cases where no real common interest exists . . . betrays the former into a participation in the quarrels of the latter, without adequate inducement or justification.'

It does not quite have the swing of 'Tell me where is fancy bred' or 'My luve's like a red, red rose'. So, down the centuries Americans have tended to shorten this unmemorable, and unlearnable, passage into a snappy single phrase: 'No entangling alliances.' When it is pointed out that this is a misquotation, that the phrase actually came from the lips of Thomas Jefferson, the sensible retort is that, anyway, that's what old George meant to say.

Now that we have the effigy and its legend pretty well established, let us come down to the man himself.

His family came from England and he was born in Virginia in 1732. His father was what you might describe as a substantial small squire, a status that made him possibly a grander figure in the Southern colonies than he would have been in the old country. Almost anybody who owned land in Virginia led a life which was a curious combination of a farmhand and an aristocrat. (I am aware that grooms and the like were all, until the First World War, elements of the aristocratic system—'all part of the same show', as a Prime Minister of England eloquently put it; but except in the rituals of blood sports their habits were not interchangeable.) Washington learned all that could be learned about the farming and management of his father's estate, which had passed to him from a half-brother who died young. He raised cattle, he was out in the fields growing tobacco, he shot wild turkey and ate it on the bone. He had taught himself a lot of mathematics and on his surveying trips he was always adding to his land. He rode by day and often by night, he brushed up against the Indians from time to time, and a scalp was as natural, I imagine, as a cow-flop.

He served in the French and Indian wars as a general's aide, had horses shot out from under him and acquired an enviable, though local, reputation for a blank refusal to panic. Then quite suddenly his health failed him and he resigned his commission and retreated, for what he thought would be the rest of his life, to a fine stretch of land overlooking the Potomac River where he had built an elegant and charming white house with a little Wren tower, a colonial façade, and a long portico supported by slender columns. (It is now a national shrine and, along with the Spanish mission at Santa Barbara, California, used to be one of the two handsomest colonial relics in America. But both of them have been refaced and at close quarters look like something out of Disney.)

He was in his bearing and looks and manners an eighteenth-century British soldier and landowner; and if he could be resurrected he would undoubtedly alarm a great many Americans by sounding and seeming more British than the British. He had, for instance, very decided ideas about the relations of one class with another. In the towns, at any rate. In the country it was another thing: he was with many conditions of men who were 'part of the same show'. Not only did he not slap backs, he made a point on becoming President of not shaking hands. He thought it was unbecoming for the President of a great state to touch the flesh of his subjects. The Senate used to bristle over this characteristic, and when he was inaugurated as President in New York—an early and transient capital—he came down the Hudson in a great barge and he clattered to the ceremony in full-dress uniform with a flourish of outriders. As he took the oath of office, the impressive silence was cracked only by the growl of a Senator from Massachusetts saying to his neighbour: 'I fear that we may have exchanged George the Third for George the First.'

You would think, then, that there was little in this reserved and lordly man to provoke the famous compliment that was spoken on his death: 'First in war, first in peace, first in the hearts of his countrymen.' Six feet three or four (the tape measures vary), imperious, self-sufficient, contemptuous of jolly human relations, his sword at his side, a big face serene to the point of complacency but pitted with smallpox, a frosty eyebrow under which rolled a sleepy blue eye, which, however, was said to rouse itself a little at the sight of a pretty woman—I think he must have been one of those people, not always appealing, whose greatness was simply the triumph of character over the flesh. Perhaps he was British enough by instinct to rise at the same qualities in his country's rulers. He had been, remember, a militiaman in the British army and had been the victim of some very overbearing officers. Not unnaturally he came to attribute arrogance to the land of their birth. He detested the strict and pettifogging restrictions on American trade that were soon to cause a war, and to cause, in fact, the United States of America. He organized the resistance in Virginia to the English Stamp Act and the Tobacco Act. He was a Virginia delegate to the first meeting of the colonies which met to decide, and did decide, to fight the mother country. He was chosen, not at that time by the mark of his obvious superiority but by a political deal, as the commander-in-chief of the rather miserable army that undertook to defend the American continent against the British.

How did it come about that in five short years he was able to break through the strong chrysalis of a Virginia gentleman and take wings and become a name which in its day combined the authority of Napoleon with the magic of Franklin Roosevelt? The answer seems to lie not in any personal charm but in his iron resolution to keep the American army united when it was all but ready to fall apart from incompetence, indifference, corruption and starvation. What an army it was! For every trained soldier there were three half-trained and ten mechanics, farmers, illiterates, half of them pressed into service or bought into service, deserting in droves, buying their way out when the going was rough.

According to Jefferson and other reliables, he often failed in the field and was not, in the military sense, a great general. But for eight years, and through many defeats and constant betrayal, he was as cool as an icicle and as impressive as God. He believed in his men long after they had ceased to believe in themselves. He fought with and for them even when the Congress thought of calling off the war. And in the famous winter of 1777 he was lucky to rescue from two thrashings by the British the ragged remnant of an army, so puny and bedraggled that the word went to Britain that the war was almost won. He pulled together a few thousand men, many times outnumbered by the crack troops of the enemy, and he camped in a rolling, bare valley in Pennsylvania. Less than half his men had arms, most of them had neither shoes nor shirts. The Congress took flight into the mountains of Pennsylvania and there was great rejoicing in London. During that winter, it is not too much to say, whatever was mortal in Washington was absorbed and elevated into the legend. He lost men from disease, desertion, treachery, and very many simply starved to death. Congress was so out of sympathy with this bitter-ender that it reorganized the War Department without his say-so. But he kept his camp at Valley Forge through the racking winter. And in the spring the French lined up with the rebels, and the rebellion held.

So Valley Forge was no victory. It was a pitiful siege. But it explains the veneration in which Washington came to be held, then and ever after, for of all the battles of the war Valley Forge was the proudest. It was the heart of the Revolution, the thing itself. No great general has ever been remembered so exclusively by such a defeat or by such a homely place name.

When he died, Napoleon was observed to bow his head, and in the English Channel the British fleet fired a salute of twenty guns.

The Assassination

24 November 1963

By now it may well be impossible to add any sensible or proper words to all the millions that have been written and spoken about the life and cruel death of John F. Kennedy. Those of us who have ever sat down to write a letter of condolence to a close friend know what an aching task it is to say something that is pointed and that touches the right vein of sympathy. But I hope you will understand that there is no other thing to talk about—not here. At three thousand miles it may be easier to speculate about policy, the new administration—not here. For I cannot remember a time, certainly in the last thirty years, when the people everywhere around you were so quiet, so tired-looking, and for all their variety of shape and colour and character so plainly the victims of a huge and bitter disappointment. That may sound a queer word to use, but grief is a general term that covers all kinds of sorrow, and I think that what sets off this death from that of other great Americans of our time is the sense that we have been cheated, in a moment, by a wild but devilishly accurate stroke of the promise of what we had begun to call the Age of Kennedy.

Let me remind you of a sentence in his Inaugural address, when he took over the Presidency on that icy day of 20 January 1961. He said, 'Let the word go forth from this time and place to friend and foe alike that the torch has been passed to a new generation of Americans, born in this century, tempered by war, disciplined by a hard and bitter peace, proud of our ancient heritage and unwilling to witness or permit the slow undoing of those human rights to which this nation has always been committed . . . Let every nation know, whether it wishes us well or ill, that we shall pay any price, bear any burden, meet any hardship, support any friend, oppose any foe, to assure the survival and the success of liberty.'

This is, of course, the finest rhetoric, worthy of Lincoln, but what made it sound so brave and rousing on that first day was the clear statement that a young man was speaking for a new generation. It concentrated in one scornful sentence the reminder that the old men who had handled the uncertain peace and the Second World War had had their day and that there was at hand a band of young Americans ready not to ignore the wisdom of their forefathers but to fight for it.

It would be hard to say more exactly or more

bravely that it was a fresh America that would have to be negotiated with, but that, as always, liberty itself was not negotiable.

Now, even in the moment of knowing that the promises of an inaugural address are bound to have a grandeur very hard to live up to the morning after, this remarkable speech, which the President had hammered out, sentence by sentence, with his closest aide and companion, Theodore Sorensen, did strike a note to which the American people, and their allies everywhere, responded with great good cheer. Of course we knew, older men and women have always known (what in their youth they blithely rattled off as a quotation from Shakespeare) that 'golden lads and girls all must, as chimney sweepers, come to dust'. But it is always stirring to see that young people don't believe it. We chuckled sympathetically then at the warning which Senator Lyndon Johnson had chanted all through the campaign: that the Presidency could not safely be put in the hands of a man 'who has not a touch of gray in his hair'. John Kennedy had turned the tables triumphantly on this argument by saying, in effect, that in a world shivering under the bomb it was the young who had the vigour and the single-mindedness to lead.

If we pause and run over the record of the very slow translation of these ideals into law—the hair's breadth defeat of the medical care for the aged plan, the shelving after a year of labour of the tax bill, the perilous reluctance of the Congress to tame the Negro revolution now with a civil rights law—we have to admit that the clear trumpet sound of the Kennedy Inaugural has been sadly soured down three short years.

Any intelligent American family, sitting around a few weeks ago, would grant these deep disappointments; and many thoughtful men were beginning to wonder if the President's powers were not a mockery of his office, since he can be thwarted from getting any laws passed at all by the simple obstructionism of a dozen chairmen of Congressional committees, most of them, by the irony of a seniority system that gives more and more power to old men who keep getting re-elected by the same states, most of them from the South. But that same American family, sitting around this weekend, could live with these disappointments but not with the great one: the sense that the new generation, 'born in this century, tempered by war, disciplined by a hard and bitter peace, proud of our ancient heritage and unwilling to witness or permit. . .', was struck down lifeless, unable to witness or permit, or not to permit, anything.

When it is possible to be reasonable we will all realize, calling on our everyday fatalism, that if John Kennedy was 46 and his brother only 38, most of the men around him were in their fifties and some in their sixties; and that therefore we fell, for a day or two in November 1963, into a sentimental fit. However, we are not yet reasonable; the self-protective fatalism, which tells most of us that what has been must be, has not yet restored us to the humdrum course of life.

I am not dwelling on this theme, the slashing down in a wanton moment of the flower of youth, because it's enjoyable or poetic to think about. It seems to me, looking over the faces of the people and hearing my friends, that the essence of the

American mood this very dark weekend is this deep feeling that our youth has been mocked, and the vigour of America for the moment paralysed.

It is, to be hard-hearted about it, fascinating—when it is not also poignant—to see in how many ways people express the same emotion. Many of the memorial photographs in the shop windows have small replicas of the Presidential standard on one side, and a Navy flag on the other, recalling the incredible five days' gallantry on that Pacific island which Kennedy himself never recalled, except to the men who were with him and survived. A young socialite, whose life is a round of clothes and parties and music, bemoans the fact that the Kennedys will leave the White House and take with them 'the style, the grace, the fun they brought to it'. An American friend from Paris writes: 'I think his death will especially be felt by the young, for he had become for them a symbol of what was possible, with intelligence and will.' An old man, wise in the ups and downs of politics, says: 'I wonder if we knew what he might have grown to in the second term.' A child with wide eyes asks, 'Tell me, will the Peace Corps go on?'

There is another thing that strikes me, which is allied to the idea of a young lion shot down. It is best seen in the bewilderment of people who were against him, who felt he had temporized and betrayed the promise of the first days. One of them, a politically active woman, rang me up and what she had to say dissolved in tears. Another, a veteran sailor, a close friend and a lifelong Republican, said last night: 'I can't understand, I never felt so close to Kennedy as I do now.' This sudden discovery that he was more familiar than we knew is, I think, easier to explain. He was the first President of the television age, not as a matter of chronology but in the incessant use he made of this new medium. When he became President-elect, he asked a friend to prepare a memorandum on the history of Presidential press conferences. He wanted to know how much the succession of Presidents since Wilson had been able to mould the press conference and how much it had moulded *them*. What he received was a plea, disguised as a monograph, to abandon Eisenhower's innovation of saying everything on the record for quotation and letting the conference be televised. He looked it over, at his usual rate (of about a thousand words a minute), granted the arguments but said simply: 'Television is now the main personal link between the people and the White House. We can't go back.' He allowed his press conferences to be televised live. He also made another decision which ran counter to the wisdom of all incumbent Presidents. No man who is in power invites a debate with an opponent who is out of power and who can speak not of the things he's done but of the things the incumbent has done wrong. In spite of knowing well that next time he would be the man with his back against the wall, he had decided that the television debate was now an essential element of a Presidential campaign.

So for three years and more, we have seen him, at the end of our day, on all his tours—in Vienna, in Dublin, in Berlin, in Florida, Chicago, Palm Beach, in—alas—Dallas, in his own house talking affably with reporters, rumpling up the children, very rarely posing, always offhand and about his business, talking to foreign students in the White

House garden, making sly, dry jokes at dinners, every other week fencing shrewdly and often brilliantly with two hundred reporters, and sometimes at formal rallies stabbing the air with his forefinger and bringing to life again, in his eyes and his chin and his soaring sentences, the old image of the young warrior who promised 'the energy, the faith, the devotion that will light America and all who serve her'.

The consequence of all this is that the family, the American family, has been robbed, violently and atrociously, of a member. When Roosevelt died, the unlikeliest people, the very young who thought of him as a perpetual President, and some of the very old who hated him, confessed that they felt they had lost a father. Today, millions of Americans are baffled by the feeling, which seems to have little to do with their political loyalties, that they have lost a brother, the bright young brother you are proud of, the one who went far and mingled with the great, and had no side, no pomp, and in the worst moments (the Bay of Pigs) took all the blame, and in the best (the Cuban crisis) had the best sort of courage, which is the courage to face the worst and take a quiet stand.

This charming, complicated, subtle and greatly intelligent man, whom the Western world was proud to call its leader, appeared for a split second in the telescopic sight of a maniac's rifle. And he was snuffed out. In that moment, all the decent grief of a nation was taunted and outraged. So that along with the sorrow, there is a desperate and howling note over the land. We may pray on our knees, but when we get up from them, we cry with the poet:

177

Do not go gentle into that good night.
Rage, rage against the dying of the light.

LBJ

28 November 1965

One of the occupational burdens of a foreign
correspondent is the request from the home office
for a piece which the home office has already
composed in its head. Many years ago, an English
magazine asked me for an article and an
accompanying photograph 'doing something
American, preferably sporting'. I was briefly
fascinated by the thought of what the editor
imagined a sporting American to be (a rodeo
rider? a Las Vegas gambler? a golfer in two-toned
—or as they used to be called, 'co-respondent's'—
shoes?). For almost at once I came on a
photograph taken by a friend on a hot summer's
day on the south shore of Long Island. At that time
I was mad about surf-casting, and here was a
tanned and lithe fellow, young and black-haired,
casting the long line with a masterful arc. I was in
shorts and my knees were buried in the froth of the
surf. It seemed just the ticket. I scribbled in a
suggestion for a caption: 'Cooke casting for striped
bass on Long Island'. Incidentally, I was in left
profile facing the ocean, which was on the left of
the picture.

When the magazine sent me a complimentary
copy, I was in right profile and the ocean was on

the right. This was not an error, though it involves a rather laborious photographic trick. I thought, Why print the negative? The editor wrote back, 'If the ocean is on your left, it will look as if you were fishing in the Pacific—very confusing.' But the printed caption alarmed me more. It said, 'Cooke fishing in Florida'. The editor had an answer for that one, too. 'The English,' he wrote on a crisp postcard, 'know certain elementary things and we mustn't upset them. The Pacific is where Hollywood is; fishing would seem a waste of time. Cowboys come from the West. Fishing is in Florida—no use puzzling them by bringing up Long Island, which is where rich men keep their yachts.'

It took me years to work up the nerve to write for a British audience about fishing. I still wanted to correct that caption, though I was undoubtedly the only living person who remembered it. I wanted to say that though they do surf-fish in Florida—and catch such inconsequential stuff as snook, permit and various snappers—it is the loot of the deep seas, the white and blue marlin, and the inshore red and mutton snappers, the pompano and other lurid and tasty monsters, for which Florida should be respected; and that it is we in the North who have the thundering surf through which striped bass as weighty as thirty or forty pounds knife their headlong way till they are practically beached at your feet, and wheel around and beat it out to sea. It was all too late to explain. No use even mentioning to a transatlantic audience that striped bass is probably the most succulent of our eating fish. If it does not swim in Europe, it's probably tasteless.

179

This early episode provided my initiation into the war between correspondents and their editors. Lately, I have had another. Very soon after Lyndon Johnson took over the Presidency I had a cable from an English editor saying, 'WOULD APPRECIATE ARTICLE ON TEXAS AS BACKGROUNDER JOHNSON STOP COWBOYS COMMA OIL COMMA MILLIONAIRES COMMA HUGE RANCHES COMMA GENERAL CRASSNESS BAD MANNERS ETC.' I promptly declined this assignment since the whole piece would have had to show that the editor was wrong at the start, and the end. If cowboys, oil, millionaires, huge ranches, and general crassness were the true background of Lyndon Johnson, or even the elementary things about Texas, clearly the editor could have written the piece himself.

My first thought was: cowboys there are, west of the Johnson country, which is central Texas, a landscape of pulverized granite planted with mesquite, very congenial to armadillos and other armoured divisions but the pasture otherwise so poor that the sheep eat the wild flowers and the goats must nibble for the rest. Goats, they say, can live where all other four-footed animals would starve. And this is goat country, and that is why Lyndon Johnson as a Congressman, or some other Congressman from nearby, would be pretty certain to be on the House Military Affairs Committee, because goats produce mohair, and mohair produces army uniforms.

All right—oil. It used to be smart to say that Texas has traded its open range for a sea of oil beneath. But it is very likely that most of the people in and around Johnson City and the Pedernales

River have never seen an oil man. The great oilfields lie to the east and the north, and to Johnson's family and neighbours they are another world. In his early days, in fact, Johnson had to fight the oil lobby on behalf of the poor farmers around him, and you could say that the unceasing struggle of the farmers against drought and floods, their need for some elementary conservation and electricity—these were the hard facts of life that first pushed Johnson into politics.

By now I hope I don't need to say that millionaires in Johnson country are as scarce as they are in northern Scotland. Huge ranches? I must say that this magazine editor had an uncanny knack for picking on the very attributes that aren't there. The celebrated King Ranch, from which this preconception springs, is in the extreme southeast of the state, right on the Gulf. It is the largest ranch there is, just under a million acres, and it is spectacularly atypical. The average Texas ranch is two hundred acres, and the ranches (meaning the farms) of the Johnson country are smaller still.

General crassness? Certainly there are crass people in Texas, as there are in Maine and Berkshire and India and France. But when I read to the end of this sorry cablegram, what came perversely to mind was a remark of the late Lord Halifax when he was ambassador to the United States. Whenever he could snatch a weekend or a few days away from Washington, he would go down to Texas and his Texas friends. It was his favourite state, and about its people he said, 'They have the finest manners of any foreign people I have ever known.'

Manners? Lyndon Johnson? In this, perhaps, he

is an original, and only a week or two after he succeeded to the Presidency, an old American statesman, an intellect and a wasp (in more senses than one), told me that 'the problem the American people are going to have with him is to recognize that his "country manners" do not preclude genuine compassion and a first-rate mind'.

So, if you are going to write a piece filling in the background of Lyndon Johnson there are some essential things that you have to picture. The granite soil, with actual high mounds of granite slabs; the heat and the barrenness of the country; the stern and tidy life of the nearby German town of Fredericksburg; the strong hold of the Methodists and Baptists on the Texas state legislature—hence no alcoholic mixed drinks are served in Texas from one end of its 800-mile stretch to another, and millionaires must tote their booze into a fancy restaurant in brown paper bags. The boyhood spent with people of Scots-Irish descent, known there as Anglos, because the other neighbours are Germans and Mexicans. The Germans are a Republican pocket on the plain, and as a boy Johnson saw many old friends suffer cruelly in the First World War because of their ties of blood.

The most important mark of this part of Texas is its classlessness, of a special, highly regional kind. Thus, Johnson could be at one and the same time a small farmer, once a very poor one, and yet be well connected as to family (his father and grandfather could be high in state government and yet be close to bankruptcy). He is a country boy with Southern talk and Western habits. He knows the Old Testament as well as he knows the soils of Texas. And throughout his childhood, college was a

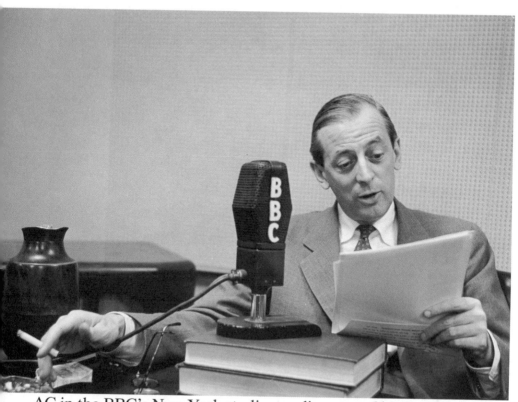

AC in the BBC's New York studio, reading one of his Letters, *circa* 1953.

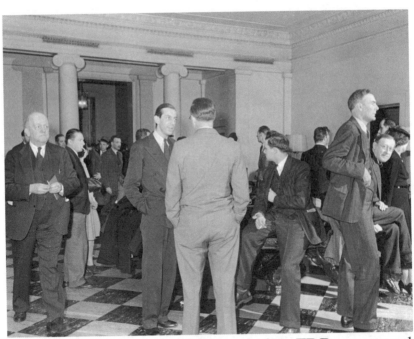

At the White House in 1941, just before FDR announced
the signing of the Lend Lease Agreement.

AC reviewing the troops along a line of New York City mounted
police in the early 1960s, probably here the Columbus Day Parade
held every October.

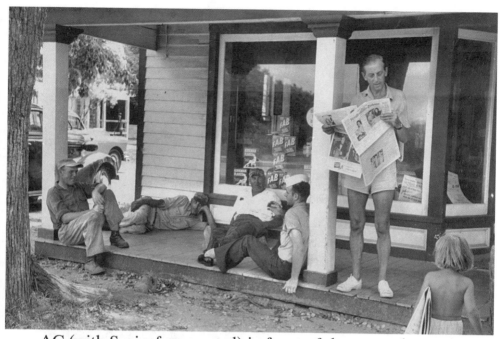

AC (with Susie, foreground) in front of the general store in Cutchogue, Long Island, going through the morning paper.

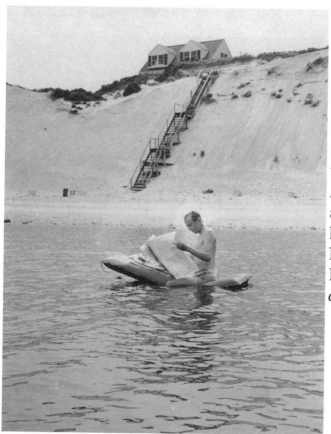

Keeping in touch and afloat with the news, AC drifts past a neighbour's house at Nassau Point, Long Island *circa* 1952.

AC filing a story to England from his teletype machine in Nassau Point while Susie waits patiently so they can go to the beach, *circa* 1952.

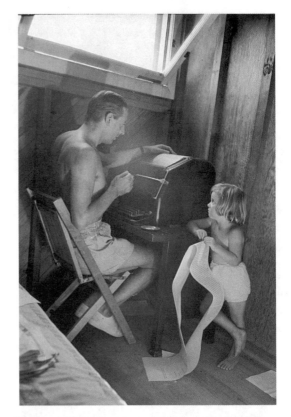

AC with his son John in a New York studio, preparing for a broadcast *circa* 1945.

AC never visited a barber shop after he met Jane. Here Janes does the honours in their bathroom at 1150 Fifth Avenue, *circa* 1952.

'Domestic Interior', at 114 East 71st Street, with AC, Jane and Susie, June 1950. The family moved to more spacious quarters at 1150 Fifth Avenue in December of that year.

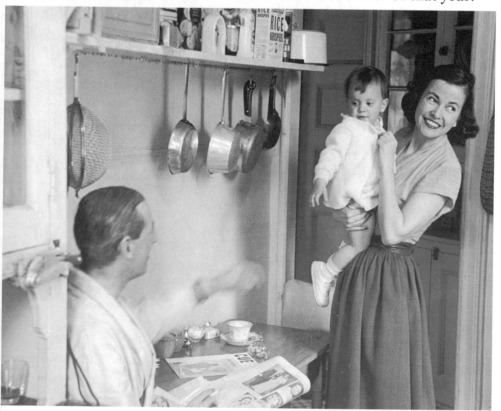

AC typically enjoying himself while discussing the Hollywood film business with colleagues in 1949.

An elegant evening with long-term friend Lauren Bacall.

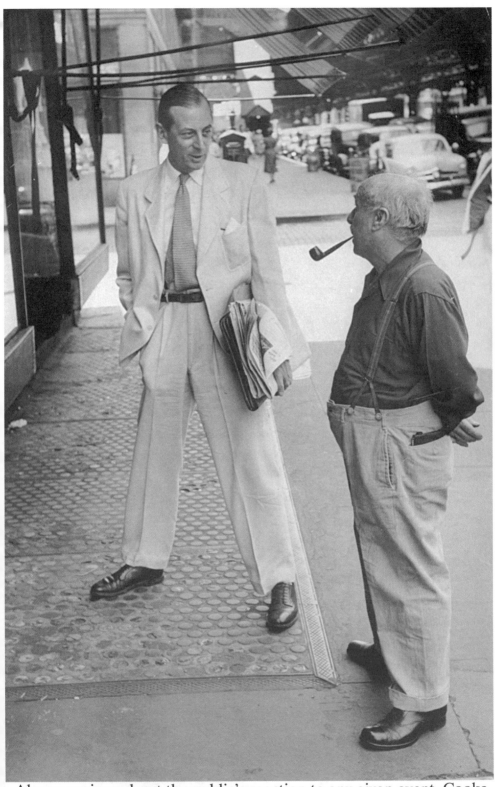

Always curious about the public's reaction to any given event, Cooke delighted in talking to the cabbie, the butcher and the man on the street.

AC with Jane aboard
Cunard's *Queen Mary*,
circa 1962.

AC delighted
and relieved to
be nearly home
and back in
New York.
Here, in
the airport,
late 1960s.

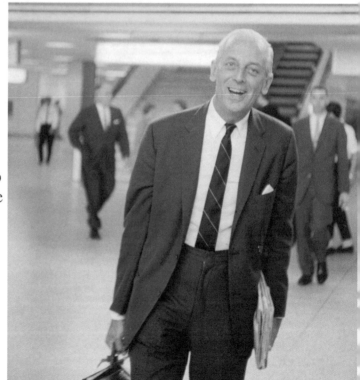

distant thing to aim at but not to take for granted. The enduring ambition of his boyhood was that of his friends: the passionate desire of a poor farmboy to own his own farm and call it a ranch. The now famous LBJ ranch is a modest place, as such things go. And when Johnson first bought it and took old Speaker Rayburn down there to show it off, Mr Sam said: 'Lyndon, you told me you'd bought a ranch, why it's nothin' but an itty-bitty farm.'

The pride of Johnson in these origins is something we shall all have to reckon with. What has already emerged from his Presidency is the force of his remark, long buried, that he was 'a Roosevelt man, lock, stock, and barrel'. Roosevelt took to the young Johnson in the pit of the Depression and sent him to his own people to reclaim thousands of unemployed young men from the streets and the farm patches. It was, Johnson later said, 'the most satisfying job I ever did have in my life'. This remark attests, I think, to the genuineness of his so-called war on poverty, which the opposition said was a cynical election-year ploy. As a Roosevelt radical he was well hated by the oil and insurance interests when he first ran for Congress. And if we say that he was allied rather with 'the ranching interests' they include very conspicuously the interest of the small farmers, the Mexicans especially, in having sheep that stayed alive, electricity for their kitchens and pumps, feed for their cattle, not to mention food for their families.

There is another aspect of this regional pride that is bound to affect Johnson's approach to negotiation both with friends and foes. He delights to look on southwest Texas as a training ground and a horoscope for the world outside. He strongly believes that if a man can learn to harmonize the conflicting interests and prejudices of Mexican bean-farmers and German bakers and Anglo retailers and Jews and real-estate men from Austin, he can approach foreigners—men from India and prime ministers from Westphalia—on the same basis. He always provokes a stranger to talk about his past and his origins, so as to gauge the real forces that commit a man's heart before his head is involved. He startled a German delegation, on its first visit to the ranch, by saying that the German demand for a milk subsidy, the Italians' concern for protecting their rice and olive oil, the Netherlands' need for a margarine tax, all composed not the dangerous battleground of the European Common Market but the common ground on which they would have to weave these necessities into a system. 'He talked to us,' said one goggling German, 'as if we were his constituents.'

It remains a great question whether this instinct for what he calls 'creative compromise' will provide the proper magic for talking to the Russians and the British about Europe, or the South Vietnamese —and maybe one day the Chinese—about South east Asia. There is another large question. It is whether a conservative country in a revolutionary mood (I mean the United States) will be willing to let 'a Roosevelt man, lock, stock, and barrel' finish the liberal revolution of Roosevelt's New Deal that was only halfway along when it was rudely arrested by the Second World War.

It is not simply to bolster your spirits on a dark anniversary that I have attempted this little session on the couch, but to warn the intelligentsia, which mourns too inconsolably the bad day at Dallas, that it should watch and wait. Lincoln, too, was considered an oaf by the intelligentsia and actually dubbed 'the Baboon' by the best-informed men in London, including the editorial writers of *The Times*. He fooled most of the people most of the time he was alive. But he didn't fool history. So it could be with Johnson.

Has the World Gone to Pot?

15 April 1966

Anyone like me who was brought up in Britain had used the slang phrase l.s.d. ever since he could remember. It was one of the last souvenirs of the Roman occupation and was the normal phrase for pounds, shillings and pence. It naturally held a fascination for the smallest tot who ever stood on the wrong side of the plate-glass window of a candy store. But the initials never had the sinister fascination they now spell out.

A letter from the federal government to two thousand university and college officials reminded me at first of the comparative innocence of my own boyhood, and then by free association of two blind men, James Thurber and Aldous Huxley. Most of all, it reminded me of a walk I took with Huxley, around Christmas time 1959, along the road and around the garden of his house high above the bowl of mountains which encloses Hollywood at its rim and Los Angeles in its huge basin. Aldous Huxley was not a poet himself but a man of fine insight into poetic experience. He was also a man who held grimly on to some rather rum superstitions, and I don't think it's unkind to say that southern California was at least one congenial room in his spiritual home.

I mention both these characteristics, one of which is a kind of parody or excess of the other, because they both applied to something he said to me as we walked high up in the hills and he began to tell me about an experiment he was making with a certain drug. It excited him greatly. He called it lysergic acid, and I presume it was an early compound of the one that is now known as LSD-25. Huxley was, so far as any ordinary person could see or sense, a blind man. He could read through very thick lenses when he held the paper almost to his eyeballs. He could, he said, distinguish intensities of light. Sometimes his eyes were better and sometimes worse but not so that an acquaintance would notice. You had to guide him on a walk and you could believe he had any sight at all only when he went into his own house and moved easily around its familiar geography. It is necessary to go into the seeming limits of his sight because he was, during our walk, talking about the essential thing in a poet, his ability to see physical things more penetratingly than most of us, and to feel more deeply.

I remember we were treading carefully along the road, and I gathered that Huxley could not possibly see more than dim shadows and shapes farther than a few feet in front of him. He had just said that D. H. Lawrence had the most acute sensitivity of anyone he had known to the texture and tactile character of animals and birds and flowers. 'Well,'

186

he said, in his gentle and intense way, 'I have found out that with this drug one can be granted for a while a kind of exquisitely heightened sensibility, so that'—he said, as the gravel crunched under our feet—'every stone or piece of gravel on this roadway, for instance, comes to look like a separate and marvellous jewel.'

In the past week or so, more than six years later, I have dared to wonder whether the drug quickened and improved the sense he had almost lost or whether it did, in fact, replace his loss with a vision. I put it this way because we have lately heard some sad and shocking testimony about the effect of LSD-25 on college students, who, in the present fashion, seem to take all sensation for their province, including the further reaches of consciousness, and unconsciousness, induced by drugs. LSD is absurdly cheap to make. It is one of the company of drugs now known as hallucinogens, and there is no doubt that in some people it produces exquisite visions. The big question is whether they are of the outer or inner world, whether in fact they heighten and deepen reality or fool the taker into believing that the kind of vision a madman sees is the real world that convention, habit, or sheer blunting of instinct hide from him. At any rate, the experience of a dose sometimes passes off with a few bad effects that are noticeable. (We ought to say 'noticeable at the time, and to the outsider'.) There now appears also to be no doubt that LSD can, and often does, induce mental aberrations and psychotic states that may last several hours or days; that it may plant a chronic psychosis, or do temporary or permanent damage to the central nervous system. Sometimes, though apparently rarely, it drives the taker to suicide, murder, or death.

It was the director of the Food and Drug Administration who sent this letter to the presidents and deans, principals and science departments of the colleges and universities, warning them of the 'extreme danger' of these 'hallucinatory drugs', in particular of LSD-25, one-tenth of an ounce of which can provide 100,000 tiny doses, each big enough, in the government's opinion, to be called 'exceedingly dangerous'.

This radical move was called for by the great prevalence of pep pills, barbiturates, and other drugs among college students. Lately, we have had scary news about the prevalence of LSD, in California especially. It is the kind of news about which it is almost impossible to make a helpful comment. Older people deplore the pathological extremes which this generation of college students seems to touch in its hunger for experience. Doctors shake their heads, but the addicts don't go to doctors unless they are thoroughly alarmed; with LSD, the government suggests, the alarm may sound too late. The hope about LSD is that it will be more often terrifying than exalting, and it will be dropped, even by neurotics who are tempted to go beyond the euphoria of pep pills and the weed grown in back gardens known as marijuana. (Marijuana is always lumped with the other dangerous drugs, but the day may come when we have to consider it as a special case. The state laws are strict against its possession, on the general assumption that it is a narcotic. But the scientists are agreed that it is not, as—for instance— cigarettes are. It spreads the time sense in some

188

people, so that an oncoming truck may seem to be a mile away instead of its actual few hundred yards. In most people, I'm told, it produces much the same sense of confident well-being and happy talk as a couple of dry martinis, which are not so far, thank God, banned from American life.)

Whenever the LSD topic comes up, most of us— if we have children of college age—are forced to ask ourselves whether we are taking a merely reflex, stuffy view of the failings of the young. We tend to lump drugs with the active rebellion of the young against what they call the establishment and we call society. I don't know the answer to this. But there is one comment I should like to make. The generation just ahead of me, which was young and dashing in the 1920s, was certainly indicted by *its* elders. It was told it had violated the whole moral code and was fast destroying family life. (If you were chic in the 1920s having children was considered naive or, since birth control was a prevailing fad, clumsy.) In this country, the brazen young defied the Noble Experiment of prohibition with a flask of bathtub gin in the hip pocket. There were, in every city, whole benches of magistrates to bemoan that the young were leading the world into decadence and damnation to the wailing of the newly revived saxophone and the shameless gyrations of the charleston.

Well, I suppose that these people, who are now in their mid-sixties or beyond, produced their quota of pleasure hounds and even drug addicts. A remarkable number of them wrote remarkable books, painted memorable pictures, composed so many charming and bouncy songs that without them any band that plays for old-time dancing (what you might now call 'square' dancing) would have to fold long before midnight. Other family-wreckers turned into statesmen, architects, businessmen, conscientious plumbers and builders, doctors, scientists, and the majority into law-abiding citizens and devoted parents who, only a few years ago, provoked the amazed admiration of their grandchildren by teaching them how to do the charleston.

The irresistible thing is to say that old people always lament the morals and manners of the young and are always wrong. The fact that is often overlooked is that sometimes the old people have been right; and the trick is to know when you are living in one of those times. An old Roman codger who lamented in the fourth century AD that the empire was going to rack and ruin was absolutely correct. A Greek doctor who, let us say, in the first century AD feared that his trade of medicine was seriously declining would no doubt have been ridiculed as a fogey. But he could hardly have been enough of a pessimist to guess that for the next twelve or thirteen hundred years, medicine would flounder in a dark age of quackery and superstition before it again enlisted the early scientific method or the insights of Hippocrates, who knew the difference between the fever of tuberculosis and the fever of pneumonia, though he had never heard of a micro-organism. Or consider an old English playgoer, in about 1630, grumbling that the best tragedies had all been written and staged in his youth. Another fogey, no doubt, but neither he nor the young who scoffed at him could possibly have imagined that no decent tragedies at all would appear in English for another two hundred and fifty years.

It's an old cliché, but annoyingly enough it's a true one, to say that Americans are obsessed with the idea that progress is inevitable, that—as a faith healer of the 1920s used to say—'every day and in every way we are getting better and better'. The belief in progress is certainly a stimulant to achieve it and is responsible for the tenacity of, say, American industrial research (applied research, to be precise) and for the national delight in new things, as well as (I've been hinting) for the complacency of seeing virtue only in what is new, whether it's a plastic or a poem or a new way of talk. But it does disguise from us the truth that civilizations have their ups and downs and all of them, at last, snuff out. Because we can 'hang' glass buildings on a steel frame does not necessarily make us the superiors of John Nash, or Palladio or Louis Sullivan. The fact that we've seen in our time—in the last thirty years only—the birth and glory of the great age of bacteriology is no guarantee that it's going to go on. As a political fact, simply, it has guaranteed the survival of more people than can be decently fed and housed.

I put the question, and I do not stay for an answer. Just in time, another medical item came off the ticker and may help us to hang on with our fingernails through this barrage of brimstone. A research scientist from the Neuropsychiatric Institute at Princeton, speaking before an impressive gathering of experimental biologists, has come up with the pronouncement that the only drug that some of us will ever take with a steady hand and a clear conscience is not only a painkiller but has very positive properties to relieve anxiety.

191

The man has been measuring brainwaves, of course, and he finds that this magic drug has more reliable and harmless effect than the tranquillizers. It is called aspirin. When it is 'buffered', he says, it will soothe you and strengthen you against 'the real anxieties of the world'.

Fortified by two of these little white placebos, I look out of my window and on to the park and, whether it is there or not, I can see the forsythia at last is out, that the cherry is starting to blossom. I have a vision of the sap rising in the trees. I am humbly grateful for the faculty of sight. And I recall suddenly that James Thurber, in his brave, crotchety way, used to maintain that writers can actually be handicapped by sight. We were sitting out on the terrace of his house in Connecticut and I asked him what he meant. 'Well,' he said, 'you are constantly distracted by the sight of the flowers and the buds bursting. I can sit here and I don't get distracted by flying birds or the sight of a pretty girl going by. Of course,' he said after a thoughtful pause, 'I can still *hear* a pretty girl go by.'

John McLaren's Folly

24 June 1966

The idea that San Francisco is a beautiful metropolis, if not the most beautiful big city in America, is one to which, I should think, most Americans and all San Franciscans are delighted to subscribe. I hate to crab our conversation at the start, but it seems to me that the appeal of the place is its cosy, small-town quality, which a huge bay and nine rambling hills cannot convert into a metropolis. San Francisco is not a beautiful city any more than a homely girl standing on a beautiful mountain top is a beautiful girl. There is a plain reason for this, and we will examine it and then pass on to something of which the San Franciscans, or more accurately the Scots, have a right to be proud.

The city, as everybody knows, was destroyed in what historians and visitors call the earthquake of 1906. There is a firm superstition among the natives which makes them refer instead to 'the fire'. San Francisco, like much of northern and central California, sits precariously on the rim of a geological fault, the San Andreas fault. On the morning of 18 April 1906, the fault gave a strenuous heave, and certainly there was an earthquake, the most damaging that has been known in North America in modern times. But whether you have in mind the enormous shudder, or the devastation of the subsequent fire (which had Enrico Caruso running out of the Palace Hotel screaming, 'It is worse than Vesuvius'), the truth is that the centre of the city was totally demolished. Its rebuilding came at an unfortunate time—I mean unfortunate in the history of architecture, either domestic or foreign. After a century of peace in Europe, and forty years of it in America, it was a comfortable, smug and earnest time, relieved by heavy whimsy in the arts, and these qualities were reflected in laborious and whimsical ideas about beauty in brick and stone. Accordingly, San Francisco is dense with thousands of the most clumsy, formidable, comical gingerbread houses and hospitals and other public buildings you can imagine.

The great thing about San Francisco is not its parts but the sum of its parts seen from a long way off. In other words, the precious thing about it is its site. Like the plain girl standing alone on the beautiful mountain top, its outline, its profile, has a dignity and charm which only rarely belong to any of its lesser attributes. The city itself is hillier than Naples, more intimate than Hong Kong. It is founded and spread over nine great hills overlooking a fine bay, and in any city that ever knew ice or snow it would have been an impossible hazard to life and limb to build houses over the hills and have streetcars or automobiles run up and down them. But San Francisco has had a flurry of snow twice, I think, in forty years; and though its nights are very often cool and clammy, the thermometer does not drop below freezing and not often into the forties. In fact, San Francisco has one of the narrowest ranges of daily temperature, winter and summer, of any city in America. So the buildings topple all over the hills, and the streetcars are pulled up by cables running through slots in the middle of the roadway, and the first necessity of an automobile is flawless brakes. When you park your car on a slanting street, you must turn the wheels to bank against the sidewalk kerb. If you do not, you get a ticket. You drive very often straight at the sky and when you come to the crest of a street that crosses a main thoroughfare you have to pause at an angle of 30 degrees or so until the crosstown traffic lets you nudge your way over the hill before you plunge down a block or two and begin the next ascent. The steepest streets have steps cut into the sidewalk, and the tourists goggle at the hills and giggle at their own attempts to walk up and down them. But the residents pant and pause at half a mile an hour and totter down a house-lined mountainside to do their day's shopping. This gives the place a solemn but rollicking air.

The land breezes are very dry and the ocean winds very clean. So it is a sparkling city much of the time, except when the fog from the ocean comes sliding in as solid as a freight train, especially in the foggy, cold days of July and August. Until the Second World War, when industry began to disfigure the whole littoral of the bay, smog was something that God in his wisdom had visited only on the vast, blowsy city four hundred and forty miles to the south—the city of the angels (a misnomer if ever there was one): Los Angeles.

Seen from any distance in the late afternoon of one of its crystalline days, San Francisco is a white city rolling over these great hills, and certainly it is unlike any other city of the United States. It is also a place of succulent and rare vegetation. And this is the miracle of the place that I want to talk about.

When San Francisco was founded, in the mania of the gold rush, it was nothing but a collection of huge sandhills overlooking on one side a great inland bay and on the other the Pacific Ocean. The earliest prints—I'm thinking of the fine ones they made in the 1850s—show fleets of decorative sailing ships in the harbour but not a tree in sight. Soon the Nobs—the makers of the earliest gold fortunes—built large houses on the highest hill, which was consequently known, and still is, as Nob Hill. Like the others it was a mountain of shifting sand. And when the winds blew in from the Pacific, the mountains appeared to move inside the orbit of their outline. It was like the Sahara in a storm, and the people staggered blindly up and down the hills holding handkerchiefs over their mouths and noses. The more chic residents patronized a shop started by a Frenchman (it is now a prosperous store) and bought from him one of his first products: a cotton-gauze mask intended to protect you from the suffocating fogs of blown sand.

This was accepted as a fact of life for twenty years or so. Then the city fathers had an agreeable new idea. They had by now acquired the essential amenities of a city—a red-light district, pretentious houses, a concert hall and a police force, in that order (after some violent years in which the most responsible citizens, outraged by the rapine and murder that infested the place, took the law into their own hands as a committee of vigilantes). Now the city fathers thought that they would have a park. This would be rather like Holland thinking it ought to have a mountain. It was plainly an impossibility.

Nevertheless, the city council set aside 1,017 acres of high flat land near the ocean which was, most of the time, a windswept desert. The fathers laboured to plant seedlings and flower beds but found that they promptly choked and died. After three years of this noble experiment, the daily newspaper of a small town in a grassy valley to the north wrote a chuckling editorial: 'Of all the elephants the city of San Francisco has ever owned, they now have the heaviest in the shape of "Golden Gate Park", a dreary waste of shifting sand hills where a blade of grass cannot be raised without four posts to support it and keep it from blowing away.' It was almost literally true. In the seventeen following years they had managed to plant and hold—with many sorts of structural braces—a thin forest of trees and some grassy spaces on the eastern, the leeward, side. In 1887 the park commission, still regarded as a bunch of visionaries, appointed a new superintendent, a Scotsman, John McLaren, a young landscape gardener, then 29 years old. The commission gave him, with his assignment, a prescription in the following gaudy language: 'Mr McLaren, we want you to make the Golden Gate Park one of the beauty spots of the world.' An English visitor to the city took home this sentence as a prime example of the American's gift for windbag rhetoric. But young McLaren was neither boastful nor amused. As he received his certificate of office, and as thousands mocked, he replied: 'With your aid, gentlemen, and God be willing, that I shall do.'

His first task was not to move mountains but to arrest them. And for that he needed what San Francisco did not have, a steady source of fresh water. Even then the salt water of the bay backed up and percolated all the surrounding land. McLaren did not ignore this disability but he fought it for a year or two. He was a Scotch type familiar to most of us, a rather grim poet of a man with the single-mindedness of a mule. He would often, as he later wrote, 'go out into the country and walk along a stream until I came to a bonnie brook. Then I'd come back to the park and try to reproduce what Nature had done.'

So he started out with what you would expect a Scot to start with: barley. It normally grows fast and dense. But not in San Francisco. He turned to native lupine. Same thing. Then he recalled the tough beach grass of Scotland, and it was the first plant to put down rapid roots and grow, on top, fast enough to give a green fringe to the dunes which the blown sand could not bury. Then he looked around for a couple of species of trees, one to hold the contours of the sand, another to build up soil as well. He found both in Australia and imported them: the tea tree and the Australian acacia. Eucalyptus, the gum tree as Australians call it, came from there too and did pretty well, though it had a habit, and still has, of blighting the growth of anything within its shade. From the nearby valleys and the canyons of the peninsula he brought in two of the loveliest of the small trees of California, the manzanita and the madrone. I make it sound as if McLaren were a slogging, purposeful type who knew what he wanted and got it. In fact, for several years he seemed to be undertaking a missing labour of Hercules. His task had its satisfactions but its despairs also. One time he planted a thousand trees, and a few months later they looked like the markers for new-formed sand dunes. He dug them all up and he tried again, and again. Fertilizer was a constant problem. It cost a lot of money to ship in from southern California, and his original budget was slimming fast. So he asked the Mayor if the sanitation department would collect and deliver to him the horse sweepings from the streets. Without too much publicity it was done.

One of his faults, as a public official, was that he was immune or allergic to political finagling—something that any man who wants anything from those in power must learn to accept and exploit. He would no doubt have been horrified at Franklin Roosevelt's remark about a big city Mayor, a gruesome character but a Democrat, from whom Roosevelt expected a landslide of votes in a crucial election. A squeamish member of the Roosevelt team was afraid that the Mayor was too crafty to depend on, and anyway he was, the man said, 'a son of a bitch'. 'Yes,' said Roosevelt, flashing his most endearing smile, 'but he's *our* son of a bitch.'

Young McLaren, on the contrary, would not truckle or hire or pay patronage to influential men he disliked. The police superintendent was one. And after some rude rebuff McLaren found three of his proudest trees had been hauled away overnight by the police from in front of their station house. John McLaren summoned his staff the same day, had the new cement shovelled away, and planted three new oaks. They stand today in front of the San Francisco police station.

But as he asserted himself, and the park began to grow into a visible thing of beauty, the San Franciscans came to think of him as a precious city asset. It was a time, remember, when rich men expected to die in their fifties and accordingly retired at 40 to live it up a little before the end came. Sixty was then the rather late, but compulsory, retiring age of all civil servants. But when McLaren got there the people of San Francisco insisted that he stay on. And when he was 70, they insisted again. After that he was given a perennial waiver of retirement. And he died, still the superintendent of the park, at the age of 95, in 1943.

Long before that time the Golden Gate Park— with its lush meadows and artful wildernesses, its sheep pastures and Japanese tea garden, its peacocks on little lawns, its waterfalls and great evergreen forests, its protected buffalo and deer, its five thousand varieties of plants, its daisies from South Africa, cypress from Kashmir, abelias from the Himalayas, its hundred-odd types of conifer, its rhododendrons from Tibet and Siberia, its playgrounds and its foxes, its dozen lakes and its myriad blackbirds—it had become indeed what McLaren promised to make it. Certainly, in my experience, the most beautiful entirely created city park.

I thought of John McLaren this week because he was doing his damnedest to hold the first trees just at the time, around 1895, when a dozen other Scots came over to teach Americans the game of golf. The United States Open Championship was held in San Francisco last week, and the great bane of the big hitters was the trees, the forty-three thousand cypresses and pines and eucalyptus planted in John McLaren's early time and tended, at one time or another, by him. Arnold Palmer, the most heroic of the new breed of America's millionaire golfers, lost the championship by driving constantly into the fronds of a great overhanging cypress. His collapse and his tragedy could all be put down to Scotland. You could say that one Scotsman gave him his living and another took it away from him.

The Well-Dressed American, Man!

30 October 1966

A few years ago, when my son had about a year and a half to go before he graduated from college, I was mildly astonished to hear myself saying to him what fathers of college boys have said for generations. 'I have a proposition to make to you,' I said. 'You've worked pretty hard and well. Keep it up for the next eighteen months and come out with a halfway decent degree and I'll give you the fare for a trip to Europe.' I was a little uncomfortable making this traditional speech, because I had not always been the father of a college boy. I am, in fact, in my fifties for the first time in my life. But I heard myself sounding like the fathers I knew in my time, all of them, I then believed, professional fathers born into middle age.

Of course, I expected my son would fall on his face in gratitude. Instead, he cocked his head and looked at me with that peculiar tenderness that 20-year-olds reserve for the naivety of their parents.

'Are you kidding?' he said. 'I'll be off to Europe a month from now.'

'Indeed,' I said, icing up very fast, 'and where do you expect to travel?' (I almost said, 'And, pray, where do you expect to travel?')

'Oh, a little time in Rome and Florence, a month or so in Paris, I guess, maybe a stretch in Tangier.'

I wondered how he expected to live on his frugal allowance. In staggered disbelief he explained to me, with great simplicity and patience, some facts of life that had been kept from me. The summer vacation before his last academic year was coming up, and the university laid on several charter flights to Europe, leave a certain date, back a certain date, at something less than half the commercial fare. My son is a cagey mathematician where rent, food and expenses are concerned and he had done a calculation on which I could not fault him. Even allowing for the cost of the transatlantic fare, he could live noticeably cheaper for three months in Europe than he could by staying in his rooms in Cambridge, Massachusetts. Uncounted thousands of American college boys and girls have discovered the same thing. Most of them, even on the home ground, live much like cave dwellers. A room as we knew it is by no means the same thing as a pad. We were, I now realize, painfully fastidious in my day. Whatever the cut of our political or social jib, we required such things as beds actually raised above the floor, curtains in windows, chairs for sitting on. These things, I am told, are now looked on as establishment fetishes. American and European college boys of today are throwbacks to the wandering minstrels of the Middle Ages. They live from hand to mouth, and friend to friend, and pad to pad. They have a universal uniform: one pair of trousers, one shirt, a guitar, a pack of Gauloises, a jacket (maybe), and a toothbrush (sometimes). The motto of my old school would serve them well. It is *Ubi bene, ibi patria*, which being roughly translated means, 'Wherever there's a handout, that's for me, man.'

All the countries of Europe, and some of Africa, are now peopled by these identical types. They rustle around the continents like cockroaches, and you can never be sure, when you see them on the Spanish Steps, or in the Uffizi, or along the docks at Casablanca, or in the streets of East Berlin, whether they are American, English, Swedish, German or even Russian. Every place they go they are at home with other wanderers from other lands. The language barrier does not exist, for I am told by a very earnest sociologist that this generation is passing beyond the need of speech into a *lingua franca* of gestures, grunts, shrugs that establish—and I quote—'a subtle and vital form of identity-communication'. No niceties of dress disturb them. On second thoughts, I'm not so sure of that. However, *our* niceties of dress are as alien and meaningless to them as the elaborate hierarchy of military orders among South American generals who have never seen a puff of cannon smoke.

Of course, today we all pretend to be unfussy and informal about clothes, and to have abandoned the social distinctions that they once used to signify. I doubt very much whether this can ever be so. I have lately been in London for a spell, and then in Devon, Dorset and Surrey, then back to New York for three days, and am now in California. I am struck by the weirdly different uniforms that the inhabitants of any one place take for granted. A man lying on a beach at Brighton would not alarm anybody if he wore a cap, a tweed coat with an open shirt (the collar folded carefully outside the coat collar), a pair of dark grey flannels, and boots. A woman coming to dinner in Surrey causes no alarm by appearing in the outfit in which a woman in Minnesota plays golf. Some of these distinctions are obviously imposed by the climate. And to prepare for the jaunt I have just enjoyed calls for some pretty thoughtful packing. Yet even here when people are in doubt they tend to disbelieve the travel-guide warnings and stay with their own prejudice. Every time we go to San Francisco, I tell my wife that she should pack warm clothes for the evening and that a fur coat is a blessing for the fog-swept, chilly nights of July and August. This is so plainly ridiculous if you were born and brought up in the East that she dismisses my advice as raging hypochondria and later complains that she has not been warned.

But providing for the weather is comparatively easy. The really subtle challenges set in when you travel between the same social strata in different countries. My last three evenings in London were spent respectively at a toney dinner party, at a cosy supper with my stepdaughter, at a 'happening' in a railroad yard in a dingy London suburb. No problem with my daughter: she is acquainted with my tastes and I with hers. I wore a suit she once admired and a tie with little tigers snarling on it, and which her friends might well mistake for a white hunter's special. At the socialite dinner party, whose hostess had casually mentioned 'black tie', I had to fake it by wearing a black business suit and a black dress tie, which I always carry against such a sudden summons to the tables of the mighty. Nobody noticed the difference, except a modern young siren with eyelashes like quills who must have seen black wherever she went. She congratulated me on the cut and style of my dinner jacket, so much 'cooler', she thought, than those old-fashioned silk facings. 'Where did you get it?' she asked. I bunched up so as to hide the breast-pocket label that said, 'New Haven, Conn.' Spain, I said. She purred.

The 'happening' was something else. I wore a suit—matching coat and trousers, that is—a necktie and a dark-blue topcoat. I looked, I was later told, like a fugitive from the Foreign Office. Everybody in sight was in jeans or stretch pants, in silver lamé, blue velvet, fuchsia corduroy, and monk's cowls, dhotis; and many of them sported beards, leather jackets, and rhinestone necklaces or beads that jangled around their thighs. They were a tolerant lot. No one, I was assured, was outraged by me. The friendly attitude seemed to be: 'If this cat wants to dress like an American ambassador, then okay, so long as he keeps his trap shut about Vietnam.'

Dressing in America is trickier, for in a country of this size each region incorporates the prejudices of a separate country. I know exactly how New Yorkers of many social types dress for winter, spring, summer and fall. I know, for instance, that it is necessary to warn a visiting Englishwoman that no New Yorker with the smallest pretension to style wears white shoes, in summer or any other time, in the city. But dressing in Hollywood so that you won't look stuffy, or flashy *in the wrong way*, is a separate trick that not one Easterner in a hundred ever masters. Because they have at the back of their minds a preconception of Hollywood—bikinis, fat cigars, picture ties, Klieg lights, two-tone shoes, Swiss silk suits, V-necks cut to the navel, summer prints of a psychedelic garishness. They know for sure that Beverly Hills is more informal than, say, London. Not so. Only in the movies. You arrive at a Hollywood dinner party in a smart blue blazer, light blue shirt, sleek slacks, a club tie and black loafers, a costume that would be entirely acceptable at a summer drop-in dinner at the Garrick Club. But in Beverly Hills you find yourself surrounded by men entirely in dark suits, white shirts and tiny patterned ties. The women, it is true, have a licence to wear evening dresses or canary-yellow slack suits. Yet I suspect that this licence too prescribes some nuances and forbids others.

Santa Barbara is only ninety miles from Hollywood but it is one social band of the stratosphere away. Although October is a hot month there, fashion obeys the calendar and dictates that it is the fall. The women put on warmer clothes, darker colours, paler shoes. At a Santa Barbara dinner the other evening there was a ravishing New Yorker present wearing a melon-pink suit of Thai silk. It became her greatly. We sat out on a terrace where it was around 75 degrees, and she stood out like a firefly in the night. She was thought by her hosts, I later discovered, to be attractive but odd.

That same evening I mentioned to my host a little detective work along these lines that I had done while driving in an airport limousine on the way from the beautiful coastline of the Carmel Bay to the Monterey airport. The only other people aboard were a handsome couple in, I should guess, their middle forties. The woman was pretty and effortlessly chic and clearly a Californian, for though the day was blinding she wore an exquisitely fitting light-brown cashmere dress and alligator shoes. Her husband, though—lover, perhaps?— was a puzzle. He had on pencil-thin well-cut slacks of a tiny hound's-tooth pattern; a dark-blue jacket;

a mini-hat—a rakish deerstalker, also of a tiny hound's-tooth pattern, and in the brim was tucked a little swirling black feather. If he had been an Easterner, I cannot think what sort of man he could have been. A very well-heeled advertising man, possibly, on holiday. But he sounded too relaxed, too professional; he looked with a steady, matter-of-fact gaze at the blue-brown headlands, the writhing Monterey cypresses, the foaming blue, blue ocean. A little wily conversation at the airport drew out from him that he was a distinguished gynaecologist—but from Beverly Hills. He could not possibly, I told my Santa Barbara host, have been a gynaecologist in the East. 'Nor,' he responded, 'in Santa Barbara either.'

To many people this may appear to be a very trivial theme in the great day of social upheaval and the equality of man. But, I am told at the United Nations, even in China the uniform of Mao Tse-tung has details that escape us which signify to the faithful that his worker's smock is not any worker's smock but the costume of the All-Highest. The Russians, once they were well over their revolution, got out a blue book for their crack regiments patterned after the blue book which once laid down for a British Guards officer the correct civilian uniform for every place and time. And my son now tells me that my own observation of Carnaby Street distinctions is naive and unseeing.

It will be said that these are snobbish preoccupations. And so they are, and important to go into, since we are all snobs. All of us draw social inferences from the way people dress. In this, fishermen and farmers are just as snobbish as debutantes and hippies. And there is no one, however regal, however humble, who is not put off by some detail of dress he personally dislikes. I well remember the morning that one of President Kennedy's aides came in wearing a button-down shirt, an item that started in America in the very early 1930s as an Ivy League fad. It remained so until a few years ago but was swiftly abandoned when it spread to bond salesmen and airline executives and then to Midwesterners, and then to cattle ranchers in convention, and finally to Englishmen. It is still retained by ageing country-club types who have not noticed that they suddenly look old-fashioned. 'For Heaven's sake,' said Kennedy to his bewildered aide, 'take off that shirt. Nobody wears those things any more, except Chester Bowles and Adlai.'

By remarking on these tiny things, John O'Hara for once cornered for himself a small but subtle and memorable view of life. For the rest of us, they can be invaluable signals and telling symptoms of what lies behind the appraising glance and the guarded handshake.

A Lonely Man

26 May 1967

On a Saturday afternoon at the end of May, a single-engine plane, looking very like something out of the early comic strips, wobbled and ducked over Roosevelt Field, one of the earliest airports around New York, and buzzed the tower. A small crowd of people on the ground looked up and waved and clapped, and then somebody unveiled a marker. And they all retired to an old hotel in one of the oldest country suburbs on Long Island and joined other crowds who had jammed the bars and the assembly rooms all day long to celebrate the same event.

It had been forty years to the day since a skinny, flat-chested, blond, 25-year-old Midwesterner had left Long Island on a most peculiar journey. He had stayed the night of 19 May 1927 in the same hotel where all the carousing and celebrating were now going on. He had ambled out on a miserable day, through rain and heavy ground mist, to an aeroplane he had built himself, at a total cost of $6,000. There were not great crowds that time. There was a wet and restless pack of newspapermen who kept sloshing in the drizzle between three planes, which were sitting there in a film of mud waiting for favourable weather to take off and have a shot at a $25,000 prize that had been put up by a New York hotel owner. There was no question which of the three competitors would make the most impressive copy. He was Lieutenant Commander Byrd, who had been to the North Pole and was already a national figure. But the lonely one, the skinny young man from the Midwest, was more challenging if only because he was so preoccupied with his plane, tinkering with it, frowning, wading back for a monkey wrench or a screw, smiling little, talking less. The reporters had all heard of him, of course. He had been a flying cadet in the Air Service Reserve, as it was then called. He had been a mail-pilot. He had made small items in the papers as a parachute jumper.

Only a week before he had flown this crate from San Diego, California, to St Louis to Long Island in the breathtaking time of twenty-one hours and twenty minutes, which was a new record for a coast-to-coast flight. They had heard about his wild ambition to make the coming flight alone. He was known as what they called a stunt merchant, a flying fool. He was about to live up to his nickname, for he decided on the wretched grey morning of 20 May that the time was now. The weather reports, such as they were in those days, said that there would be fair skies over most of the Atlantic. He decided to risk it. He arranged his long limbs in the tiny cockpit, pulled his goggles down, and splashed off through the rain puddles on the runway. He wobbled into the air and bounced back on the ground again; up again and then down. At the end of the runway, to everyone's relief, he was airborne. None too soon, for he just managed to clear the telephone lines at the end of the field.

I suppose, at 8 o'clock on that May morning, not one American in a thousand was preoccupied with his name, and in most other countries not one person in a hundred thousand had ever heard it. The wire services noted that he had taken off alone, in a home-made plane, with the mad ambition of being the first man to cross the Atlantic alone. I can't recall ever having read about anyone who swooped so suddenly into world fame. It is strange to look back to the morning papers of 20 May and hunt for the first stories about him; and then turn to the evening papers and get the impression that Alexander the Great had reappeared on the earth and was headed straight for you. It was not necessary to know anything

210

about flying. The farmers rang through to the nearest newspaper office, and the telephone switchboards were clogged on three continents. Stockbrokers and parsons and racing touts and new brides and politicians and intellectuals and steelworkers had been galvanized in a few hours. By what? There had been transatlantic flights before. There had been the dramatic close call of Alcock and Brown. As long ago as 1919 a British dirigible had flown thirty-one men from Scotland to Long Island and turned around and flown back again. Only three years before, two American army planes had crossed by way of Iceland, Greenland and Newfoundland.

There were two new things that combined to stir the imagination of people everywhere. He was not going to hop islands or countries. No Newfoundland to Ireland for him. He was going for the whole stretch: New York to Paris. And he was going alone.

He had not publicized these dramatic facts, though they were known to the sponsors of the prize. But what catapulted the populations of America and Europe into a two-day delirium was the shock of the news, not that he was going to take off but that he had already gone. That night, there was a championship bout in Yankee Stadium (Sharkey was fighting Maloney). Before the fight started, the announcer stood in the ring and bawled at an audience of forty thousand fans and asked them to rise and pray for the flyer. Like some vast chorus in an open-air performance of *Guys and Dolls*, they stood and bared their heads. By then, nobody knew where or how he was.

Today, we should hear about him every mile of
211

the way. But he had no radio, no radar, no sextant, only an instrument panel slightly less impressive than the dashboard of a modern car. You remember when John Glenn fired his retrorockets, and we heard a scramble of talk about heat coming up from somewhere? And the long crackle of radio waves and he'd gone? You remember we'd been told that the fearful heat of re-entry could bore through the nose of his capsule—and for five minutes there was the chance that he'd been burned to ash? Five minutes! This boy was lost to us for nearly thirty hours. It was the agony of Glenn diluted but stretched over a day and a night. Then the headlines boomed that he'd been seen over Ireland, then that he was crossing over England. Then he was over the Channel. Then the night fell. From his own account, he experienced the most enraging episode of the flight. He knew he was over France but he did not know the way to Paris. He sputtered along in a daze of exhaustion and at last he recognized Paris. Now he had to find Le Bourget. After half an hour more, which he later said felt like another night, he was struck by a curious broad shaft of fog, a sort of pathway of diffused light. Of the hundred thousand Parisians who were thrashing around down there, a hundred or more had cars and they'd been told to turn their lights on. This was his rudimentary glide path. And he came on it and bumped in and trundled to the edge of the field. And then an ocean of humanity broke around him. 'I', he said, 'am Charles Lindbergh.'

There was never any need, anywhere in the world after that, for the next forty years, to introduce himself. I was at a party in Nairobi two years ago, a diplomatic affair, and the main room of an ambassador's house and the terrace outside were flashing with all degrees of political grandees. But they were as excited, in a subdued way, as a gaggle of teenagers in the lobby of a hotel housing the Beatles. I sensed this restless curiosity but I didn't know the reason for it. Pretty soon a dark, fragile, handsome woman came in and at her side was a very tall, very clean, very tanned, white-haired man with the same boyish face, now matured and fully modelled. It was, of course, Lindbergh. Diplomats don't normally rush at a great man for his autograph, because it's impolite and because they are always rather hoping that somebody will rush at them. There was no fuss, no vulgar staring. The Lindberghs fell in with a little group, but at their coming there was a kind of rustle of pleasure, a palpable feeling among these eminent men that they were really hobnobbing with the famous.

By now the gruesome and the distressing periods of Lindbergh's life have been forgotten—the kidnapping of his child, the obscene trial, the exile in England, and the later incarnation as the hero of the isolationists, the cat's-paw of an American nationalist party. This weekend, it was nothing but the unique flight of 20 and 21 May, forty years ago.

You mention it today to people who were alive at the time and, as with the death of President Kennedy, they will tell you at once where they were when it happened. I was in school in England, and the morning after the great night scene in Paris, our science master skipped the lesson and recalled his own heroics in the Battle of the Marne. The geography master took on a special glow of pride

213

and demonstrated over and over again that he was the living expert on the geography of the North Atlantic. Everybody paid Lindbergh the most naive and sincere form of tribute: they wanted to be in on the act.

So, on this Saturday morning, the crowds milled around the Garden City hotel on Long Island, and till long past midnight they toasted Charles Lindbergh. He was not there. He had turned down the invitation. He is an acutely shy man with an acute loathing of crowds. Perhaps the first huge night at Le Bourget was a trauma. He was thoroughly secluded, across Long Island Sound, in Connecticut. At 65 he has three absorbing interests. He is the technical adviser to a famous airline. He has long been interested in the construction of an artificial heart. And all the rest of the time he spends between here and East Africa. His great concern is to preserve, in the jet age, the lonely leopards and the wildebeest and the gazelles of the Serengeti Plain.

Vietnam

22 March 1968

There was once a British ambassador to this country, a good man, now dead, who—like most of his predecessors, with the blinding exception of Lord Bryce—had much trouble understanding the difference between a parliamentary system and a federal system. He could not understand why the Cabinet didn't sit in Congress, nor why the legislature and the executive were completely separate. No one, I'm afraid, had explained to him the Founding Fathers' pressing fear of a military dictatorship, of a king with a private army, and the precautions they took to frustrate it by setting up the President and the Congress as natural enemies. Or you can say that they set up the President as the chief executive of the state and then provided for a permanent pack of watchdogs to check his every move. The ambassador wrote down in his journal this conclusion: 'This leaves the President's press conference as a poor substitute for the regular cross-examination of ministers at question-time in the House of Commons.'

Well, the President's press conference does seem to be the obvious counterpart. It is obvious but it is wrong. And many an American Cabinet officer could wish it wasn't. For occasional exposure in the House of Commons to a rasping question or even a guffaw is not to be compared, as a form of executive torture, to an all-day inquisition by a standing committee of Congress. The Congressional inquiry, I'd say, is the nerve system of what Americans like to call 'the democratic process'. And nowhere is it seen to more terrifying effect than in the cross-examination of a Secretary of State by the Senate Foreign Relations Committee. This committee has the power to reject ambassadors and treaties proposed by the President.

In the spring of 1968, then, it was anxious to recall the President to his constitutional duty to seek the 'advice and consent of the Senate' on a war that had got away from both of them: the undeclared war in Vietnam. So the Secretary of

215

State, called as the President's understudy, was subjected to the third degree by the representatives of the people. If that sounds a little lurid or sentimental, let me remind you of the cast of characters that sat like a court of judges there and challenged Secretary Rusk from ten in the morning to six-thirty one day, and from nine to two the next.

The lives and labours of these men may not represent (as advertising executives like to say about their wives) a 'cross-section of the American people'. But they made up an impressive sample of the variety of the millions who chose them. There was a farmer from Vermont, a mining engineer from Montana, a Rhodes scholar from Arkansas, the schoolteacher son of a hardware merchant from South Dakota, an electric-products manufacturer from Missouri, a stockman from Kansas. The mining engineer wound up as a professor of Latin American and Far Eastern history. The electric products man was a former Secretary of the Air. The schoolteacher was also a famous fisherman. There were six lawyers, not too many to reflect the preponderance of lawyers who sit in Congress and who do, after all, make the laws. None of these men had been in the Senate for less than twelve years; the farmer had been there twenty-eight years and two others for twenty-four years. Five of them were veterans of the First World War. One saw action in the Second in Burma and China. Another was a survivor of the Normandy invasion. Two of them had, and have, enough ordinary vanity not to give their ages in the *Congressional Directory*. If you think of them in this variety you will be less inclined to imagine a cartoonist's Star Chamber of Neanderthal men bearing the tag 'Senate

Committee'.

Secretary Rusk had resisted this call for two years. But there was a well-substantiated rumour that General Westmoreland wanted another two hundred thousand troops. And suddenly the world expressed its distrust of American policy by losing its confidence in the dollar. So the Secretary yielded and agreed to go before the committee and talk about the administration's request for foreign aid. But the committee had brought him in to expound and defend the administration's policy on Vietnam, the excuse for ignoring the main theme being that you can't guess how much money will be left over for any other dependent country until you've gauged the expense and the probable scale of the war in Vietnam. For two days Secretary Rusk was questioned and quizzed and lectured to and pleaded with by a committee whose old ratio of hawks to doves was significantly shrinking. The role of Chairman Fulbright as a scold and ironist could now be presumed. So could the ringing patriotism of Senator Mundt of South Dakota and the troubled curiosity of young Senator Church of Idaho and the holy wrath of Senator Wayne Morse of Oregon, God's favourite maverick.

But at these sessions only Fulbright and Morse stayed with the usual script. The others were sufficiently disturbed to think aloud with more honesty and eloquence than they had shown before. And all of them maintained an unfailing gravity and courtesy such as men do when they are scared, when they are losing an attitude and acquiring an anxiety. Nothing was more startling than Senator Mundt's forlorn suspicion that elections in South Vietnam were not alone worth the ensnaring of half a million Americans into the continental bog of Southeast Asia. And a bugle sounding the retreat is not more ominous than the confession of Senator Symington, a resolute hawk, that he was now a prey to misgiving. Senator Symington had been saying for years that the war had better be won or written off, since the day was coming when the United States would have to weigh the cost of it in gold that wasn't there. He has always been indulged by his colleagues and friends as a man riding a comical hobby horse. This time, he had the sad satisfaction of being taken seriously.

We have not talked lately about Vietnam, whereas once we talked about little else, because everything that could be said has been said. Families, friends, and the workers at the same bench either ran with their own kind or resigned themselves, as so many bad marriages do, to a kind of despairing truce. But now we were measuring, with quite a new sort of alarm, the eleven and a half billion dollars in the Treasury that covered our stock of gold against the twenty-six billion a year that was being spent on Vietnam. And, at last, the American casualties in Vietnam surpassed those of Korea: a turn which, I suggested a year ago, would be the hardest test of the people's tolerance of the war.

So we were shaking ourselves out of the stupor and the truce, and starting all over again with the fundamental questions. How had it come about? Was it indeed a crusade or a vast miscalculation? Would Asia crumble to Communism if South Vietnam fell? Was it the wrong war in the wrong place, or the right war in the wrong place? Was the

218

United States the only man in the boat rowing in time?

A hundred books and a thousand editorial writers have recited and disputed the political origins of the war and enlarged on the human tragedy of its conduct. What matters, or will come to matter to most people, I think, is not any new balance we can strike in the old argument; but the realization that America, which has seldom lost a war, is not invincible; and the very late discovery that an elephant can trumpet and shake the earth but not the self-possession of the ants who hold it. So when I say how did it come about, I am not thinking of splitting the hair between the SEATO treaty's pledge to resist 'aggression' and the American protocol that stipulated 'Communist aggression'. I mean, how did the American people move from their early indifference or complacency to the recognition of a nightmare?

Well, the war crept up on us with no more menace than a zephyr. South Vietnam was only one of many strange place names that joined the noble roll-call of countries which America, in the early glow of its world power, swore to protect and defend. If Russia, that atomic monolith, could be scared off Iran and Greece and Turkey and foiled in Western Europe, it never crossed our minds that we couldn't intimidate Asian Communists who fought with sticks and stones. Certainly it would have been churlish to deny these brave little countries the handful of American 'technicians' they needed to train their armies. (We presumed, without doing much detective work, that—as with Belgium and Finland at other times—the democratic credentials of Thailand, Pakistan, Laos,

Cambodia, Vietnam and the other signatories could be taken for granted.) In 1962 we moved troops into the Mekong Delta and the Pathet Lao withdrew. And that took care of Laos.

Johnson came in, and for a year or more the shadow of Vietnam failed to darken the bright procession of legislation he drove through the 89th Congress. It dawned on us very slowly that the American technicians were turning into American soldiers. Then we admitted that the men were off to the rice paddies and not the desks and hospitals behind the lines. The draft felt the chill, and the college boys, and the Vietniks were born. It was not with most of them a conscientious objection to war itself. Most, I think, would have admitted that Hitler had to be stopped and that Korea, the first United Nations war, was a good war. But they were baffled by the morality of this war, which killed more civilians than soldiers and devastated the land we were sworn to protect: a war in which there were no attacks at dawn, no discernible lines, and few human restraints either of rules or weapons. 'Napalm' and 'fragmentation bombs' came into the language and sickened us, though our own 'strategic bombing' of Dresden in the Second World War had been worse than Hiroshima, and millions of women and children had been routed from their homes in Europe too. War, the administration could only remind us, was hell. So we piled up the forces and piled on the force and dropped more bombs than all the bombs dropped in Europe and Africa in the Second World War. The American forces rose from thirty thousand to fifty, then to a hundred thousand and then to half a million. And the latest word was that perhaps seven hundred thousand might in truth fulfil the promises of the generals, whose estimates of when and how the turn might come had dreadfully paralleled the expert predictions of the French generals before them.

These and many other doubts and disasters were aired and tossed before Dean Rusk. The administration's position had something of the straightforward grandeur of Bach, if only Bach had been the tune that were called for. The theme was that the war in Asia was a continuation of the European struggle, first against Hitler, then against the Russians. The United States was pledged to resist aggression against free nations. If one pledge was betrayed, then the other wards and dependants would panic and succumb to Communism. The countries of Southeast Asia are a stack of dominoes and if one falls so will they all.

Down the years, the administration has offered us many warning historical examples of what happens to a strong power which yields to an aggressor bit by bit. The favourite analogy is Munich, and it has been reinforced by the old tag about nations that know no history being doomed to repeat it.

But many people have looked at this analogy and rejected it, as they have rejected, also, the analogy of Korea, where there was a clear aggression, so defined by all the sitting members of the United Nations Security Council. The New Left has a bad-tempered analogy of its own in the white man's treatment of the Indians in this country: the determination to obliterate him for his own good and resettle him on permanently protected 'enclaves' of bare land on which no white

221

man could exist. I myself keep thinking of Napoleon's disastrous adventure in Haiti. The ideology and the excuse for this overseas expedition were quite different from ours. On the contrary, Napoleon moved to denounce and destroy the extension of self-government to the natives. But strategically, the adventure so far from home has a lesson for us. To put down the native peoples he dispatched an expedition of seven warships and forty-five thousand of his crack soldiers; which, at the time, must have seemed every bit as formidable as our half-million and their bombers. But there was a native general, Christophe, who revived a tactic used originally by the Tunisians against the Arabs and later known as a 'scorched earth' policy. More successful still was his practice of 'guerrilla warfare', so called. Not all the armament and skill of the most modern army in Europe could suppress these roving guerrillas, who were friends by day and enemies by night, who never stood and made a front, who could live on the forage of the fields, and take yellow fever or leave it, who pounded prepared positions and dissolved into the earth. A ragged native population whipped the best of France. It was enough to turn Napoleon against any more campaigns at four thousand miles and to decide him against conquering North America; with the happy result, for us, that he sold the huge reaches of the Louisiana Territory to Jefferson for $15 million.

These analogies are dangerous to press, because you are always faced with a situation in which what is new hurts more than what is familiar. Still, I think that the view of the United States as

Napoleon in Haiti is better than the view of Ho Chi Minh as Hitler in Europe.

There is one awful possibility that was put to me, when the war was only beginning to warm up, by the late Pandit Nehru. It is that a Western power, finding itself deep in Asia, might simply refuse to believe, as the Romans did, that its Roman might could possibly be disabled by a primitive people. 'You see,' said this bland Indian, 'the trouble with Westerners is, they hate to lose face.' It was too early in the game to reflect that a Texan might hate it more than anybody.

Yet it seems to me that anyone who ridicules the domino theory is obliged to say how and why it is wrong, and to suggest some better way of, as Dean Rusk put it, 'organizing the peace' either through the United Nations or through some alliance that can guarantee preponderant power. Preponderant power—that has always been the true deterrent, in spite of the Christian rhetoric that breathed so piously through the preamble to the Treaty of Westphalia (1648) and through the preamble to the Charter of the United Nations (1945). All these favourable balances of power have expressed that power through their willingness to use their ultimate weapon. With the British it was the Navy, and it was through their Navy that they could patrol the seven seas, put down wars in Asia, confine all big wars to Europe, and backstop for landbound allies. Today the United States is the world's greatest power only through its nuclear power. But, what is never acknowledged, the universal taboo against the use of this power disarms America at a blow and leaves it a large and rich but far from omnipotent power, capable of fighting one or two unconventional wars with conventional weapons.

This, it seems to me, is the real American position in the world today and the reason why its best aims are frustrated. The United States has one hundred and thirty-two military bases abroad and solemn treaty 'commitments' to come to the aid of forty-three nations if they are attacked or, what is more likely these days, disrupted from within. The earnest and gentle Senator Church put his finger on this Achilles heel by asking the Secretary if the great conflict was not between 'commitment and capacity'. In other words, America may be right, but is she able?

How did it come about that this country, led successively by a soldier, then by an alert foreign affairs student, and then by the shrewdest of politicians, committed itself to play St George to forty-three dragons? We must go back, I think, to what I called the 'early glow' of American world power, in the early 1950s. That is when the pledges were given, and when the cost of them was never counted. The Communists, not to mention the nationalists, and the millions of Asians who simply want to see the white men leave their continent for good, had not attempted a test of American power. As late as the day of Kennedy's inauguration, the United States was still flexing and rippling its muscles for lack of exercise. And on that day, the President delivered himself of a sentence, magnificent as rhetoric, appalling as policy. Secretary Rusk, very much moved, recited it to the committee as the touchstone of America's resolve: 'Let every nation know, whether it wishes us well or ill, that we shall pay any price, bear any burden, meet any hardship, support any friend, oppose any foe to assure the survival and the success of liberty.'

This is fine to read but fatal to act on. It may be the wish of a strong nation to do this, but in reality it will not support any friend or fight *any* foe, or support the burden, say, of a civil war in its own land, in order to rush to the aid of forty-three friends and fight forty-three foes. Vietnam, I fear, is the price of the Kennedy Inaugural.

A Bad Night in Los Angeles

9 June 1968

It does not seem nearly so long ago as thirty years that the trade of the foreign correspondent caught the fancy of the Hollywood producers. And for good reason. Hitler was on the loose, and Europe was crackling with crises and atrocities, and some of the best American reporters of the time—John Gunther and Vincent Sheehan and Ed Murrow—always seemed to be on hand. They came to look like heroic agents of the American people, who were fascinated and repelled at long distance by the violence of Europe and who, I must say, indulged a good deal of self-righteousness in parroting the ancient American lament about 'old, sick Europe'.

Well, I was saying, the foreign correspondent was in vogue. And soon Hollywood created a romantic stereotype of him. First, in the Boy Scout version of Joel McCrea in a trench coat; and then in the subtler variation of Bogart, who acted so

225

tough and seemed as tricky as Goebbels but who—
for all his smoker's cough and his cynical appraisal
of passing females—was secretly on the side of all
good men and true.

This attractive stereotype was not only larger
than life but luckier than any journalist living or
dead. He followed unerringly in the tracks of
dictators and tipped off foreign ministers marked
for *anschluss*. He was behind a curtain when a king
signed an instrument of abdication. He knew the
man who shot the prime minister. He decoded the
vital message that gave the date of the invasion. He
was always where the action was.

In life, it is not like that. Only by the wildest
freak is a reporter, after many years on the hop,
actually present at a single accidental convulsion of
history. Mostly, we write the coroner's inquest, the
account of the funeral, the reconstruction of the
prison riot, the *trial* of the spy, not the hatching of
the plot.

On the night of Tuesday, 4 June 1968, for the
first time in thirty years, I found myself, by one
casual chance in a thousand, on hand: in a narrow
serving pantry of the Ambassador Hotel in Los
Angeles, a place that, I suppose, will never be
wiped out of my memory as a sinister alley, a
Roman circus run amok, and a charnel house. It
would be false to say, as I should truly like to say,
that I am sorry I was there. It is more complicated
than that. Nothing so simple as a conflict between
professional pride and human revulsion, between
having the feelings and having to sit down and
write about them. Yet, because I saw it for once not
as an event to comment on but as a thunderbolt
assault on the senses, my own view of the whole

226

thing, now and later, is bound to be from the stomach up to the head. Visceral, as we say. I don't imagine that if your hand falls on a live wire you are in any condition to measure the charge or judge the sense of the public safety regulations or moralize about the electric company's dereliction of duty.

So my view of this miserable episode is probably strange and I ought not to ascribe to anybody else the shape or colour of the opinions that floated up later from my muddled sensations. I warn you about this, because I feel unmoved by some ideas that others feel strongly, and on the other hand I have some fears that others may not share. So, since this is a more personal talk than I could have hoped, I had better tell you how it came about.

On that Tuesday afternoon, I was in San Francisco, on one of those jewel-like days that are revealed when the wrapping of the morning fog has been lifted. I had no great urge to fly to the vast spread of Los Angeles. On the contrary, I had hoped to spend the day padding down the fairways of the Olympic Club, which run like cathedral aisles between superb stands of cypresses. But it was election day, and Los Angeles is now the hub of California politics, if only because, of the fifty-eight counties of California, Los Angeles County alone accounts for 48 per cent of the vote. For the purpose of an election dateline, San Francisco, four hundred-odd miles away, was not much better than New York City. So it had to be done. I was going to have to report the general atmosphere of the winner's camp and the loser's.

I had seen scores of these election night entertainments. They are amiable but blowsy

227

affairs. But to give me a fresh view of a ceremony that had staled by familiarity, and also to make some compensation to a hostess who had offered me a bed, I had asked her if she would like to mooch around the town with me and see what we could see. She was agog with anticipation, for just as a foreign correspondent thinks a movie actress must have a fascinating life, so a movie actress thought a correspondent's life must be glamorous in the extreme.

So, high in the Santa Monica hills, amid the scent of the eucalyptuses and the pepper trees, we sat for a while after the polls closed and waited for a sign of the outcome. You don't have to wait long in these computer days. The Oregon result was exactly predicted by the Big Brain twelve minutes after the polls closed, when the returns already in were less than 1 per cent. Somehow, the Brain was having more trouble with California. Party politics are, for various historical reasons, very loosely organized in that state and, for one thing, its northern end tends to contradict the verdict of the South. So when the early returns from the North showed McCarthy in a commanding lead it proved nothing. Los Angeles County, with its heavy working-class vote and its swarms of Negroes (or blacks, as we are now more respectfully meant to say), and its Mexican-Americans, was fairly certain to go heavily for Kennedy. Pretty soon, the gap between McCarthy's tally and Kennedy's began to shrink and it became clear that, saving a miracle, McCarthy would not be able to withstand the avalanche of Los Angeles votes that began to move in for Kennedy. The computers were silent, but the writing was on the wall.

Just before eleven, then, we took off for the McCarthy hotel, and there was no doubt when we got there that the college boys and the miniskirt girls and the wandering poets and the spruced-up student leaders and the chin-up McCarthy staff were whistling in a graveyard. There was a rock band that whooped it up all the louder to drown out the inevitable news. They would pause a while, and another ominous statistic would be flashed, and an emcee would shout, 'Are we downhearted?' And the ballroom crowd would roar its defiance of the obvious.

The Ambassador, a comparatively venerable hotel miles away on Wilshire Boulevard, was the Kennedy headquarters. And that was the place to be. We took off, and so did lots of other people, so that when we turned into the long driveway we lined up behind scores of cars containing all those sensible people who love a winner. At last we got into the hotel lobby and a tumult of singing, cheering, and happy hobnobbing. Election parties give out innumerable tickets and badges to keep out the rabble, but no one is more aware than a winning candidate that on such occasions the rabble are the people. So you can usually drift with the multitude and nobody asks for a credential.

It was not so at the Ambassador. Guards and cops blocked the entrance to the ballroom, and I doubt that a passport and a birth certificate and a personal recommendation from Senator Kennedy could have got you in. My own general press credentials were useless. The lobbies were too packed to lift an elbow and too deafening to talk in. My companion and I screamed at each other through the din of all these happy people and we decided that the whole safari had been a mistake. We turned and started down the corridor for the outdoors and for home.

On our left, about fifty feet along, was another door to another room and a pack of people trying and failing to get through. There was a guard shaking his head continuously and pushing people back and behind him a young Kennedy staff man turning down everybody. This man shouted over the bobbing heads, 'Mr Cooke, come on, you can get in here.' We were folded in through the mob and emerged, as from a chute, into an open place: a cool, half-empty room, a small private dining room of the hotel stripped and fitted out as a press room. There were newsmen I knew and a radio man untangling cables, and a swarthy photographer in a sweatshirt locking up his cameras, and one or two middle-aged women and a half-dozen Western Union girls, and a fat girl in a Kennedy boater, a young reporter in a beard and, I guess, his girl.

It was a perfect private way through to the ballroom. But one of my reporter friends said, 'You don't want to get in there. It's murder in there. Anyway Pierre [Salinger] has promised that when Bobby gets through his speech he'll come through in to this room and talk with us.' It was an unbelievable break. We sat down and had a drink and heard the telegraph girls tapping out copy and tried not to wince at the television set in a corner that was tuned up to a howling decibel level.

A few minutes later the television commentators gave way to the ballroom scene, and Bobby was up there with his beaming helpers and his ecstatic little wife, and he was thanking everybody and saying things must change, and so on to Chicago. It

230

was about eighteen minutes after midnight. We were standing outside the swinging doors that gave on to the serving pantry he would come through, on his way from the ballroom to us. These doors had no glass peepholes, but we'd soon hear the pleasant bustle of him coming through greeting the coloured chef and various waiters and bus boys who had lined up to shake his hand.

Then. Above the bassy boom of the television there was a banging repetition of sounds. Like somebody dropping a rack of trays, or banging a single tray against a wall. Half a dozen of us were startled enough to head for the doors, and suddenly we were jolted through by a flying wedge of other men. It had just happened. It was a narrow lane he had to come through, for there were two long steam tables and somebody had stacked up against them those trellis gates, with artificial leaves stuck on them, that they use to fence a dance band off from the floor. The only light was the blue-white light of three fluorescent tubes slotted in the ceiling.

We heard nothing but a howling jungle of cries and obscenities and saw a turmoil of arms and fearful faces and flying limbs, and two enormous backs—of Roosevelt Grier, the football player, and Rafer Johnson, the Olympic champion—piling on to a pair of blue jeans or chinos on a steam table. There was a head on the floor streaming blood, and somebody put a Kennedy boater under it, and the blood trickled down the sides like chocolate sauce on an iced cake. There were splashes of flashlights, and infernal heat, and the button eyes of Ethel Kennedy turned to cinders. She was wrestling or slapping a young man and he was

231

saying, 'Listen, lady, I'm hurt, too.' And then she was on her knees cradling him briefly, and in another little pool of light on the greasy floor was a huddle of clothes and staring out of it the face of Bobby Kennedy, like the stone face of a child's effigy on a cathedral tomb.

I had, and have, no idea of the stretch of time, or any immediate sense of the event itself. Everybody has a vulnerable organ that reacts to shock, and mine is the stomach. My lips were like emery paper and I was feeling very sick and hollow. I pattered back into the creamy, green genteel dining room. And only then did I hear somebody yell, 'Kennedy's shot, they shot him.' I heard a girl nearby moan, 'No, no, not again!' And while I was thinking, 'that was in Dallas', a dark woman suddenly bounded to a table and beat it and howled like a wolf, 'Goddam stinking country! No! No! No! No! No! No! No!' Another woman attacked the bright television screen and the image of the placid commentators, who had not yet got the news. My companion was fingering a cigarette package like a paralytic. I sat her down and went back in again. Everybody wanted to make space and air, but everybody also wanted to see the worst. By now, the baying and the moaning had carried over into the ballroom, and it sounded like a great hospital bombed and in panic.

It may have been a minute, or twenty minutes later, when a squad of cops bristling with shotguns burst through the swinging doors of the pantry our way with their bundle of black curly head and the jeans, and the tight, small behind, and the limp head, and a face totally dazed.

*   *   *

Well, the next morning, when I saw and heard the Pope in his gentle, faltering English, I still could not believe that he was talking about the squalid, appalling scene in a hotel pantry that I had been a part of and would always be a part of.

I don't doubt that such an experience is a trauma. And because of it, and five days later, I still cannot rise to the editorial pages and the general lamentations about a sick society. I for one do not feel like an accessory to a crime. And I reject, almost as a frivolous obscenity, the notion of collective guilt, the idea that I or the American people killed John Fitzgerald Kennedy and Martin Luther King and Robert Francis Kennedy. I don't believe, either, that *you* conceived Hitler, and that in some deep unfathomable sense all Europe was responsible for the extermination of six million Jews. With Edmund Burke, I don't know how you can indict a whole nation. To me, this now roaringly fashionable theme is a great folly. It is difficult to resist, because it provides emergency resuscitation to one's self-esteem. It deflects the search for a villain to some big corporate culprit. It offers cheap reassurance, cut-rate wisdom, but is really a way of opting out of the human situation: a situation that includes pity for the dead Kennedys and the living, compassion for Sirhan Sirhan, and sympathy for the American nation at a time when the vicious side of its frontier tradition (to which it has owed its vigour and variety) is surging up again, for reasons that no one has accurately diagnosed.

I said as much as this to a young friend. And he replied, 'Me too. I don't feel implicated in the murder of John or Bobby Kennedy. But when Martin Luther King is killed, the only people who know that you and I are not like the killers are you and I.'

It is a tremendous sentence and exposes the present danger to America and its public order. The more people talk about collective guilt, the more they will feel it. For after three hundred years of subjection and prejudice any desperate black man or deluded outcast is likely to act as if it were true: that the American people, and not their derelicts, are the villains.

Making a Home of a House

26 January 1969

It obviously takes a little time to be able to judge the political style of any new President, because he suddenly has more power inside the White House than he'd ever guessed. But less power outside the White House than he'd hoped.

In the meantime, there are other changes, from one White Housekeeper to the next, that are more likely, I believe, to fascinate more people than those who are interested only in political programmes. I mean, quite simply, the way the man lives, or is made to live by what we call 'maintenance' and once called a wife. What he does with his day, the gadgets and objects he likes to have around him, the sort of midnight snack he chooses to steal from the icebox.

Five Presidents and thirty-five years ago, the

chief White House usher brought forth a book of reminiscences covering nine Presidents and forty-two years in the White House. 'Ike' Hoover, as he was familiarly known, was a sharp-eyed man who had quiet but definite ideas on dignity, eccentricity, what was becoming in a President and what was not. His book is a mine of offhand observation not unlike, I imagine, the notebooks that Dickens kept on names, characters, foibles, for novels he died too soon to write. Ike Hoover's is a proper book and anyone looking for keyhole confidences or coy sexual innuendo is going to be disappointed. Ike Hoover would have despised such stuff. Nevertheless, what stays in my memory more than all the Cabinet crises or the state dinners are his small observations about character and taste. He never hesitates to draw comparisons. Such as, that Wilson was the only President who cared for the theatre (though Harding 'liked vaudeville'), and that nearly all of them were voracious readers of detective stories. As for diversions, he records— without irony—that whereas for Wilson it was 'much motoring, golf, and solitaire', and for Harding 'golf, poker and lots of company', Coolidge indulged in 'some smoking, sleep and jigsaw puzzles'.

Ike Hoover puts down whatever comes to mind always with propriety but never with censorship. It will be hard to forget the offhand note that Herbert Hoover seldom noticed the staff and never said 'Good morning', 'Good evening', 'Merry Christmas' or 'Happy New Year'. Ike Hoover also seemed to feel a historian's responsibility to deliver a final judgement on every man he served. He announced that 'The nine Presidents whom I have known seem to me just about average men.' But having obliterated them under a blanket of ordinariness, he then pulled them out again and assigned them marks for human qualities that meant much to him. Egotism? Coolidge had most, Hoover least. Self-control? 'Those who saw Coolidge in a rage were simply startled for life.' Laughter? Taft was a hearty laugher. Hoover, he says, never laughed at all. Fondness for the ladies? 'Theodore Roosevelt was a man's man, through and through. Taft was a ladies' man, pure and simple. Harding was a sporting ladies' man.' Food fads? 'Harding liked fancy food . . . Roosevelt would make a whole meal on pork and beans . . . Coolidge enjoyed cheese and would eat it by the slice like pie . . . Hoover just ate.' Sleeping habits? Teddy Roosevelt never slept by day, Taft 'could sleep at any old time', Wilson could take a nap 'when he had large affairs to deal with . . . [he could] go right to sleep as soon as he lay down on the couch. It was part of his plan of self-control.' The report on Calvin Coolidge amounts to a revelation. He went to bed at ten and got up between seven and nine. 'In the afternoon he would without fail take a nap lasting from two to four hours, going from one-thirty to . . . sometimes five o'clock.' I have forgotten many things about Calvin Coolidge, but I shall not readily lose the picture of a President of the United States who on principle slept between eleven and fifteen hours a day.

Well, Ike Hoover is long gone, and we shall never have the pleasure of his clean but odious comparisons between, say, Truman and Eisenhower. Even though we've had a spate of

236

memoirs and torrents of gossip, we still don't have as memorable a domestic picture of the newcomers.

A few of us were sitting around the other evening indulging a fantasy that millions of Americans must have been enjoying in secret this week: what would you do if the impossible office came your way? What's the first thing you'd do if you moved into the White House? A pretty brunette with a fine chin knew at once: 'I'd get rid of those damn Remingtons.'

Frederic Remington was an American painter and sculptor of the old West, born just at the right time, the year of the outbreak of the Civil War, to see the last upsurge of the old boisterous life on the plains. If he'd been born out West, he no doubt would have taken for granted the old corral, and the trail herd, and the branding, and the buffalo range, and the occasional Indian massacre. But he was born in New York State and, following the rule that no true believer is so bigoted as a convert, he did over two thousand seven hundred paintings and drawings of horses, cattle, cowboys, Indians, soldiers, and horses, horses, horses. They were done with almost painful realism, every hoof and muscle and lariat and nostril painted as if by a photographer who was not satisfied with the print until he had pencilled in all the creases. Yet Remington prompted in strong, simple men the thrill of recognition that comes to yachtsmen when they see a painting, good or awful, which reflects the sunset light on ballooning sails.

Today, Remington's pictures bring incredible prices. Two of them were loaned to the White House at the insistence of President Johnson and hung in a room outside his big office. It was a compulsory routine, if you were a visitor to Johnson's White House, to be led at the end out of the office and planted in front of these broncos and urged to admire them. The President would look at them as other men look at a Rubens or a photograph of their grandmother, and a tear would form in the corner of one eye. He would sniff like a gusting wind and brush away the tear with the back of a hand the size of a cod.

Now, if one thing is more certain than another in the transfer of power from Johnson to Nixon, it is that the style and flavour of White House family life will change. It always does, of course, though there have been new occupants too timorous to change anything for a while. Mrs Truman was one. For six weeks, she nibbled away at cold, hard dinner rolls of a kind surely very familiar to English-speaking and French-speaking people. But she'd been brought up in Missouri and inherited the Southern taste for hot, crumbly rolls. It was only on the command of President Truman that her recipe was passed on to the chef, and the Trumans reverted to breaking the bread of their fathers.

I don't suppose any of us would dare to say yet what changes the Nixons are likely to make. In spite of the loving work done on the Nixon image by advertising men and similar plastic surgeons we really know very little about his tastes and private prejudices. He was so anxious for so long to be all things to all men that he seemed to have no preferences whatsoever. In, for instance, food. On his campaign trips his enthusiasm was carefully prepared for the regional food that came his way.

In Idaho, he simply craved a baked potato. In the state of Washington, he couldn't get enough apple and boysenberry pie. In Maryland, he drooled to get at the crabs (and in that, we must admit, he was at one with the best crab-fanciers on earth). In his native state of California—which grows an alarming variety of food—he knew enough to be pretty spry. Praise an orange in Merced County, for example, and you're likely to lose the votes of all the Armenians who pack apricots. When in doubt he settled for plastic hamburgers everywhere, and in southern California, his home ground, he made a big thing of wolfing chilli con carne in the Mexican districts, even though it is a Texas and not a Mexican dish. But now he's in his own large home, and he can do what comes naturally, and it must be an immense relief.

First thing he did was to throw out those Remingtons, or rather send them back politely to the museum. Within twenty-four hours, he struck some other blows for liberty that wiped out the more theatrical memories of the Johnson reign. First, he announced that he's not comfortable working in a large, pretentious office. The President's office is a sumptuous and beautiful white oval room. It has two or three superb portraits of earlier Presidents, some elegant eighteenth-century furniture, and a great sofa, in front of which Johnson planted a massive white console. It looked like the computerized dashboard of a nuclear submarine, with many winking lights signifying all the people at home and abroad who were dying to phone the President. He used to gaze at it fondly, as a Roman emperor might have gazed at the roaring Colosseum begging him to elevate his thumb or invert it. A way off, and facing the sofa, were three television sets, each tuned to a different station, for if ever there was a man yearning to know what the world was saying about Lyndon Johnson on three networks, not to mention Telstar, that man was Lyndon Johnson.

Well, the console has gone, and so have the television sets. Mr Nixon hastened to remark that he was not against television. He just wants to turn an IBM headquarters into a home. The Oval Office will be used for ceremonial occasions. Mr Nixon has taken over a small office, where he can put his feet up and—a moving touch—have a fire, with the air conditioning turned way up, even on the blistering days of midsummer.

These changes will be applauded, I believe, by both the citizens who voted for him and by those who didn't. Nixon is a small-town boy, and in spite of the trappings of power that have surrounded him since he came to the Vice Presidency sixteen long years ago (he has been at the top or close to it as long as any politician in American history) he likes small surroundings and homely things. There is an anxiety among some old courtiers from Camelot that the Nixons will tear down the French eighteenth-century wallpapers, and dispose of the fine paintings, and otherwise reduce to a suburban 'den' all the other elegant fixings with which Mrs Kennedy did over the White House in the splendid Federal style. There's no sign of this at the moment.

But a President has considerable say in how he wants to have the house look while he's in it. Theodore Roosevelt, another New York convert to the muscle-flexing life of the Far West (and the jungles of Brazil), did over several rooms into menageries of moose and bison heads. His successor couldn't wait to ship them away and be free to walk through the place standing up straight. Harry Truman loved to sit in an old rocker in the evenings and face the lawns behind the White House. What he missed was a porch to rock on, so after a squabble with Congress and the architects (who said the second floor would look like a big Missouri back porch), he had some construction done under the back portico. It looked like a big Missouri back porch.

And how about the Vice President? Agnew is his name. In spite of the usual promise that he will be given vast new sovereign powers, he is tucked away in a tiny office he has commandeered from a secretary. He thus gives substance to Mencken's definition of a Vice President: 'He is a man who sits in the outer office of the White House hoping—to hear the President sneeze.'

Telling One Country about Another

2 March 1969

A year or two ago, I had an invitation to go and talk to the cadets at West Point, which is the Sandhurst or St Cyr of the United States. The letter was signed by a general. It was the first time a general had invited me to anything, though more years ago than I care to say I did get a letter from the President of the United States which began: 'Greetings!'—with a cordial exclamation mark, too.

241

The general even sent a car to drive me up the Hudson. If I'd been going to talk to the Arts Club, or whatever, of Long Beach, California, I'd have put on a pair of golfing slacks and a blazer. But I was not going to be found guilty, at West Point, of what my headmaster called 'the supreme act of rudeness: casualness' and I decked myself out in a suit and a tie bearing the three cocks (the cock crowed three times) and weeping crowns of Jesus College, Cambridge. This badge offered the only possibility open to me of pulling rank. I also practised saying 'Yes, sir', 'No, sir' and 'Not at all, sir'.

When I got up there, I was the one who was called sir. The commanding general, it happened, was about five years younger than I and on the verge of retirement. He wondered if there was anything he might do to make me comfortable. This alarming deference made me think back to an afternoon, in 1962, aboard the USS *Kitty Hawk*, a super aircraft carrier. I was along with the White House press corps at a demonstration of missile firing being put on for President Kennedy. When it was all over, and the twilight was dropping over the Pacific, I was nearly knocked down by a hefty slap on the back. It came from the Admiral of the Pacific Fleet. 'Hi, there!' he said, 'You old bastard.' I had known him twenty years before as a humble lieutenant, and we had had one or two memorable raucous evenings together.

There seem, indeed, to be fewer men around than there used to be to whom I feel I ought to defer. By the same token, there are more and more men, going from grey to white at that, who come to me and seek advice. It is a mixed compliment.

I now get calls from incoming foreign correspondents who wonder how to go about acquainting themselves with the Presidency, the Congress, investigating committees and the rest of it. The other day, one of them asked me to tell him the main differences between reporting the America of today and the America of thirty years ago. It is worth a passing thought or two.

To begin with, I could say, and truly, that the job is always the same: to say, or write, what you see and hear and relate it to what you know of the country's traditional behaviour. 'Traditional behaviour' may sound a little clumsy. But I'm trying to avoid the trap of what is called 'national character'. Whenever you are really baffled, it is always safe to put it all down to national character. I have come to think that a strong belief in national character is the first refuge of the anxious. For the moment, we'll let that pass.

A foreign correspondent, then, is both an interpreter and a victim of his subject matter. He must be aware of his own changing view of the country he's assigned to. And the danger here is that of assuming that the longer you stay in a country, the truer will be your perspective. As the Pope said to the earnest visitor who wondered how long he ought to stay in Rome to know it well: 'Two days, very good. Two weeks, better. Two years, not long enough.'

More important still, the reporter must always have in mind the settled view that his readers or listeners hold of the country he's writing about. The home reader, whether a simpleton or an intellectual, a Socialist or a Tory, wants—like a tourist—to find what he's looking for. He doesn't

243

want to be startled out of his preconceptions. It is the correspondent's job to startle preconceptions. And, I must admit, sometimes to say that they're right.

There was, twenty-odd years ago, the instructive case of a Hungarian refugee from his Communist country. He had been a Communist himself, till he saw Communism in action. Then he escaped to Britain. He was a journalist, a brilliant intellectual, and a Jew. When, after the Second World War, the British Labour government had to try and establish a policy for Palestine, a British editor decided that this man was the ideal outsider to report on the anarchy and ill-will that had set in between the British and the Jews. The editor gently suggested that it would be a fine thing if he could incidentally expose the 'lies' that the Palestine Jews were spreading abroad. The 'lies' included the notion that Mr Ernest Bevin, the Foreign Secretary, in trying to hold on to Palestine, and the support of the Arabs, and the goodwill of the Jews, was attempting an impossibility that was involving him in ruthless treatment of the Jews. The Hungarian was told to spend a few weeks feeling his way into the situation and then to begin filing his series of articles. He stayed a month, five weeks, six weeks, and nothing was heard from him. When the editor cabled, 'What happened? Where is the series?' he cabled back, 'Sorry, no series, all the lies are true.'

Luckily, no such bad blood has soured the relations between Britain and the United States in the past thirty years, except during the first three or four years of the 1950s, when the British view of the late Senator Joseph McCarthy blew up the only blizzard of disgusted mail I have ever received. But, more recently, there have been delicate problems involved in reporting a first-rate power that was once a second-rate power to a second-rate power that was once first-rate. For many years after the Second World War, Britons refused to acknowledge their fading influence. And for a blazing month or two the most unpopular American in Britain was Dean Acheson, simply for having expressed his glimpse of the obvious: 'Britain has lost an empire and not yet found a role.'

When I arrived in Washington in the late 1930s, I was one of only four British correspondents. Today, there must be forty or fifty, if you count reporters on particular assignment, and the enlarged radio and television staffs of the BBC and the British commercial television companies. This trek followed a simple law of politics: the best reporters, like the best chefs, gravitate toward the centres of power. (The Australians today complain, as Americans did fifty years ago, that the foreign press corps in their country is unreasonably small.) When Britain really ruled the waves, in good King George V's glorious reign, London was the capital of foreign correspondence. The Foreign Office briefings were attended by a pack of correspondents from nations big and small. And the Foreign Office, being the repository of all wise and relevant information, felt no call to bandy debating points with the press. The Foreign Office distributed handouts, no questions asked. It did not justify its policies. It announced them. And I remember how American correspondents, newly arrived in London, used to fume in their impotence when they found it was not possible to have a

245

private word with a Cabinet minister. To have invited him to lunch would have thrown him into a coronary.

A young Texan, a journalist, who is now a distinguished American magazine editor, stayed with me in London when I was back there in the early, dark spring of 1938. He was an inquisitive and typically courteous Texan, and one night he had a message from his New York office asking him to look into a rumour, a correct rumour as it turned out, that the Nazis were about to invade Austria. It sounded pretty melodramatic to me, but in those days we were not yet accustomed to the idea that gangsterism was a working technique of international politics. My friend mulled over the cable from New York and his instincts as an Associated Press stringer got the better of him. He asked to use my telephone and he rang up the Foreign Office, an impulse which to me was as bizarre as phoning Buckingham Palace. When the FO answered he asked to talk to Lord Halifax, who had just then become the Foreign Secretary. I was agog with admiration. I was at the time a political innocent, a film critic, but I knew my Hitchcock movies well enough to know that that was exactly how Joel McCrea in a raincoat went about his business.

It was soon obvious that my friend was having a rough time with the other end of the wire. 'Yes, sir,' he kept saying in courteous variations, 'I know it's very late in the evening, but this is not the sort of rumour the Associated Press can just forget.' Somehow, he managed to get Lord Halifax's home number, a remarkable feat in itself. He re-dialled and there was a crackle and a pause and a respectful fluting sound from the other end. It was the butler, who had a strangulated moment or two while, I imagine, he was being revived by the rest of the household staff. At last, he pronounced the definitive sentence: 'I'm sorry, sir, his Lordship is in his bath.'

This is still not an approach I'd be inclined to take, though in failing to be so brash I no longer feel merely courteous: I feel I'm neglecting my duty. Because I now take for granted the ease of access to people in government in America. Americans had, and have, a quite different feeling about the press. In many countries, and Britain used to be one of them, a reporter is a potential enemy. The Americans, however, feel it is better to have a friend in print than an enemy. And this, too, is a great danger, for nothing castrates a reporter so easily as flattery. But the main thing is, the politicians tend to look on you as a camp follower through the maze of politics, and if they can help you find your way out, without trading the Pentagon secret file, they will do it. Nowadays, of course, even dictators have to pretend to welcome cosy conversations with television interviewers.

America, from the beginning of my time, was an open book to a reporter. The people were there to mix with, and the landscape and its troubles and pleasures, and a reporter with the most modest credentials could get to talk to everybody from the Governor, the local Congressman, the Chamber of Commerce, the saloon keepers, the local madams. Huey Long stretched out on a bed barefoot in the Roosevelt Hotel in New Orleans and picked his toes while he enlarged on the glorious future he had in mind for Everyman and Everywoman in

Louisiana. I once asked the late Governor Talmadge of Georgia how the (since abolished) 'county unit' system worked in his state. He sucked his teeth and ordered up a car, oddly—it seemed to me then—a humble jalopy. We jumped in and he drove me into the corners of three counties that fringed Atlanta. In each of them he dropped in on a couple of farmers on the pretence of needing to relieve himself. When we were back in the city, he said, 'I got myself six unit votes right there, and them students and doctors and Commies in Atlanta can shout themselves hoarse—it's more votes than they have.' Once, I was driving across Nevada and noticed from the map that I was close by Hawthorne, and that it was the site of the US Naval Ammunition Depot. I asked to look in on it, and I did. I am a little awestruck now to reflect that a Japanese reporter could probably have done the same right up to the eve of Pearl Harbor.

In the 1930s you required no confidential sources to straighten you out on the condition of the country. The country was racked by Depression. On several trips around the United States, in the South more than anywhere, I was physically nauseated by the people I saw in the country towns and in the workless cities: the absolutely drained look of mothers nourishing babies at shrunken breasts, the general coma of the rural poor, with the telltale rash of scurvy or pellagra on the back of their necks. Today there is very little, if any, scurvy or pellagra in the South, because they varied the crops and learned about green vegetables, and the cities turned to textiles. They were no longer doomed to plates of rice and corn and potatoes and hominy grits—a feast, whenever it was a feast, of nothing but starch.

The first year I drove around the whole country, about one family in four was on the breadline or just above it. Yet, while we totted up the grim statistics, we wrote little about these things for foreign consumption. The foreign consumers too had their silent factories and marching miners, and they had bemused and stumbling leaders. The great news from America was that the country was galvanized by the new President into a prospect of greener pastures. The story was the exhilaration of the Roosevelt era: the public works, the dams and new housing, the first national network of concrete highways, the poor boys planting millions of trees. These things excited us more than the conditions they were meant to cure depressed us. If 30 or 40 per cent of the population was then at some stage of need, today only 11 per cent falls below the government's rather generous definition of a subsistence income of $2,200 a year. And though that may sound like small pickings, there has never been a time in this country's history, or perhaps in human history, when more people in one nation were better off, never a smaller percentage of two hundred millions who could be called poor. Yet there is less complacency, I believe, than there ever was. As I talk, the cities tremble and the countryside groans over the shame of it.

In case my drift is being misunderstood, let me say that this trembling and groaning is a good thing too. If God observes the fall of one sparrow, it is right in a prosperous time that we should feel not only that we are our brother's keeper but that our brother is the whole of society. I think it must be the first time in history that the so-called civilized nations have felt this way. Why? Are we more humane, more sensitive than we used to be? I think not. The world's population of the starving and near-starving at the height of the Victorian age must have been beyond our imagining. But the point is, the Victorians had to imagine it, or read the fine print, or take the progressive magazines or dig out—from some encyclopedia—the infant mortality rates. Statistics make few people bleed or weep. Today all of us, in a castle or a cottage, can see every night the warped skeletons of the children of Biafra. Thirty students up at Columbia University paralysed for a time the education of several thousand, and it looked and sounded, on the evening news, like the siege of Mafeking. A hundred cops go berserk on an August night in Chicago, and next day it's the scandal of the world. Television, whatever its faults and banalities, is the new conscience—or nagger—of mankind. I am frankly relieved to reflect that in the early Hitler days we had no television. The news dispatches of brave men had to be read by choice. The television scene of Nazism, as filmed by the devilishly skilled Leni Riefenstahl, could have recruited millions of disciples. It might, of course, have made people stop and listen to Winston Churchill, who went on and on, a croaking old orator, about the threat of a frightful regime he had evidently pictured in his mind.

This, I am sure, is the single greatest change that has come over our society's awareness of what is going on everywhere. The sight of violence has quite likely upset our sense of proportion just as badly as the assumption of general calm upset it by default. If so, we are upset in the right way.

The effect on the foreign correspondent has been revolutionary. All newspaper reporters, whether they know it or not, are competing with the television news, which has a daily audience bigger than the most famous newspaper correspondent ever dreamed of. The sheer pungency of television, of the thing seen, invokes not meditation but partisanship: that is to say, instant ideology. The newspapers, to stay solvent, try to match this emotional appeal. The result is that—in Britain, for example—the best papers are more and more turning into daily magazines of opinion, and the worst make the crudest, the most blatant, appeal to the seven deadly sins.

Consequently, while the scope of a foreign correspondent has not been narrowed (he's still expected to take all knowledge for his province) the reader's expectations of him are narrower, more ideological. When I began, it was possible to present the awkward complexity of a political story without any side being taken. And then to move on to any number of what were called 'colour' pieces: on the landscape, the livelihood of a region, sport, odd characters, the history of this custom and that place. Today, you write about these things and the partisan oldsters say you are fiddling while Washington or Chicago burns. The young say you've got a hang-up on whimsy.

A year ago, I was talking to a forum of Californians about the rape of their beautiful landscape by the developers. The tidal wave of new arrivals. The mania for city ways. The universal obsession with industry as the only true form of progress. When it was over, a handsome, 19-, 20-year-old girl came up to me and said, 'I understood most of it except for one thing.' What's that? I said: She said, 'You have a thing about trees, don't you?' That's right, I said.

In these talks, and at the risk of seeming callous or whimsical, I propose to go on having a thing about many other matters than Soviet expansionism, and the plight of the cities, and the nuclear arms race, and who—after the next Presidential election—is going to be the lord and master of us all.

Pegler

29 June 1969

I'd like to tell you about an outrageous man who was one of the best American humorists of any time and even at his worst handled the American language with a freewheeling audacity that has rarely been matched since Mark Twain.

Westbrook Pegler died suddenly the other day and I was saddened. I am puzzled to say why this should be so. I was never close to him, he was 74, he'd been sick in more than a physical way for years, and he had not been seen in print much in a decade or so. Scurrility was his trade, you might say, and in the 1930s and 1940s, it was a breathtaking thing to see how close he could sail to the wind of the libel laws. Long before the end, he lost all skill in coming about when the wind was raging. He grossly libelled an old newspaper friend by describing him, among other repulsive things, as a coward, a war profiteer, a fugitive from the

252

London Blitz in the bowels of comfortable hotels, 'an absentee war correspondent', and he wrote also that the man had once gone 'nuding along the road with a wench in the raw'. This spasm of whimsy and malice cost Pegler's employers $175,000 in the biggest libel settlement awarded up to that time.

He was always a scornful man, but after that his scorn turned rancid and he babbled on and on about old enemies, about both President and Mrs Roosevelt long after they were dead. His last years seemed to have been spent in fuming total recall of all the Presidents he had watched, from the first Roosevelt to John F. Kennedy, whom he called 'a mean, ratty, dough-heavy Boston gang politician'. Towards the end, even the monthly magazine of the John Birch Society found his last piece, on Chief Justice Warren, too raw to print.

You would think that here was the case of a great talent gone to seed. And as a man, certainly, he was for years simply thrashing in deep water and making incoherent sounds before he went under. Why, then, should I have felt sad at his going? It is because, I think, of a fact of relativity not mentioned in Einstein's theory. Some people are so bristling with life that when they have been dead for years they still seem to be on call, whereas many sweet but pallid people who are up and about have nothing more to offer.

Pegler, newspaperman, is the man I am talking about, and he had a lion's share of the vitality that outlasts its time and place. Picture him first. A big hulking man but erect as a guardee, with glimmering blue eyes that flashed an ultimatum to all simple believers and all secret slobs. A grim, mischievous Irish mouth. Two shaggy, forked

253

eyebrows, to stress that the message—via Western Union—came from nobody but Mephistopheles. Plainly not the kind of reporter to be brushed off by a handout, or a telephone call, or a Presidential 'no comment'.

He was what they used to call a muckraker, and in his middle years he was the best. Once, over a drink in Denver, when I asked him what he was doing so far from his den in Connecticut, he said he'd heard that a couple of insurance companies had suddenly shown alarming fat profits. 'The trail led out here,' he said, 'and I thought I might come and—sink a pick. Could be pay dirt.' I imagined every insurance man in the West out of bed and doctoring the books.

When, soon after, he appeared in Hollywood to look into the way the motion picture unions worked, his hosts should have been warned. At that time, a man named Willie Bioff was the labour boss of the movie unions and a man highly thought of by the bigwigs of the New Deal. Pegler threatened nothing and nobody. He mooched around the studios and the houses in Beverly Hills and dingy offices downtown, and picked up a private scent that led him to Chicago and on to other, obscurer, towns in the hinterland. He pored over police blotters and old newspapers and tramped off to interview this anonymous old man and that forgotten old madam. And after six months of pick-sinking, he wrote a series of searing columns. The first began with the firecracker of a sentence: 'Willie Bioff is a convicted pimp.' Period. By the time Pegler was through, so was Bioff, whose shady past Pegler had reconstructed with the tedious accuracy of one of those picture puzzles in a hundred bits and pieces that emerges at last as the Taj Mahal. Bioff went to jail. So did the national president of a building employees' union, and the prison gates closed behind him on the whining phrase: 'I've been Peglerized.'

Pegler was born in Minneapolis, a skinny little runt, irascible at his first gasp. He delivered newspapers as a boy in the paralysing northern winters, and one day he was shoving his little wagon along in Chicago when the Arctic wind whistling in across the lake blew his papers away, and while he was chasing them his route book too took off in another direction. He was disgusted. He tore off home and when the route boss called him up and said, 'You're fined three dollars,' he shouted back, 'Oh, shut your face!' And that was the end of his first job.

He was the son of a newspaperman and he never thought there was any other trade to follow. He started, at 16, as a $10-a-week cub reporter and described himself as 'a raw kid as freckled as a guinea egg'. He was transferred to St Louis and at 22 was in London as a fledgling foreign correspondent. Then he went into the Navy in the First World War and after that turned sports reporter and in no time showed that he had a rowdy, biting style that was to make him a star. He moved up to a sports column, and when nothing much was happening he wrote about this and that and found himself sounding off about the cost of living, the gangsters and the man in the White House. In 1933 he set up shop as a national columnist with no illusions about the pretensions of the breed. He called all columnists 'myriad-minded us . . . experts on the budget who can't balance an expense account, pundits on the technological age who can't put a fresh ribbon in their own typewriters, and resounding authorities on the problems of the farmer who never grew a geranium in a pot'.

The first fifteen years of his column were the great years. He wrote about everything with the unsleeping scepticism of a man in the bleachers who had watched many a dumb-bell turn into a national hero on the baseball mound, who had seen many a horse race fixed and who was therefore quite ready to believe that a labour leader, a Governor, a Secretary of the Treasury or even a President might be no better than he should be.

He refused to be dazzled by the vocabulary of the sociologists or distracted from his own horse-sense by the hushed pronouncements of the Walter Lippmanns and the Arthur Krocks—what he used to call 'double-dome' commentators. Mussolini, for instance, at one time had very vocal admirers and detesters in the United States, but the role of his Blackshirts in the Spanish Civil War was thought to be a topic for exclusively military experts. To Pegler it was all very simple: 'In most invincible legions, the front rank is regarded as the post of maximum peril and honour. But at Guadalajara, when Mussolini's brave Blackshirts encountered the enemy, the men in the rear rank found themselves overwhelmed by the impetuous dash of their comrades in the forward positions . . . it is reliably reported that most of the Blackshirts casualties were caused by hobnails.'

Off in Florida covering some labour conference, he took a day to explore the expensive magic of deep-sea fishing. He was not impressed. Listen to

256

this: it might be out of *Life On the Mississippi*.

> We were going after tarpon and they kept
> telling me the water was absolutely reeking
> with all kinds of fish with queer names like
> dace, mace, plaice, reach, peach, gudgeon,
> mullet, grommet and shovel-nosed duebills
> . . . we anchored in the barley water beside a
> channel and rigged up a lot of tackle with
> hooks the size of those on which they hang
> half-cows in butcher shops . . . we didn't catch
> any fish on the first day or the second . . . the
> third day we were burned as red as fire
> engines and the mosquitoes were coming up
> in clouds . . . I can't play golf either . . . when I
> was a kid, I was a punk ball player. Poker—
> the same story. I try to live right and follow
> the instructions, but it never makes any
> difference. Maybe this is what makes me so
> mean.

Well, in time Pegler's meanness got to be a
national scandal, and the obituary writers made
much—too much I think—of his almost psychotic
hatred of the Roosevelt family, and his ornery
conviction that practically all Americans of Slavic
origin were probably Communists. In life, in fact,
he was most of the time, and in a private room, an
amiable and surprisingly soft-spoken companion.
But the path to his prose led through the bile duct.
He had a perverse love of demoting all current
heroes in a single phrase. Vice President Henry
Wallace was 'old bubble-head'. J. Edgar Hoover,
when everybody thought of him as the national
scourge of all evil men, was put down as 'a

nightclub fly-cop'. Mayor Fiorello LaGuardia, the plucky Little Flower to the citizens of New York, was to Pegler 'the little *padrone* of the Bolsheviki'. And though it may seem odd, his devotion to Franklin Roosevelt till America got into the war was an expression of this same contempt for people in power, for he saw Roosevelt as the champion of 'the hired help' against 'the meanness of a complacent upper class'.

He was brought up in the tough and talented school of Chicago reporters when Chicago was the best newspaper town in the country. And when he came East, he carried with him this air of being a prairie lad permanently unfooled by the rich, the genteel, the powerful and all foreigners. He must have adopted the manner early on, possibly as a small fry's defence against the jeering reminders of his gang that his father (a diligent and respectable Cockney immigrant) was English, and his mother was Canadian: Irish-Canadian but still Canadian. Like many other Midwesterners, Pegler was specially on his guard against any beguilements that came from England and the English. But unlike some Midwesterners, he was not exasperated by an English story that defeated the usual American preconceptions.

There was an unforgettable evening just after the Second World War when I was dining with a Midwesterner who had made a fortune in New York as an advertising tycoon. He was the son of a poor parson and he remained a lifelong rural Republican, and a fervent anti-Royalist with a very pat view of Europeans as the lackeys of kings and courts. The only other guest was Pegler. I had just returned from London and the bleakness of

England in the winter after Harry Truman had abruptly cancelled the blessings of Lend-Lease. In material comforts the British were, if anything, worse off than they'd been during the war. But I had been struck, as all visitors were in those days, by a new and rousing social equality that the war had—you would almost say—enforced on the country: an equality of want. Pegler and the tycoon politely doubted it. I told them how I'd been invited by the Lord Privy Seal, no less (fifth in line of precedence after the king) to look over the bomb damage to the House of Commons and other ancient memorials. They visibly sniffed at my dragging in such a title. I couldn't think why I'd been chosen for this flattering grand tour until the Lord Privy Seal began to speculate aloud about the type of Englishman who might be best qualified to be the next ambassador to the United States. I said only that I wished for once he could be plain Mr Somebody, and not knighted beforehand, since Americans were fuzzy about titles and tended to think that even a knight was an eighth earl accustomed to whipping the peasants. Pegler and the host glared at their plates as if to challenge me to produce one common man in a society so notoriously class-ridden. Well, so what did Lord What's His Name say to that? He replied, I said, 'Ah dawn't want to goa to't friggin Stairts, we've got a bloody sawcial revolution goin' on 'ere.' (The Lord Privy Seal was a poor boy from the woollen mills of Yorkshire.)

There was a long bristling silence. Then the tycoon said grimly, '*The Prisoner of Zenda* was the last good book to come out of Europe.' The tycoon glowered while Pegler bellowed. He told me much later he'd never forgotten it.

It's true that Pegler often got angry about many foolish things and never forgot a grudge. But just as often his indignation was nobly directed against unfashionable targets and sometimes his scorn made Dean Swift read like Lewis Carroll. He bucked the Ku Klux Klan when it was dangerously powerful, and he belaboured the ruthlessness of union leaders when their power was sacrosanct. He wrote withering pieces out of Nazi Germany, which was more than many resident correspondents did, but when Hitler was everybody's Evil Eye and Stalin was his benign counterpart, Pegler saw Stalin as at least an equal monster. Defending the American police in the gangster days against invidious comparisons with Scotland Yard, he pointed out the comparative amateurishness of English criminals and the probity of English courts, and ended with this blazing sentence: 'So the British hang their simpletons and Scotland Yard takes credit for another triumph, all to the great inferential disgrace of the American cops, who have to fight it out with Dillingers and Harvey Baleys and Vincent Colls and crooked lawyers, low-grade governors, sentimental juries and courts beneath contempt.'

If the spiritualists are right, and Pegler is somewhere within the sound of these words, he is certainly tearing at his robes and bashing in his harp. But those are the kind of opinions for which he is to be honoured. All you can do with the talent is envy it.

'Eternal Vigilance'—by Whom?

19 October 1969

The other day I had a long talk with an attractive young American. The conversation divided between long sarcastic monologues on his part, and grunts of approval—more often of doubt—on mine. He was bemoaning, as we all should, the noisy and smelly flood of scandal and corruption that fills the papers these days, defaces the brightness of the television screen, and makes television commercials seem more smug and fatuous than ever. We touched on street crime, on the army sergeants swiping huge profits from overseas service clubs, the continuing proof about risky short cuts in the manufacture of automobiles, the deep inroads the Mafia is making into big and respectable business. And so on and so on.

What bothered me was that he put all these things down, not to the corruption of any class but to 'middle-class values' in themselves. Before we come to that, I'd like to say that it was not only the substance of his jeremiad that upset me, the blanket indictment of a whole country. It was the muddy language that drooled from his lips. Nobody burgles a house any more: 'A kid I know was burglarized.' None of the statesmen we brought up ever met or tangled: they were involved in 'a confrontation'. He talked of 'interface' and 'feedback'. People were either 'committed' or 'alienated'. I said goodbye and went off. I believe he thought I was shaken and impressed. I was glad

I'd not said what I was tempted to: that the whole burden of his song had been sung long ago—'It's the rich what gets the pleasure, it's the poor what gets the blame.'

I suppose that one way of explaining this unpleasant get-together (confrontation?) was the so-called 'generation gap'. Well, in some things it is a fact, and always will be. In many more disputes, and strained relations, the generation gap is a lazy excuse for the age-old suspicion between parents and children. And today, certainly, there is a widening gap between the language the generations use. I throw it out as a suggestion merely that this may be due to the sudden eruption, in the past twenty years or so, of technology—the passing over, into ordinary speech, of the special vocabularies of advanced mathematics and computers, and the new and respectable status now given to the ghastly language of sociology and psychology. Most of the horrors that now befog the speech of students and politicians, not to mention advertising men, are a special lingo that the layman doesn't understand: like 'input', 'orientation', 'parameter'. 'Parameter' is a good example. In mathematics, it means a quantity constant in a given case, but one that varies in different cases. It is used by politicians and pundits to mean no more than limit, or boundary.

No wonder they talk about a failure of 'communication' (another stopgap word between two thoughts) when they spend so long using words like 'communicate' and 'verbalize'. Only a year ago, I heard a qualified psychiatrist declare that his 2-year-old was already talking. But he didn't say it that way. He said, 'Children of his age group don't usually verbalize at this stage.' Especially if there's a verbalizing sibling in the familial situation. A gabby brother, that is.

Well, by way of thoughtful reacting, I can only say that things are bad and they'll probably get worse. There's just one point I'd like to make to people who despair of American society—and I have to confess it's a point I often forget myself. In a self-governing Republic—good government in some places, dubious in others—three thousand miles wide, eighteen hundred miles long, with fifty separate states which in many important matters have almost absolute powers—with two hundred million people drawn from scores of nations, what is remarkable is not the conflict between them but the truce. Enough is happening in America at any one time—enough that is exciting, frightening, funny, brutal, brave, intolerable, bizarre, dull, slavish, eccentric, inspiring and disastrous—that almost anything you care to say about the United States is true. You can make a case for thinking this the best, the worst, the most abject, the most alert democracy ever invented. Of course, this reflection doesn't help people bleeding in a riot or languishing in a sloppily run hospital at an outrageous daily rate. The great need for anyone in authority is courage. And the requirement for a reporter, an onlooker, is horse-sense and the ability to strike a true balance. I don't know any good reporter who would confidently claim these qualities.

Yet there is one whole class in America, and that is the largest, which claims them and thinks of itself as the balance wheel of the American system. It is nothing more or less pretentious than the middle

263

class. In America, it is not only huger—proportionately and absolutely—than anywhere else. It is not simply a large group of people who qualify by reason of income and social habits. It includes all the people who aspire to be in it, or think they are already there. In nearly forty years, I have never heard an American say, 'I am a working-class man.' I have often heard people say, 'So-and-so is looking out for the ordinary guy like me', but that's not quite the same thing.

In all the great conflicts of the past ten years—of race, student rebellion, street crime, pornography —the middle class has not been much heard from. It has been, in fact, the besieged, the ridiculed victim—of the black leaders, the student leaders, the film makers, the intellectuals, all leftists and many liberals. Yet middle-class standards, as they were planted and have grown everywhere in this country, are the ones that have kept America a going concern. It is time to grit the teeth slightly, prepare for a shower of eggs, and say what those standards are. Fair wages for good work. Concern for the family and its good name. A distrust of extremes and often, perhaps, a lazy willingness to compromise. The hope of owning your own house and improving it. The belief that the mother and father are the bosses, however easygoing, of the household and not simply pals. A pride in the whole country, often as canting and unreasonable as such patriotism can be. Vague but stubborn ideas about decency. An equally vague but untroubled belief in God. A natural sense of neighbourliness, fed by the assumption that your neighbour is much like you and is willing to share the same lawn (hedges are rare in American towns) or lend you a mower, a hammer or a bottle of milk.

Did you ever hear of qualities less heroic? Helpless laughter must be bellying up from almost any group of young people who happen to be hearing this recital. But there are signs, tentative and fumbled signs, that these people—who for too long have been called 'the silent majority'—are tired of being laughed at and frustrated. In desperate times, the meekest people show alarming symptoms of defiance. And, in the early races for the autumn elections, I notice that policemen are being elected as the mayors of cities. It should not yet give us cause to splutter. It is possible, I dare to say it is common, to find policemen who are fair, brave and level-headed.

However, it doesn't seem to me a good thing that the middle class, weary of violence and mockery as it may be, should turn to policemen as rulers, any more than that we should turn the government of the military over to the military. If war is too important to be left to the generals, the government of the people is too serious to be turned over to the police.

There is a more disturbing sign of the turning of the worm. Some cities are beginning to form vigilante committees. The most famous instance of this drastic remedy for lawlessness and disorder happened in San Francisco in the first furious years of its life as an El Dorado, after gold had been discovered nearby. San Francisco had been a shanty town on whistling sandhills. Then suddenly hundreds, and shortly thousands, of people from many states and several lands, came hurtling in to pan the rivers and get rich quick. The vast majority never made it but stayed. The garrison down the Peninsula deserted. The farmers quit. The shopkeepers closed down, and the laundries. The lucky new-rich sent their shirts to Hawaii—or even to China—to be washed.

When the ordinary, and pretty rude, services opened up again, the town was a combination of a doss house, a street bazaar, a mushrooming suburb and a brothel. At nightfall gangs roamed the streets, invaded stores, taverns and houses and beat up the inmates, especially if they were foreigners, and robbed them and quite often shot them. In two months, among a population of only twenty-five thousand, there were over a hundred murders, and no one had been executed. In the end, the silent majority rose up, held mass meetings, elected officials and formed what was known as the Vigilance Committee of San Francisco. In short order they tried, condemned and hanged all the notorious criminals they could catch.

Inevitably, the lust for justice, and quick justice, can be as insatiable as any other lust. When California came into the Union, it became possible within a year or two to suspend the committee and hand the law over to the State government. Not all San Franciscans thought this was a sensible, or even a decent, thing to do. In a report I have in front of me, written in 1856, the author has this to say about the Vigilance Committee of that year. It is quite an end-of-term report:

Scorn and applause, exoneration and abuse, indignation and sympathy, have been the expressions of the civilized world in speaking of the Vigilance Committee of San Francisco. To law-loving and worthy people, it did seem

266

strange that such an organization which usurped, as it were, the laws of the land and inflicted the severest penalties, should exist without molestation at this time . . . yet from this power California recognized her only protector of life and property, her only security for peace and virtue. Such was the object of the Society of Vigilantes. The remedy was violent but the result was good.

The other day, the *Wall Street Journal* carried a long report on the growth of vigilante societies around the country. At present they take the form of night patrols. They mean to make the streets safe. Mostly, they go unarmed. But in some small towns they tote guns, and in others they are sufficiently in league with the police to ride around in police cars. In one place their targets are robbers or muggers, in another Negroes or radicals or homosexuals. Most of them protest that their aims are innocent. Conceivably, these are simple and just men who, like the sheriff's deputies in the old Western towns, feel they must fill in for the failure of law and order. Needless to say, the courts and the police and the Governors in most states are dead against them. Vigilantism is at best a mischievous pretension, at worst a seedbed for civil chaos.

It is a small, and understandable, but ugly symptom. It would be a tragic thing for America if the middle class, the silent majority, provoked by some appalling wave of rioting and violence, found its voice and used it not to preach but to improvise law and order. Those last three words have become a catchphrase, used by the Right to argue for arbitrary restraints on the freedom of people you don't like. But the phrase has been taken up too by the Left, as a sneering put-down of ordinary people who question violence and the abuse of 'peaceable assembly'. I say, a plague on both your houses. Any society that hopes to be stable must surely yield its most passionate prejudices in the cause of getting law and order by consent of the majority. The only alternative is to get a very tough form of law and order imposed by a powerful minority. Sometimes, a minority of one.

The 1970s

The Letter from Long Island

4 August 1970

We have just seen for the first time a film made in Japan exactly twenty-five years ago. It is about what happened on that fine, hot August day to the city of Hiroshima. It was shown here now, I suppose, as a bleak reminder, and a commemoration of the 120,000 dead or injured. Two things struck me all through the film. One was the remarkable bravery—or phlegm—of the cameramen. The other was the thought that this gross nightmare should have happened to a people who have always been noted for their delicate fine touch, whether in the growing of a tree or the making of an optical lens or, as here, following the tracery of a score of wounds on a single human being.

It was enough to lacerate us, and it started up again the controversy, which will never be settled, about President Truman's decision to drop the bomb in the first place. Without raising more dust over the bleached bones of Hiroshima, I should like to contribute a couple of reminders. The first is that the men who had to make the decision to pass on to the President—General George C. Marshall and the Secretary of War, Henry L. Stimson—were just as humane and tortured at the time as you and I were later. And secondly, that they had to make a choice of alternatives that I for one would not have wanted to have to make for all the offers of redemption from all the religions of the world.

271

What the President and his advisers did not know, and what we rather confidently know now, is that by August 1945 the Japanese were at the end of their rope. The plans were going forward for a step-by-step invasion of the Japanese home islands, where the Japanese had a million men under arms, apart from another three million if the worst happened in the rest of the Far East. The best estimates, put together by the staffs of Marshall and Stimson, were that an invasion would require five million American men, that it would probably not succeed until 1947, and that the casualties, of Americans, the fighting Japanese and Japanese civilians, would amount to something between one and a half and three millions. When the invasion was being planned, the bomb had not been tried. But once it went off in New Mexico, the question was whether the Japanese should be given an ultimatum and a warning 'technical' demonstration, on uninhabited land, of the bomb's power. The atomic scientists in New Mexico delivered their opinion: 'We can propose no technical demonstration likely to bring an end to the war; we see no acceptable alternative to direct military use.'

With that judgement in their hands, Marshall and Stimson and Co. looked over the proposed targets. They ruled out the old cultural capital of Kyoto and in the end decided on Hiroshima, as the headquarters and main arsenal of the Japanese army defending southern Japan; and Nagasaki, a seaport and a centre of the war industry.

I suppose we must all have wondered, in a distraught way at some time or other, how it all started. To be painstakingly historical about it you could, of course, take it back far beyond Einstein and Rutherford and the quantum theory. If you really got going, you could find yourself in the fifth century BC with Empedocles, who worked on the assumption that an atom is the smallest indivisible particle of matter. But let us leap, say, twenty-five centuries forward to the spring of 1939 and the slowly dawning idea, in the minds of a few physicists, that an atomic bomb might be made. It was left to a scattered band of Jewish refugees from Germany—some in Sweden, most in the United States—to realize that the bomb might get into the wrong hands, namely Hitler's. Three of these refugees, all Hungarians, lived here in the obscurity that is the lot of scientists whose speciality is so exotic that neither the statesmen nor the public knows that it exists.

These three men were named Szilard, Wigner and Teller. They kept up with what was happening in their work abroad through letters from old friends, Jews mostly, who had been driven out of Germany into Belgium and Britain and Sweden. By the winter of 1938–9, the three began to hear that the Germans were working on something called 'the uranium problem'. In March 1939 an Italian physicist, Enrico Fermi, had actually called on an American admiral in the Navy Department and had touched on the possibility of an atomic bomb. Evidently it was an interesting, wild, passing thought, like the possibility at some remote time of a man landing on the moon. Neither the Navy nor any other branch of the government gave it another thought. Then the three heard that a meeting of physicists had been called in Berlin to discuss the possibility of using something called 'nuclear fission' to drive an automobile.

Maybe they were reassured about the German intentions. But not for long. The summer came on and they had a letter from a woman scientist in Sweden who told them something that, even if it had been circulated in the Foreign Offices of London and Paris, let alone the American State Department, would have meant nothing at all to anybody outside businessmen with an interest in metal stocks. Germany had suddenly banned all exports of uranium ore from Czechoslovakia, which it occupied. There was only one other European country that stocked uranium ore: Belgium, which got it from the Belgian Congo. Szilard, Wigner and Teller, it is safe to say, were the only trio of friends anywhere in the United States who were alarmed by the news. They felt they must get the warning word to somebody in American government. This was a problem. They were unknown refugees; only Wigner was an American citizen. They had cause to distrust the military mind, because of its ingrained habit of preparing to fight the last war. They had no more standing with the White House or the State Department than any ordinary person who writes a crackpot letter to the President. (The Secret Service and the FBI between them screen several hundreds of such alarms every week.) They saw what was ahead. And suddenly they thought of 'the Old Man', who was world-renowned and who, if he wrote to the Belgians—that was their first idea—might be able to get them to hold on to their stocks of uranium. They must get to the Old Man.

So it began, on a drenching hot midsummer day in July 1939. Two of the refugees, Szilard and Wigner, woke one morning and got out a map of

Long Island. They knew that the Old Man had rented a cottage for the summer from one Dr Moore. That's all. They had been lately so out of touch with him both in their work and their social contacts that they didn't know where the cottage was. Long Island is a hundred and twenty miles long and choked with place names, English and Indian. But the Old Man had named it on the telephone. Wigner was his associate at Princeton. He looked over the map. It was something with a 'P'. Way down on the south shore of the island, he saw the name—Patchogue. That was it. So they drove off. They got out to Patchogue and asked in stores and gas stations for the whereabouts of Dr Moore's cottage. Nobody had ever heard of him. They got back into the car and sweated over the map. Could it be, said Szilard, looking up across the bay to the North Fork of the island, could it be Peconic? 'Peconic,' said Wigner, 'that's it, I remember.' So they drove north and east forty-some miles, along the North Fork, and came to the minute town of Peconic, which to this day consists of one small saloon and the clearing of what was then a crumbling wooden railway shelter. Dr Moore, please? Dr Moore was unheard of.

It was one of those hideous northeastern midsummer days, of a grey leaden sky, and the wet heat up in the nineties, and the map was like a towel in their hands. They were irritable and pretty much in despair and they turned, to drive the hundred miles back to the city. Less than two miles from Peconic, on a two-lane road, you have to come back through a one-street town called Cutchogue. They stopped at Mr Kramer's drugstore to get some trifle or other. They saw a boy, about 7 years old, standing in a corner with a fishing rod in his hands. The Old Man was a great fisherman. 'Sure,' said the boy, 'he lives in Dr Moore's cottage.' He climbed in and he led them over a causeway and along a narrow peninsula called Nassau Point and they came to the cottage.

The Old Man came out in his slippers, and they told him their news. They had a hot hour explaining to him what it all meant, or could mean. Szilard, with whom I checked the facts of this trip years later, said he was surprised to realize that 'the possibility of a chain reaction had not occurred to the Old Man'. But they convinced him, and together they agreed that the best thing to do would be to write a letter to the Belgian government and send a copy of it to the United States State Department. Then Wigner and Szilard drove back to New York.

And there they began to have more misgivings. The Belgians might not respond. The copy might vanish in the yawning files of the State Department. They began to grow tense over the likelihood of a long delay. Maybe they should persuade the Old Man himself to write to the President of the United States, no less. They made discreet inquiries of other friends, other refugees, and came on a German economist who knew a banker who was a personal friend of President Roosevelt. Maybe the banker could be the courier. They sat down and drafted a much bolder and simpler letter.

And on 2 August, they drove off again. 'They', this time, were not the same couple. Wigner had gone on his holiday in California. Szilard, a scientific brain beyond our comprehension, couldn't drive a car. So Szilard invited Teller to drive him down the island. With no fear, this time, of losing the way. Not Patchogue, with a 'P', not Peconic, but Cutchogue with an 'ogue'. An easy mistake. Our weekend guests make it all the time.

The Old Man was ready for them, and they went from the porch into his study and read him both a German draft and an English translation they had typed. At last the Old Man nodded, and put his pen to it. Next step, on to the middleman banker and the White House.

It read:

> Nassau Point,
> Peconic, Long Island.
> August 2nd, 1939

F. D. Roosevelt,
President of the United States,
White House,
Washington, D.C.

Sir:

Some recent work of E. Fermi and L. Szilard, which has been communicated to me in manuscript, leads me to expect that the element uranium may be turned into a new and important source of energy in the immediate future. Certain aspects of the situation which has arisen seem to call for watchfulness and, if necessary, quick action on the part of the Administration. I believe therefore that it is my duty to bring to your attention the following facts and recommendations:

In the course of the last four months it has been made probable—through the work of Joliot in France as well as Fermi and Szilard in America—that it may become possible to set up a nuclear chain reaction in a large mass of uranium, by which vast amounts of power and large quantities of new radium-like elements would be generated . . . by which, my dear Mr President, it might be possible to unleash an immense destructive force.

The President got the letter from the banker, but not before the following October, and maybe he thought it interesting enough, though mysterious. Not until two years later, in the fall of 1941, did he appoint a committee—of the Vice President, and the Secretary of War, and General Marshall and two scientists—to look into it. He put aside some hundreds of dollars in executive funds for this study, which, later on, were increased to the tune of over $2 billion.

The Old Man, who put his signature to the Nassau Point letter, was, of course, 'A. Einstein'.

Give Thanks, for What?

25 November 1972

A week ago I was on one of the islands that the English had a rough time settling, because it is whipped at all times by high winds around a rocky and treacherous coastline. It is made of coral, which is not hospitable to swarming algae. So the sea around it does not present the usual blue-grey goulash that slops up against the islands of the North Atlantic. It is clear water, and even on overcast days it's of a light and shimmering aquamarine or turquoise colour. This beautiful sheen disguises the many perils of the rocks and helps you to forget the winds and the fact that in the late summer the island is in the path of the hurricanes that are brewed in the tropical Caribbean. I am talking about Bermuda, which Shakespeare vividly and accurately called the 'vexed Bermouthes'.

Well, I was rambling over the hills and dales of a hundred-odd acres of this island thoughtfully set aside for the pursuit of a little white ball with a liquid centre. I was accompanied by one of the most celebrated brooders in America, a man who denies himself the pleasure of chasing the ball for about 363 days in the year because, like the unflagging Calvinist he is, he feels a prior obligation to his job as a journalist of the most awesome kind: a daily preacher whose duty is, in the good old phrase, to 'comfort the afflicted and afflict the comfortable'. I cannot think of any more forgivable auspices under which to play any game whatsoever. Playing a round of golf with this man is as comfortable as drinking double martinis with Billy Graham.

His routine of self-sacrifice would not be praiseworthy in a golfing duffer. In fact, to most of us, wrestling with the problems of inflation or foreign policy is a good deal easier than guiding the damn ball into a hole 425 yards away. But this old Scot (and the fact that he has spent the last fifty years in this country has not pacified his conscience in the least, he is still the dour little—well, large—preacher from Clydeside)—this old Scot was once, I believe, the junior golf champion of Ohio. He was, in other words, at one time that forever forbidding figure, a scratch player. (For the uninitiated, may I say that golf is one game in which you do not start from scratch.) James Reston began on the sports desk of the Associated Press. In his late twenties he heard the call of John Calvin or John Knox or John the Baptist, it doesn't matter which, and turned to politics during the London Blitz, and then to Washington. Since when he has been urging us, on a syndicated basis, what to believe about Europe, the Soviet Union, Cuba, China and all fifty of the United States.

If all Mr Reston's powerful sermons were lost, he would still be a large footnote in history. Because, on his visit to China (it was typical of him that he got there before Mr Nixon) he came down with appendicitis and had the useless organ removed by a top team of Chinese surgeons (they may be seven thousand miles away but they know that you don't leave the appendix of the chief columnist and vice president of the *New York Times* to a horse doctor). While he was under the anaesthetic influence of acupuncture, he wrote it up, and when he could amble around, he and his wife were allowed to watch several operations, during which—so he claimed—the patient who'd just had a brain or a lung removed said, like the boy in *Pickwick*, that he 'wouldn't lie there to be made game of, and he'd tell his mother if they didn't begin'.

So Mr Reston returned with the glad tidings of the wise men from the East who stick needles in you and lo, you feel no pain and, practically before the bandages are wrapped, you get up from your bed and walk. The news of this miracle was syndicated in papers around the world, and in this country we are now in the full flush of the belief, or the fashion, or the superstition, that there is no human ill that cannot be cured in a trice by a Chinese sinking in a needle. Many an American doctor, and non-doctor, is already preparing to moonlight with acupuncture and pick up a little pin money, so to speak, on the side.

I've built up Mr Reston's considerable credentials as a seer and prophet—not beyond his due—because I wanted to assure you that I don't spend my time loping around a golf course with heedless bums. We would fall silent occasionally to ponder the nasty stance required to pitch to a pulpit green from squirty crabgrass. But we would then get down to the business in hand and fall in together (as, we are told, the British ambassador and the Emperor Franz Josef used to do while in pursuit of the stag in the old days) and ponder tremendous matters. Even when Mr Reston is pursuing the little white ball, he is pursued in turn by a deadline.

Much on his mind, that beautiful afternoon, was a column he had to write on the eve of Thanksgiving. What, he wanted to know, had we cause to be thankful for? It was a problem. He stood to the ball, reminding himself to imitate the immortal Bobby Jones, whose swing was said to have 'the drowsy beauty of a summer's day'. Reston then unloosed the tornado of his caddie swing, which has all the drowsy beauty of a pneumatic drill. 'Well?' he said. 'Come to think of it,' I said, 'I

281

can't think of anything we can be grateful for.' I moved over to my ball and performed my own ritual swing, which I have often thought bears a striking resemblance to Tom Weiskopf in the take-away and to Henry Cotton in the finish. A recent series of stop-action pictures, however, shows a man who, at the top of the backswing, is either taking off a sweater or putting on a lifebuoy.

'Come now,' said Reston, fluffing a three-foot putt, 'there's a lot of things to be thankful for.' 'Name one,' I said, and dispatched the thing ten feet into the back of the cup. 'Well,' he said, and he now had his pipe out, which is always an impressive accompaniment to a stalling mind. Come on, come on. 'Why, sure,' he said, ambling off down the next fairway like Barnacle Bill the sailor. All I could think of was the demonstrable fact that Mr Nixon, like him or loathe him, had done something that no Eisenhower, Kennedy or Johnson had done before him. He had not conquered inflation but he had held it remarkably in check. The economists knew it, and praised him. The bankers knew it, and rejoiced. Even the liberals knew it, and grunted reluctant approval. More important, the housewives knew it, and they had voted for him.

I was giving Reston time to digest his column. He brooded some more and put two balls in the drink of a long water-hole. Which is ridiculous in a former scratch player, though playing twice a year does not tend to maintain the handicap at a single figure. Then I teed up majestically, thought about Thanksgiving, and with incredible accuracy placed two balls in exactly the same grave as his. After that, we jokingly decided it was only a game and, anyway, we were still wondering what to thank the

Lord for.

Mr Reston's column appeared duly on the eve of Thanksgiving and it betrayed no smitch of strain, no hint of the writhings that had seized him as he peered all over the rolling course looking for blessings to count. He put up a brave show. There may be five millions unemployed, but there are eighty-two millions in jobs. More than half of all American families, families not individuals, have an annual income of roughly $12,000. Vietnam, they say, is close to a ceasefire. The campuses have cooled. There is, he believes, 'a calmer atmosphere between the races and the generations'. America may be relatively less powerful than she was but there is 'less danger and fear of a major clash between the nuclear powers than at any other time since the start of the Cold War'. Mr Nixon, he believes, has at least 'bought time to arrange a kind of truce between the Communist and the Western worlds'.

In the main, I believe that this is, with one big reservation, fair enough. Nobody ever expected a Republican President to introduce compulsory price and wage control in peacetime, but it seemed to work. A Democrat and an economist, who takes a generally dim view of Mr Nixon, has just written: 'He hasn't mastered it, but it's working, and that's something when you look at South America (Chile has reduced its inflation in the past year from a hundred per cent to eighteen per cent). And in Europe, the British inflation is disastrously out of hand.'

Also, one has to grant, if there had been a Democrat in the White House, the liberal press would be sounding hosannas for the courage of the visits to Moscow and Peking and the shrewd recognition that they both need money and trade and good crops more than they need arms. (The Russians are doing very well building their own mammoth navy, thank you, and the Chinese move on deferentially, with charming smiles, towards their own nuclear capability.)

My reservation is about the calm between the races and the generations. I devoutly hope it is so. But I cannot see how the widening gap between the prosperous majority and the poor and bitter minority will keep the minority from protest. All the groups that raised Cain in 1968 are still there. The colleges may appear to be beginning to share authority with the students, if that's a good thing. True, a black boy has a better chance of going to college here than practically any boy in Western Europe. Yet, one black boy in three between the ages of 16 and 22 has no job and very little prospect of ever getting one. The cities groan quietly, and the President promises not to soften them by 'throwing dollars at problems'. The powerful malcontents—the young, the black, the radicals, the Mexican-Americans—who were told to work within the system tried it with McGovern and it got them a stone. We may have cause to give thanks, but we should leave as an open question whether militant America is calming down once for all or whether it is pausing. Anyone who has ever been in the eye of a hurricane knows the blessed feeling of relief when the damage is done, and the clouds are scudding, and the blue is breaking through, just before everything goes leaden and hissing again, and the fury is let loose from the other side.

This is just to say that I think there's a danger in

the present lull of overlooking the hazard in front of our eyes. As Reston and I teed up on that long water-hole (we had to carry about 160 yards before the dry land) the caddie said, 'Forget the water, just pretend it's all smooth grass.' It would be nice to do this, looking out across the United States and seeing only the green haven beyond the drink. We shouldn't forget, though, that both of us, disdaining the briny deep in front of us, drowned in it—twice.

The Duke

31 May 1974

'When it is finished,' says the guidebook, 'it may well be the largest cathedral in the world.' I am always leery of sentences that contain the phrase 'may well be'. But it is certainly a very large cathedral: namely the Episcopal Cathedral Church of St John the Divine on the Upper West Side in New York City. Its foundations were laid in 1892. They've been building it ever since, and the end is not yet.

On Monday, 27 May 1974 St John the Divine housed a ceremony that would have flabbergasted its architect and its early worshippers. Every pew was filled, and the aisles were choked, and there were several thousands listening to loudspeakers out on the street. And when the ten thousand people inside were asked to stand and pray, there was a vast rustling sound as awesome, it struck me, as that of the several million bats whooshing out of the Carlsbad Caverns in New Mexico at the first blush of dawn.

It is not the size of the crowd that would have shocked the cathedral's founders (they might have taken it jubilantly as a sign of a great religious revival). It was what the crowd was there for. A crowd that ranged through the whole human colour scale, from the most purple black to the most pallid white, come there to honour the life and mourn the death of a man who had become supreme in an art that began in the brothels of New Orleans. The art is that of jazz, and the practitioner of it they mourned was Edward Kennedy Ellington, identified around the world more immediately than any member of any royal family as—the Duke.

The Duke's career was so much his life that there's very little to say about his private ups and downs, if any. He was born in Washington, DC in 1899, the son of a White House butler, and perhaps the knowledge that Father had a special, protected status inside the white establishment had much to do with the Duke's seeming to be untouched, or untroubled, by the privations and public humiliations we should expect of a black born in the nation's capital. Certainly, he must have thought of himself as belonging to one of the upper tiers of black society. But his upbringing could be called normal for any of the black boys who were to turn into great jazzmen. I'm thinking of men like Earl Hines and Fats Waller, the sons of coloured parsons or church organists who, almost automatically as little boys, were hoisted on to a piano stool. The Duke took piano lessons but also took to sketching and thought of a career as an artist. This dilemma was solved by his becoming a sign painter by day and running small bands by night.

What got him going was the nightly grind and the daily practice. It is something that nightclub habitués seldom credit, it being assumed that while classical pianists must follow a daily regimen, people like Ellington, Hines, Waller, Tatum simply have a 'natural gift' and just rattle the stuff off on request. Nothing could be more false. I remember ten, fifteen years ago running into an old and engaging jazzman, a white who was employed in a poky little jazz joint in San Francisco. Muggsy Spanier, a sweet and talented man who had had a long experience of the roller-coaster fortunes of a jazzman: one year you are playing before delirious crowds in a movie theatre or grand hotel, three years later blowing your brains out before a few listless drunks in a crummy roadhouse off the main highway in some place called Four Forks, Arkansas, or New Iberia, Louisiana. Just then Muggsy was in a lean year playing in a small band with Earl Hines, who was also at a low ebb (this was before Hines, the father of jazz piano, had been discovered by the State Department and the Soviet government, or been rediscovered by a new generation). Well, Muggsy had left his trumpet in this dreadful nightclub and found he needed it, on his night off, for some impromptu gig or other. So he had to go into the nightclub next morning, always a depressing experience, what with the reek of sour air and spilled alcohol and the lights turned down to a maintenance bulb or two. He told me that one of the unforgettable shocks of his stint in San Francisco was coming from the bone-white sunlight into the smelly cave and squinnying

287

through the dark and seeing Hines sitting there, as he did for two or three hours every morning, practising not the blues or 'Rosetta' or 'Honeysuckle Rose' but the piano concertos of Mozart and Beethoven. To the gaping Muggsy, Hines looked up and said, 'Just keeping the fingers loose.' To be the best, it's a sad truth most of us amateurs shrink from admitting, you have to run, fight, golf, write, play the piano every day. I think it was Paganini—it may have been Rubinstein—who said, 'If I go a week without practice, the audience notices it. If I go a day without practice, I notice it.'

This digression is very relevant to the character and the mastery of Duke Ellington. He was at a piano, but he was there as a composer, day in and night out. For a man of such early and sustained success, it is amazing that he not only tolerated the grind, after one-night stands, of the long bus rides through the day and the pick-up meals, but actually cherished them as the opportunity to sit back and scribble and hum and compose. He did this to the end.

I knew all the records of his first period when I was in college, from 1927 through 1932. And when I first arrived in New York I wasted no time in beating it up to the Cotton Club to see the great man in the flesh. But apart from a nodding acquaintance in nightclubs, and becoming known to him no doubt as one of those ever-present nuisances who request this number and that, I didn't meet Ellington alone, by appointment so to speak, until the very end of the Second World War. I went up to his apartment on the swagger side of Harlem. There is such a place, in fact there are as many fine shadings of Negro housing through the hierarchy of Negro social status as there are shadings of pigment from the high-yaller to the coal-black. Ellington was at the top of the scale, in a large Victorian building looking out on a patch of greenery.

The date had been for two in the afternoon. In my mind's eye I had the picture complete: the dapper figure of the Duke seated in a Noël Coward bathrobe deep in composition at a concert grand. For those were the days long before band leaders got themselves up in gold lamé and sequins. The big band leaders wore dinner jackets. The Duke wore white tie and tails, and was as sleek as a seal.

Well, I was shown into a large and rambling apartment with a living room that had evidently seen a little strenuous drinking the night before. Off from the living room behind curtained French doors was a bedroom. The doors were open and there in full view was a large bed rumpled and unmade. Beyond that was a bathroom, and out of it emerged what I first took to be some swami in the wrong country. It was the Duke, naked except for a pair of under-drawers and a towel woven around his head. He came in groaning slightly and saying to himself, 'Man!' Then *his* man came in, a coloured butler, and they went into the knotty question of what sort of breakfast would be at once tasty and medicinal. It was agreed on, and the Duke turned and said, 'Now.' Meaning, what's your business at this unholy hour of two in the afternoon?

The breakfast arrived and he went at it like a marooned mountaineer. To my attempts to excite him with the proposal I had come to make, he grunted 'Uh-huh' and 'Uh-un' between, or during, mouthfuls.

At last, he pushed the plate away, picked up his coffee cup and sat down and slurped it rapidly and nodded for me to begin again. I had come to suggest that he might like to record a long session with his band for the BBC. This was, remember, the peak period of his big band, and I suggested that we record him not, as we now say, 'in concert', but in rehearsal. He shot a suspicious glare at me, as if I'd suggested recording him doing five-finger exercises. But slowly and warily he began to see my problem and to respect it. Simply, how to convey to a listener (this was before television) the peculiar genius of the Duke, since it was unique in the practice of jazz music. Which was somehow to be, and feel, present at the act of creation when it was happening to the Duke standing in front of the band in rehearsal. Everybody knows that the best jazz is impossible to write down in the usual musical notation. You can no more make a transcription of Hines playing 'I Can't Give You Anything but Love', or, worse, Art Tatum playing any of his cascading variations on 'Tea for Two', than you can write down three rules for the average swimmer to follow in doing the two hundred metres like Mark Spitz. Jazz is always improvisation done best by a group of players who know each other's whimsical ways with such mysteries as harmonics, counterpoint, scooped pitch, jamming in unison. Alone among jazz composers, the Duke's raw material was the tune, scribbled bridge passages, a sketch in his head of the progression of solos and ensembles he wanted to hear, and an instinctive knowledge of the rich and original talents, and strengths and perversities, of his players. They were not just trumpet, trombone, clarinet, E flat alto sax, and so on. They were individual performers who had stayed with him for years, for decades. One of them, Harry Carney, played with the Duke on his first recording date in 1927, and he was with him on the last date, in Kalamazoo, Michigan, last March. In 1927, Ellington had created a weird, compact, entirely personal sound with his band. It was weirder still and richer, but it was just as personal at the end.

Eventually, the Duke appreciated that what we wanted was not just another performance. He agreed, and we had a long and unforgettable session, in a hired studio on Fifth Avenue, where we recorded the whole process of the number dictated, the roughest run-through, with many pauses, trying this fusion of instruments and that, stopping and starting and transferring the obligato from one man to another, the Duke talking and shouting, 'Now, Tricky, four bars!' and 'Barney, in there eight.' And in the last hour, what had been a taste in the Duke's head came out as a harmonious, rich meal.

The Duke was nicknamed as a boy by a friend who kidded him about his sharp dressing. He was an elegant and articulate man and, as I've hinted, strangely apart from the recent turmoil of his race. Not, I think, because he was ever indifferent or afraid. He was a supremely natural man, and in his later years devout, and he seemed to assume that men of all colours are brothers. And most of the immediate problems of prejudice, and condescension, and tension between black and white dissolved in the presence of a man whom even an incurable bigot must have recognized as a man of unassailable natural dignity. He had a childlike side, which—we ought to remember—is recommended in the New Testament for entry into the kingdom of Heaven. He was very sick indeed in the last few months. He knew, but kept it to himself, that he had cancer in both lungs. A week or two before the end he sent out to hundreds of friends and acquaintances what looked at first like a Christmas card. It was a greeting. On a field of blue was a cross, made of four vertical letters and three horizontal. They were joined by the letter 'O'. The vertical word spelled 'Love' and the horizontal 'God'.

He has left us, in the blessed library of recorded sound, a huge anthology of his music from his twenty-eighth birthday to his seventy-fifth. He began as a minority cult, too rude for the collectors of dance music. For much, maybe most, of his time he was never a best-seller. He never stuck in the current groove, or in his own groove. He moved with all the influences of the time from blues to bebop and the moderns and transmuted them into his own, and at the end his difficult antiphonies and plotted discords, the newer harmonic structures he was always reaching for, were no more saleable to the ordinary popular music fan than they had ever been. Most people simply bowed to him as an institution.

In 1931, a college room-mate of mine who was something of a pioneer as a jazz critic, on the university weekly, was graduating, and he wrote a farewell piece. He recorded the rise and fall—during his four-year stint—of the Red Hot Peppers, and the Blue Four, and McKinney's Cotton Pickers, and Bix and Trumbauer. He ended with the phrase: 'Bands may come and bands may go, but the Duke goes on for ever.' Ah, how true! We thought it a marvel that the Duke had ridden out all fashions for four long years. In fact, his good and always developing music lasted for forty-seven years. And we have it all.

So, I am inclined to paraphrase what John O'Hara said on the death of George Gershwin: 'Duke Ellington is dead. I don't have to believe it if I don't want to.'

The End of the Affair

11 April 1975

Throughout the nineteenth century and on into our own time, military disasters were reported to the home front as, at worst, military setbacks. Thanks, I suppose, to strict censorship at the front and the unquestioned existence of official secrets acts and such, which concealed the unvarnished truth for so many years that by the time it was open for inspection, the people at home had other things on their minds. It was left to the historians to analyse and thrash over the ashes of once burning issues.

I think of the ill-fated expedition to Dakar in the Second World War, and the ill-conceived British landings in Norway. True, they caused a rumpus in the House of Commons, since the brave invaders quickly came home again. But there were no nightly pictures on the television to show, for instance, our men landing in Norway without skis, on the assumption of generals bred in a temperate climate that the men were going off to fight a rifle-to-rifle battle in Surrey or on the fields of northern France.

The enormous catastrophe of the Dardanelles campaign in the First World War was, I well remember, reported to us as a difficult but heroic undertaking. And when it failed, the tiptoe evacuation of all our forces was glowingly represented as a triumphant success. In those days, they did not publish the human cost. Only the schoolboys of a later generation learned to be dazed by the news that Gallipoli cost each side a quarter of a million casualties. And those of you old enough to remember Dunkirk will recall how the relief at the evacuation of so many men from beaches under aerial bombing was turned by the government of the day, by the newsreels, and then by Hollywood, into a glorious thing. Until Mr Churchill brought us to our senses with a speech in the House of Commons in which he bluntly declared, 'It is a colossal military disaster . . . wars are not won by evacuations.' But there can never have been a time like that of the mid-nineteenth century, not in Britain anyway, when the romantic legend of our brave chaps out there was so deliberately separated from the reality. The dreadful idiocy of the Battle of Balaclava was celebrated—by the Poet Laureate no less—as an act of epic valour: 'Theirs not to reason why/Theirs but to do and die.'

Well, the United States has just suffered the most unmitigated defeat in its history, and we know it. The cost, in casualties, and money, and pride is being counted *now*. And everybody is arguing 'the reason why'. What Kennedy started with the quiet infiltration of 'military technicians' is about to end, fourteen years later. It would no doubt have ended much sooner if the United States hadn't believed in the beginning that it had a duty to stem the advance of Communism in Asia and, what turned out to be more fateful, believed it had the capacity to do it. The most unrepentant hawks will maintain on their deathbeds that the United States did have the capacity, by a general invasion of North Vietnam or by the use of tactical atomic weapons. But none of the four Presidents who bore the burden, and the curse, of the Vietnamese war was ready to do that. All of them knew that if America could keep its treaty commitments only by means of even a limited nuclear bombardment, America would be a monster's name everywhere on earth.

So the country is just now in a stew of recrimination. No doubt in time the arguments will straighten themselves out and people will come to take up one of two positions, which won't necessarily be closer to the truth because they've been over-simplified.

The most striking thing to me about this turmoil of public opinion is the way, while the Right is holding its ground, the Left is shifting its ground. The leftist and liberal commentators who have been against the American presence in Indochina more or less since the beginning have always tended to stress the corruption of the South Vietnamese government and the brutality of its treatment of prisoners and political dissidents, but has always turned a blind eye towards—or refused to credit—the Hanoi government's brutal treatment of prisoners and political dissidents (if any were ever known to speak up). The Left has always said that if the United States got out, and if South Vietnam capitulated, then the people of South Vietnam would receive their conquerors with relief and, after thirty years of nothing but war, would settle down peaceably to be ruled by them.

But now that we've seen thousands of bedraggled and wounded civilians fleeing from their homes and jamming every escape route to the south, the Left is saying how shocking that we didn't evacuate these people sooner instead of leaving them to the mercies of the oncoming armies. This shock implies a belief in something that the leftists and the liberals have never been willing to concede: that vast numbers of the population of South Vietnam have been and still are terrified of the Communists and want to get out.

In other words, since the United States is no longer there as a military force, it has got to be blamed for something. And it is now being blamed for deserting the South Vietnamese in their hour of need. Some reporters, especially foreign correspondents who throughout the war have been privileged to enjoy the luxury of neutral high-mindedness, have written dispatches burning with indignation at the thought of President Ford playing golf while babies were being bundled into planes and flown to camps in the United States (and—something I've not seen in an American paper—to homes in Britain and Australia).

Well, it was maybe a tactless time for the President to be practising his backswing, but the inference of these angry men is that President Ford and his advisers callously refused to send in planes, and the old Marines, to arrange a mass evacuation when the Central Highlands were about to be overrun. But neither the President nor the Pentagon, nor an American military mission on the spot, seems to have been given much notice of President Thieu's independent decision to abandon the Central Highlands. The White House and the Pentagon seethed with their own sort of indignation when it happened, and had to improvise a makeshift Dunkirk operation. Naturally, they said hard words about President Thieu. And their anger gave him a god-sent excuse to declare that the United States had betrayed its ally.

In turn, the conservatives here who have gone on thinking of President Thieu as the poor man's Chiang Kai-shek were only too eager to pick up his accusation and turn it, not so much against President Ford, whom they've come to consider a well-meaning drifter, as against the Democrats' majority in Congress. Certainly, if the retreat of the South Vietnamese could have been held up by more millions of dollars from Congress, then those Democrats in power are to blame. At this point, the country is heard from. Over 70 per cent of the American people are convinced that South Vietnam and Cambodia would be lost, sooner rather than later, no matter how much money the Congress voted.

Meanwhile, less positive people—middle of the roaders, weary newspaper students of the long war—are going back to see where the rot set in. Who was to blame? President Johnson blamed the doubters for having little faith. President Nixon called his opponents traitors. President Ford is going back to Kennedy's line—a rather forlorn battle cry so late in the day: that the United States has 'solemn commitments' and must honour them. He blames Congress. And he's helped by Henry Kissinger who sees, in the Congressional echo of public sentiment, a dreadful determination 'to destroy our allies'. Others again, looking pluckily on the bright side, say that the administration is making a fundamental error in confusing the collapse of Indochina with America's real interests. They say that to let Vietnam go is no proof that the United States would let Japan go, or Israel, or Europe.

However, it is possible to recognize a pall forming over all this dissension in the reports that are coming in from Thailand, and Malaysia and Israel and other places whose governments— rightly or wrongly—are beginning to wonder whether the United States is an ally you can depend on. Hardly reported at all are the fears of the Australians, to whom what we call the Far East is the Near North, against which they had better prepare their own defences.

And through this bedlam of charge and counter-charge, a still small voice rises, from people who were once dogmatic, and from people who are merely puzzled: what if, after all, the domino theory is correct?

I'm All Right, Jack

21 May 1976

Somewhere, in Shakespeare certainly, but maybe also in some simple nursery rhyme, there must be a wincing reminder that when a small painful thing happens to you and me, it blots out a catastrophe that staggers the headlines. Nobody has made a keener comment on it than James Agate in a passage of his 'Ego' diaries. He had been to watch a day in the trial of an architect's wife and her lover. She was 38. The chauffeur-lover was 18. Came the day when the husband was hit over the head with a mallet. The couple was on trial for his murder.

It sounds like a humdrum, squalid business—except, of course, for the accused couple. Anyway, Agate was in court when the woman was asked what was her first thought when her lover came to her and told her what he'd done. She replied, 'My first thought was to protect him.' It's the sort of surprising line that a dramatist would give his right arm—a dollop of his royalties, anyway—to have thought of. Agate remarked it was the kind of thing that Balzac would have called 'sublime'.

In the following days, Agate couldn't get the woman's reply out of his mind. And just then, there was an immense earthquake in Quetta, in India. Agate wrote in his diary: 'This trial has moved me immensely, probably because I saw part of it, while the dreadful affair at Quetta makes no impression. The 20,000 said to have perished might be flies. I

299

see no remedy for this; one can't order one's feelings, and to pretend different is merely hypocrisy.'

I imagine that we all have secret ways of compensating for this awkward truth. I make it up to myself by admiring immoderately those people—hospital volunteers, the Salvation Army, most of all people who work every day with the disabled: the people *who do something about it*, even though they obviously have lives and troubles of their own. I think I was saved from living the life of a secret slob by my father-in-law, an austere old New England puritan. When I came back to the United States for keeps, he explained to me—as you might to a child about to receive its first weekly allowance—how 'we Americans' divide the breadwinner's salary: 'You try to pay between a fifth and a quarter of your income for rent, never more than a quarter, and you set aside 10 per cent of your income for charity. The rest goes for food and savings.' For a time, I followed this punctiliously, for I had applied for citizenship and took it to be a requirement of the Constitution. Later, I regret to say, rents went up, and so, but not for a long time, did the income.

Well, the past two weeks have reflected once again the embarrassing truth that the downfall of a dictator is significant, but a toothache is an emergency. I ought to be talking about Dr Kissinger's decision to resign as Secretary of State after the next election. I ought to go on about the recent earthquake in the Soviet Union, which had a force one-third as great again as the 1906 San Francisco earthquake. There is a lot of room for comment in the fact that the Russians have been

300

very tight-lipped about it. But Dr Kissinger and the Russian earthquake fade away like ghosts at dawn before the sentence shouted at me during the past fortnight by my wife whenever I am on my way out. 'Don't go out,' she'd scream from some distant room, 'without taking down the garbage.'

What is this? Am I moonlighting as a spare-time dustman—or, as we slangily say in the United States—a sanitation department employee? Of course not, though there must be scholars and clerks and other members of the sedentary professions who are greatly tempted by the report from San Francisco that the dustmen of that city successfully struck for a guaranteed high wage of $27,000 a year.

No, what has been happening here is a strike of handymen and the other 'maintenance personnel' of our apartment houses, or blocks of flats. (By the way, although I'm always maintaining, in the presence of Americans, that the British still hold to Anglo-Saxon English in contexts which Americans fog up with pompous Latinisms, I am bound to say that it is the British who have succumbed to the euphemism of 'industrial action'. In America, they still strike.)

Well, the men who keep things humming in the big apartment houses walked out two weeks ago. So it was left to the tenants to run the lifts, stoke the furnace, stack the garbage, sort the mail, guard the front door and work in shifts round the clock keeping tabs on all visitors and demanding to see their identity cards, if any. If not, the house phone rings and a voice—plainly not that of the regular doorman—says, 'There's a gentleman down here who claims to be Mr Tim Slessor and says he has a date with you.' And you answer, according to mood, 'Send him up,' or 'Throw the bum out.'

It was a trying time for us tenants. But we learned some useful things. A friend of mine phoned me one morning. He'd been running his elevator for four hours that day. He said, 'D'you know something? It's not true that being an elevator man is an unskilled job—you have to know all about the weather.'

Well, it's over now. The strike ended at 4 p.m. and at five the men were back in uniform helping old ladies out of cabs, carrying bags, handing out mail and recognizing friends and tenants without peremptory challenge. They struck—as almost everybody does these days—for more pay and a shorter working week. They didn't get what they asked for, since it's well understood that the first increase they demand (it's always 'demand') is like the first price a Persian quotes to you when you admire a rug. You simply walk round the block, get a second price, go out to lunch, come back and settle for the third price.

In most strikes today, the non-striking people on the outside, commonly known as the public, make an assumption, I think, which a friend of mine in California tells me is very naive. I find it hard to label his profession, since it is a comparatively new one. Not quite a labour lawyer but a contract adviser or, as he puts it, a hassle soother. Sometimes he's hired by a company, sometimes by the union, either to draft the next contract or, if things are already out of hand, to help settle a strike. Most of his adult life has been spent in bargaining between the two contending parties about such things as time and a half, pension

302

payments, redefining overtime, pregnancy benefits, a new recreation ground, redundancies (another British euphemism, by the way, for men you no longer need).

According to this cunning negotiator, the naive assumption we all make is that in every strike the dispute is between the employer and the employee, a conflict which is dramatized in the newspapers either as a fight between the ruthless union and the company going broke, or between the ruthless boss and the ground-down faces of the workers. He says this is 'a bunch of—er—nineteenth-century ideology'. He says that almost invariably both sides *want* the strike. Generally, to prove their need of recompense—more wages or a fairer profit margin—to some third party: the government, the city council, or even the consumer himself. Well, it was strongly hinted in our apartment strike that both the union members and the landlords were eager to prove to the state government in Albany and the city fathers of New York City that rent control has to go.

I think I'm right in saying that no other city in America still retains the rent control laws that were imposed nationally during the Second World War. There are many thousands of apartment houses in this city—rundown buildings, modest blocks of flats, handsome big apartment buildings—which must conform to the rents set by a city control board. This board yields, about once a year, to the landlords' plea that their costs—of fuel, insurance, staff, maintenance in general—far outrun the biggest rents they are allowed to charge. The rent control board yields them an extra seven and a half per cent a year. And though I ought to keep my mouth shut, I must say I feel a little sheepish when I run into a young couple in an uncontrolled building who pay for two rooms what I pay for eight. When a baby comes, they do not tie pink ribbons, they wring their hands.

If they are in 'the professions', they go to their boss and say, in some dudgeon, 'An electrician earns more than I do.' They become—what miners become, and nurses, and truck drivers, and all of us when we feel the pinch—'a special case'. In fact, it sometimes seems to me that an ever-soaring inflation rate was guaranteed the day that the ordinary citizen, who is against both inflation and strikes on principle, started to say that his case was different.

Until ten or twenty years ago, I think it was as true in America as in less affluent countries, the socially sanctioned scale of wages has held since the nineteenth century. I say *scale*, not wage rates. It was an unwritten law that working people, so called, could earn only a certain maximum, which stopped short of the general level of wages paid to the professions. This is so obvious that it's either not worth saying or it's one of those simple discoveries that nobody thought of before Aristotle. It's so obvious, anyway, that nobody seems to have said it. We have gone on, down all the years during which labour–management relations have grown more complex and more acrid, talking about the labourer being worthy of his hire, while the industrial and craft unions have been developing a wholly new view of their monetary worth to society. While the professions— the learned professions especially—have gone on living on the old assumption that being upper- and not lower-middle class, they must be living better than the average skilled factory worker. They slowly and sadly learned that it is not so, that they—along with the old and the pensioned professionals—are the worst victims of inflation. It is odd that the more educated should have done nothing to define or justify their relative worth, while the less educated—with the help of such as my labour negotiator in this country, and the shrewd shop steward in other countries—have done everything.

No Cabinet Officers Need Apply

24 December 1976

One of the most curious but absolutely dependable chores of political journalism in the United States is undertaken around Christmas time once every four years. Whenever we are only a month away from the inauguration of a new President, the papers are full of speculation about who is likely to be a Cabinet officer, and of profiles of people who've already been picked. I say it's a curious custom because the American Presidential system is not a Cabinet system. This is something that Cabinet officers usually discover, to their chagrin, rather late in the day. The system puts all the responsibility for a riot, say, not on the Secretary of the Interior (the British Home Secretary) but on the President. A cruel budget is not attributed to the Secretary of the Treasury but to the President. If there's a public outcry about selling wheat to

Russia at bargain prices, the howls are piped into the White House, not into the Department of Agriculture. And so on.

But there is one Cabinet appointment just made that has set off a tremendous uproar, especially among the blacks. The concern is not particularly ideological, though while Mr Carter says that the new man has a 'superb' record on civil rights, the black leaders say he has a very dubious record indeed. What has aroused the blacks is a provocation which I don't think would come up in other white democracies. The appointee is Mr Griffin Bell to be Attorney General, who—as the head of the Department of Justice—is therefore the chief law enforcement officer of the United States. Mr Bell is an Atlanta lawyer and a close friend of Mr Carter. The sin with which he is charged stresses once again the vigilante role of the American press that makes the life—the private life and public life—of any man or woman an open book. To sharpen the contrast with Britain, say, let me put it this way. When you hear that John Wallaby has been made Foreign Secretary, or Richard Stretchford Chancellor of the Exchequer, do you instantly wonder how many companies he has shares in? Are you impatient for the newspapers to list the clubs he belongs to? Do you, every now and then, expect questions to be asked in the House, and have them followed by a regretful little speech from the Prime Minister withdrawing the appointment? I think not.

Well, Mr Bell had been Attorney General designate for no more than twenty-four hours when the diggers of the press dug up the hair-raising fact that he was a member of two private clubs in

Atlanta that have no blacks or Jews as members. What amazes the politicians is that Mr Carter should not have routinely questioned his appointees about such affiliations. Because when it comes out, it always triggers a shock wave, which always subsides when the appointee regrets the insensitivity of his past life and resigns from the club or clubs. Which Mr Bell, after a little self-defensive hectoring, will undoubtedly do.

When Mr Carter heard about the sin of Mr Bell he said rather wanly that he 'hoped' all his Cabinet officers would give up their membership in any society that discriminated against minorities. (In California, it may soon become a scandal if you belong to a club that does not admit Chicanos, that is to say, Mexican-Americans, whose vote is large.)

This has brought up in the minds of many people the question of whether it is legal today to form a club with any sort of exclusive membership. Well, yes, it is, no question. You can form an Irish-American club, or a rifle club, or a tennis club, or a drinking club *provided* you don't meet in a building, or on land, or employ services, owned by your city, your state, or by the federal government. All the test cases that have come up before the Supreme Court since its integration decision of 1954 have challenged the right of exclusivity of any organization that is supported in any way by public funds: schools, restaurants, buses, toilets, housing projects, recreation grounds, clubs and so on. The grounds here are always the same, and the Supreme Court has reiterated them again and again: that such discrimination violates the Fourteenth Amendment to the Constitution, which says, 'No state shall make or enforce any law which

307

shall abridge the privileges or immunities of citizens of the United States . . . nor deny to any person within its jurisdiction the equal protection of the laws.'

No one, I think, has yet tested the right of private clubs to exclude people on the grounds of race, religion or whatever. And I doubt they're likely to. Mr Bell's clubs were privately owned. Like most such clubs everywhere, they were organizations of congenial people who shared a certain interest, people who are like-minded, like-coloured, alike in their enthusiasms or even their prejudices. Senator John F. Kennedy belonged for years to a private and very exclusive club in Washington which, in the most gentlemanly way in the world, quietly excluded Negroes. When he became President, he resigned at once. Similarly, Mr Bell is not up against the law. He's up against the strong public feeling that anyone who chooses to become a government official, dedicated to the service of the whole country, should not be associated with any group that bars any sort of American.

We had, a few years ago, a prime example of the power of the press to embarrass any public man with ambitions to govern into shedding a lifetime's fellowship with his own kind. When Mr Nelson Rockefeller came out for the Presidency, the press discovered overnight that he was a member of an exclusive New York City club that had never had a Jewish member and never seen a Negro, except one bearing a tray. 'What?' cried Mr Rockefeller, 'no Jews or Negroes?' He was shocked to his marrow and he got out at once. It then came out that one of his sons—I believe it was the littlest and

308

the last, a toddler—had a sizeable block of shares in the club. Well, I never—said Mr Rockefeller, and scrupulously and immediately sold it.

Within a matter of days, Mr Richard M. Nixon let it be known that he too was thinking of the Presidency. So the press obliged by discovering that he was a member of a famous golf club in New Jersey that might have heard of Jews or blacks but had never seen one out on the course or on the receiving end in the clubhouse. Mr Nixon's approach was, as you might expect, less hasty, more thoughtful, more humane. Mr Nixon said 'Ah, yes,' he was well aware of the discrimination but he was 'working from within' to end it. This admirable crusade, which he had naturally not publicized, was brought to an abrupt end when—within a day or two at most—Mr Nixon resigned.

This, by the way, was the club that was chosen, in 1967, as the site of the US Open, the American national golf championship. I remember it well, because I was called on by my paper to cover the championship at the last minute. It seemed that our golf expert, the eminent Pat Ward-Thomas, was detained in Britain on other business. This put me in a bind. The Security Council of the United Nations had been meeting night and day over the Arab–Israeli war. Its last session finished considerately at three in the morning of the day the United States Open was to start. And I recall the puzzlement on the face of the most artful of American sports writers, a prose demon named Red Smith, when he saw me on that first morning, before the play had begun, bent over my typewriter in the press tent banging out a couple of thousand words. What could I possibly find to write? Then

309

he looked over my shoulder, saw that the dateline was 'United Nations, NY' and he relaxed with an 'Oh, that. I thought you knew something the rest of us didn't.' This was my last dispatch on the Middle East.

The tournament was played in one of the most drenching heatwaves even of an American summer on the infernal Eastern seaboard. On the last, the fourth, morning of the championship, it was 112 degrees inside the press tent. At some sweating pause, in mid-morning, two or three of us were standing around looking up at the scoreboard that blanketed one wall of the tent. The scores are recorded cumulatively, so you can see at a glance who is leading. You look first for the players whose scores are up there in red: the ones who are playing the course under par. At the end of the last round, there was only one name in red. It was that of an unknown, a fellow named Marty Fleckman. As we were goggling over this, and hoping for some official to come through with a quick, potted biography of this redoubtable Fleckman, an old stockbroker who cuts a considerable figure in the administration of American golf, an old gaffer not famous for his tact, followed our gaze and barked out, 'Who is that Fleckman in the lead? Is that that Jewish boy from New Orleans?' 'The same,' somebody said. Somebody else said, 'Boy, wait till the Arabs hear about this!' Red Smith said wistfully, 'Forget the Arabs, wait till the club hears about it!' This funny remark is something which, in the United States today, you'd have to be careful to pick your audience for.

The ironical thing about discrimination, against Jews in particular, is that it is practised with the

310

quietest tenacity by white professing Christians of the genteelest kind. It's a rueful thought, at this time of the year, that they would have been the first to blackball the founder of Christianity himself.

Christmas in Vermont

31 December 1976

I spent a four-day Christmas with my daughter in northern Vermont after flying out of New York City on one of those brilliant blue winter days that ring like a bell. There was not a smidgen of snow anywhere. But very soon after we flew over Long Island Sound and into Connecticut, the smears were lining the roads, and by the time we were over Boston every lake and pond was a white rectangle and the forests were as leafless as a storehouse of telegraph poles, the towns collections of little wooden boxes strewn around bare ground. Then the real snow came in, first fringing the mountains then blanketing them, and as we veered and banked over the white-peppered evergreens the only bare land you could see was the long curving ribbons of cement, of the federal highways snaking through a planet of snow.

When you're not used to it, it's always a shock to get out of a plane and feel that somebody's slapped you in the eyes with a towel. This is simply the first adjustment to the blinding northern light. I went padding towards the tiny airport taking deep breaths of oxygen as sharp as ammonia. I was met by my daughter and son-in-law and grandson, a grinning Brueghel trio if ever I saw one. It had been 14 below zero when they woke up, and though it had gone up to a suffocating 20 above, their outlines were thickened by the snow boots and the billowing pants and those parkas that look like balloons but weigh about an ounce and are warmer than all the wool and sweaters in the world. My family, in short, looked like the first family of spacemen out there to greet a wan man-creature from remote New York.

With suspicious casualness, my daughter told me to put my bag in the back of the station wagon. I found it was impossible, because rearing up there and making a frightful honking sound were two of the fattest geese outside the *Christmas Carol*. About twenty minutes later, when we'd arrived at the graceful little white wooden eighteenth-century box they call home, I should say not more than ten minutes after we'd arrived, the two fat geese honked no more. They had departed this life, having had their necks wrung by my son-in-law and my son—a flown-in refugee from another distant planet, California. I didn't see these two for the next hour or two, which is just as well for a squeamish city type, since they'd been busy cleaning and plucking the birds against the Christmas feast.

The kitchen, which on any working farm is the centre of things, was dense with odours and tottering with platters and bowls, and my wife and daughter up to their elbows in parsley and onions and forcemeat and chanterelles, and pans bubbling with morels (plucked, according to a sacred tradition of my children, from dark corners in the woods by the light of a waning moon). The only time I ever saw anything like it was in rural France when I was invited to see what was brewing in the recesses of one of those country restaurants that manage to snag three stars from the Parisian dictators of such things.

My daughter and son-in-law lead a hard—but on these occasions and strictly to an outsider what looks like an idyllic—life. The food is not everything in some families but it happens to be my daughter's passion. And why not? After all, she has a lot of time hanging on her hands. She gets up before six, feeds, dresses and civilizes two small children, then goes out to see to the chickens and—in summer and fall—the raising of the fruits and vegetables. All that's left is to clean the house, stack the wood for the stoves, clean the barns, shovel the knee-high, fresh snow into parapets so as to be able to get to the big sleeping polar bear which tomorrow, the next day maybe, will turn into an automobile. Ferry the 4-year-old over the ice and snow to school, and put in an hour or so campaigning for the public (non-commercial) television station. So this leaves her ample time to prepare three meals a day, which are never snacks, at any time of the year. The first night, we started—started, mind—with a platter of smoked bluefish, one of a dozen thirteen-pounders her husband had caught in the summer off the end of Long Island. We smoked them within hours of the catch and they froze beautifully. After that came the irresistible piece of resistance: venison. Ten days before, my son-in-law had shot a doe and I'm happy to say I was not on hand to watch him and my daughter spend the next six hours skinning, de-gutting and butchering it before leaving it for the

313

statutory week or so to hang.

I ought to say that I've had venison in farmhouses in Scotland and in lush restaurants in London and Paris. And, with an immense to-do and gaudy promises of food for the gods, in Texas. Texas does not, like any other region, simply have indigenous dishes. It proclaims them. It congratulates you, on your arrival, at having escaped from the slop-pails of the other forty-nine states. Welcome to Texas, and the incomparable three dishes of the Lone Star State: venison, chilli con carne and rattlesnake. (To the goggling unbeliever, they say—as people always say about their mangier dishes—'But it's just like chicken, only tenderer.' Rattlesnake is, in fact, just like chicken, only tougher.)

Well, about venison and its hunters and preparers, I can only say that they all wag their fingers against their noses and confide to you, as a privileged guest, their dark and secret recipes for hanging and cooking and having it 'come out just right'. And it's always smelly and gamey and a little tough. In a restaurant, you can let the whole thing go with a sickly nod at the waiter. But the Texans are nothing if not considerate and eager hosts. They always beg you to tell them truthfully if you've ever eaten venison like that. The true answer is yes, unfortunately, always. But they are kindly people and you have to think up some variation on old Sam Goldwyn's line when he was pressed for an opinion by a brother film producer who'd just shown him his latest masterpiece in a sneak preview. 'Louis,' Goldwyn used to say, looking the man square in the eye, 'only you could 'eff made a movie like thet.'

Well, I want to tell you that that first evening I had naturally assigned the venison to Christmas Day and the big feast. I started to slice into a very fine tenderloin steak. It was so tender you could have eaten it with a spoon. But a round of uh-ums alerted me, rather late, to the fact that this was the venison. With delicate chanterelle sauce. A salad with raw mushrooms. Then Susie's fat and creamy cheesecake, with some of the fruit of the two hundred and seventy strawberry plants I'd seen her putting in earlier in the year, up to her knees in mud on some idle day. Just to keep things in the family, the wine was a remarkable claret from the vineyard my stepson farms in the beautiful Alexander Valley eighty miles north of San Francisco.

Well, it went on like that. And on Christmas Day, we had the geese, succulent and very serene in death. And a billowing cheese soufflé. And from time to time, there wafted in from the kitchen the scent of the four sorts of bread my daughter had baked. I once said to her, 'Any day now, Susie, you'll be making your own soap.' It was too late. She'd done it.

At the Christmas feast, with old Thomas Beecham whipping his orchestra and principals into proving once again that he is the Handel master of all time, I was asked to turn it down a shade while my son-in-law—a New England version of Gary Cooper—proposed a toast. He is not a gabby type, and this extraordinary initiative must have been inspired by the Alexander Valley grapes. Anyway, he said he didn't know what a proper toast should be but all he could think of with—'well, pride I guess you can call it'—was the

315

fact that everything we'd eaten in three days had lived or roamed or been grown right there, or in the woods that rise from the long meadow that goes up to the hills. Nothing, as they say in New England, had been 'store boughten'. And, he ended, 'If it doesn't sound pretentious'—wriggling at the fear that it might be—'I think we should drink to the bounty of nature.' A very weird thing to toast in the last quarter of the twentieth century, when you can hardly buy a tomato that hasn't been squirted a chemical red, and chickens are raised in little gravel cages, and since they are immobile from birth and failing fast, must for our protection be injected with antibiotics and God knows what. (I know a very knowledgeable food writer in France who says he now recalls that the last time he tasted a chicken—a real free-range chicken—in a restaurant was in 1952.)

That evening we sang carols, in close if creaky harmony, with the 4-year-old Adam piping 'God Rest Ye Merry, Gentlemen' right on pitch. Next morning, I woke up and he was out on his skis. They are small skis and he got them a year ago. He was plumping up the hills and skimming down them with the poles helping him on the turns. And I thought, what an extraordinary childhood. He was born in 20 below zero (outside; of course he was born inside). Winter brings about 100–120 inches of snow. May is the squishy month, when the thaw sets in. Summer bangs in with 90 degrees. Fall is a fountain of scarlet and gold, and inky forests of evergreens on the mountains. And here, at 4, he's skiing over the deep and crisp and even like a Disney doll. And this is all the life Adam knows.

One day he will grow up and, I'm afraid, taste of

the forbidden fruit. One day, he will read the *New York Times*. And Adam will be out of the Garden of Eden, out of Vermont, for ever.

Mr Olmsted's Park

8 July 1977

My workplace is a study that has the great luck to be perched on the fifteenth storey of an apartment house that looks out over the reservoir and the enclosing trees and meadows of Mr Frederick Law Olmsted's Central Park.

Olmsted was a remarkable Connecticut Yankee who wrote the classic, and still the fairest, account—on the verge of the Civil War—of life in the slave states of the South: *The Cotton Kingdom*. During the war, he ran the Union's sanitary commission. But before that, after a lively knockabout career, he had settled down as a landscape architect. When the city fathers of New York were thinking, in the 1850s, of having a city park, and when—naturally—the real-estate men and the cement contractors and the politicians were trying to guess at the likely location and buy up every acre in sight, Olmsted's plan won out over the plans of thirty competitors. Maybe, I suspect, because Olmsted brought great relief to the realtors by placing his park on empty, bosky ground way out of town. In fact, Oliver Wendell Holmes, the father of the great Justice, wrote a satirical essay wondering why Olmsted should have christened the proposed park 'Central' Park, since

317

it would be about two miles north of where everybody lived.

Olmsted had out-foxed them all. He privately, and correctly, figured that the next great lurch of residents would be north of the limit of populated Manhattan, which in the 1850s was the streets in the Forties. By the time the park commission had voted on the site and ordered the twenty-year job to begin, it was too late for the realtors to do more than buy up the surrounding fringes of what would become a precious breathing space in a jungle of cement and steel. Olmsted showed remarkable foresight in other ways. His original plan allowed for meadows and a lake for recreation, for a wriggle of footpaths, for carriage paths, and for so-called 'transverses' that would at three banked intervals allow the invisible passage of crosstown horse-buses. When the internal combustion engine arrived, nothing radical was required to adapt the original plan to the 1920s or the 1970s. The carriage paths and the transverses were paved over, and today the automobiles skim their winding way through the trees and meadows and the buses and trucks cut through and under the bridges without entering the park. Olmsted went on to lay out three more parks in New York, and the grounds around the Capitol in Washington, and those around Stanford University in California, and the now splendid lake front of Chicago. His masterpiece, to my mind, is the little-known but exquisite estate of trees, lakes, lawns, and rolling hills that now houses Emory University bang in the middle of Atlanta, Georgia.

Well, as I was saying, I have the luck to look out on Olmsted's first great work and, in moments of

318

furious idleness, when I am trying to work up a little creative thought, I stare at the stark trees of the winter against the snowfields, or the heartening fuzz of the breaking spring, or the rioting forsythia and dogwood and cherry, and then the vast blobs of the summer's full foliage before the yellows and scarlets of the fall come on. I am just at the height of a plane coming in for a steady landing, but I am low enough to sit and envy the kids down there—in winter the little Brueghel dolls scudding downhill on their sledges, but now—in the steaming mid-summer—tossing balls, lolling under trees with girls, gobbling ice-cream cones and, on the diamond off to the right, playing baseball.

Which gave me an idea. What has occurred to me, sitting here and weighing several leaden statements of the world's rulers—of Mr Brezhnev and Mr Carter and Mr Sadat—is that all the people I've ever known who are able to maintain an absorption with politics in the summertime don't play, or even watch, games. Of course, they can't stop governing through the summer—though in the blissful days before the United States became the Big Guy, the Congress of the United States managed it. But because great statesmen are almost wholly unfamiliar with games, they are unacquainted with such simple truths as that you win one, lose one, and begin again. This incapacity makes them fail to realize that politics—government, too—is a game.

I remember in the bitter Presidential campaign of 1932, in the pit of the Depression, when President Hoover was saying that prosperity was just around the corner, and Governor Roosevelt was saying that Hoover and his kidney had betrayed America, the rhetoric got so sharp and malicious that Will Rogers, the cowboy philosopher, wrote one of his three-sentence columns saying: 'Who do these fellas think they are, telling us who owns the Republic, and who is ruining the people? If we lost both of them, we'd get along. Why don't they shut their traps and go fishing?' Such was the popular prestige of Will Rogers that within days the news agencies received two photographs and printed them. One was of Roosevelt hauling a swordfish over the stern of a yacht. The other was of Hoover fly-fishing in a creek.

I hope it's not flippant to wish that Mr Sadat and General Dayan and Mr Carter could find some game they all played—cricket, say—and work up a healthy sweat and then sit down and talk about the future of the occupied territories, and the security of Israel, and the possibility of a Palestinian homeland. Instead of looking at the elements of the game, they all hammer away at a thesis. Which is to say, they are obsessed with their own ideologies. They are like a man who agrees to play a game but only on the understanding he shall win. Consequently, they have no disposition to begin by saying what and where are you prepared to lose? We've just had a particularly depressing example of what happens to idealists, ideologists, or—as we now say—ideologues when their ideology is reinforced by fear.

Let's admit that the problem of limiting the manufacture, and stockpiling, of nuclear arms is immense and maddeningly complex, and hard to simplify. You may remember that one powerful speech of Mr Carter—which had much to do with his election to the Presidency—insisted on beginning to limit nuclear arms and then working with the Russians to scrap them all. The Russians responded to this by saying that Mr Carter was saying just what they'd been saying all along. At the same time, to show the wickedness of Mr Carter's Republican opponents, who were always equated with 'the imperialist, war-mongering ruling classes', the Russians disclosed to their astonished people that thirty cents in every American tax dollar went for arms. What the Russians didn't tell their people was that: first, in Kennedy's day, it was closer to sixty cents in the dollar and, second, that they themselves accounted for rather more without any Russian being aware of it.

But the Americans, from the beginning of the SALT talks, have laboured under the hobbling difficulty of a democratic press, which lays out all the facts, supposed facts and rumours, and leaves them open to all sorts of benign and malign interpretations. During the Presidential campaign, the Democrats were quite willing to let the Russian characterization of the Republicans stand. Then along comes Mr Carter, who—the Russians delightedly recalled—had promised during the campaign not to go ahead with the B-1 bomber, which is superior to anything the Russians have. However, a couple of weeks ago, the word got out that he would, after all, go ahead with the B-1. The Russians said they knew all the time it was a campaign promise. Then he *did* ban it. Now the Russians say this only shows how foxy he is, and probably he'll manufacture it in secret. But so he won't be thought to be a fall guy for Russian bullying, Mr Carter says that, by the way, he *is* going ahead with the air-launched cruise missile, which is years ahead of the Russian missile. This had been agreed upon, but now the Russians are howling that America has in the White House an even more warlike, imperialist leader than Nixon.

This is what in diplomacy is blandly called an impasse. Now the administration announced that it has successfully tested a neutron bomb, and must therefore put up its umbrellas against a downpour of abuse not only from the Russians but from its liberal critics. Useless for Mr Carter to explain that the new bomb would greatly reduce the area of contamination in its job of killing off a military force inside a circumscribed place. What the Russians are going to say, and the liberals are saying already, is a phrase overwhelmingly attractive to ideologists, because it is so sharp and tangy. It is that at last we have a 'clean' bomb: one that protects the real estate but murders the inmates. As far as thought—and sarcasm—can reach, it's going to be a very tough ideological game to win.

In this impasse, I look out on Mr Olmsted's park again. And what do I see? Not people tossing balls, lolling under trees with girls, gobbling ice-cream cones, or playing baseball; all of which are honourable occupations. I see joggers. To be frank, I see them every morning, winter, summer, in sleet and Arctic cold, in the brisk fall and the furnace of the summer: these panting, slanting figures, in shorts and T-shirts, jogging, jogging, jogging around the long circumference of the reservoir. They are all very earnest, and so they are all ideologues. For earnestness is the only soil in which ideology can grow.

They used to make me feel guilty. But no more. Because I have to hand a copy, flown in here overnight, of the London *Times*. And in it is a short letter which, as far as I'm concerned, disposes once for all of the insanity of jogging. I don't know if there is a medical consensus about jogging, though in California—as you'd expect—there are psychiatrists, physiotherapists and other druids who, for a fat fee, promise to supervise your jogging by way of curing loneliness, depression, arteriosclerosis and hypertension, and restoring hair, fallen arches and failing marriages. I incline, myself, to the wisdom of three doctor friends of mine, one in San Francisco, one in Baltimore, the third in New York. The San Franciscan says that to jog over the age of 50 is madness, too much of a strain on the heart. The Baltimorean—who keeps his windows shut night and day, winter and summer—says more people have died of what they call 'fresh air' than any other noxious gas. The New Yorker, a man of great experience and some important original research, says that two martinis will cure anything.

Well, however that may be (and these are medical findings we should by no means dismiss without exhaustive testing), I can only say that the gentleman who wrote to *The Times* made a simple point worthy of Aristotle or Sir Isaac Newton: that is to say, he discovered an obvious thing which many people may have been dimly moving towards but which nobody ever said before. Let us not be coy about the identity of this great man. I have never heard of him, and it is possible that not many people have ever heard of him outside Blackheath—which is where he writes from. But I put his letter in a file of human wisdom that contains such gems as Aristotle's 'A play has a beginning, a middle and an end', Dr Johnson's 'Much may be made of a Scotsman if he be caught young', Mark Twain's 'The human being is the only animal that blushes, or needs to', and H. L. Mencken's definition of self-respect: 'The secure feeling that no one, as yet, is suspicious.'

The great man's name is Mark Godding. And this is his admirable brief chronicle: 'Sir— Regarding the current enthusiasm for jogging to extend one's life, may I point out that if one jogged ten miles a day then, having lived to the ripe old age of eighty—one would have jogged for approximately nine years . . . Is it worth it?' Here in a nutshell is revealed the absurdity of seeking to prolong life by a process that shortens it, by nine years, during which you might better have been reading, playing games, flirting, shutting windows or drinking martinis.

A year or two ago, a doctor in California planned a book on How to Avoid a Heart Attack. Before he'd finished writing it, he had a heart attack. The main thesis of the book was that human beings fall into (yet another) two opposing types—A and B. A is highly strung and, therefore, subject to heart attacks. B is placid, less subject. Recently, this doc was approached about jogging. 'Well,' he said, 'I really hate to have a jogger for a patient. Because a jogger is, by definition, a type A.'

PS About ten days after I broadcast this talk, I had a letter from London. It said: 'Dear Mr Cooke, I was very pleased that you mentioned me in your talk. Would you kindly send me your autograph? Sincerely, Mark Godding (aged 15).'

The Retiring Kind

9 September 1977

Americans, successful Americans most of all, are always talking about 'getting out of the rat race'. The rat race can mean any working routine that has started to bore you. I've heard this ambition voiced—bitterly, wearily, wistfully—by businessmen big and small, lawyers, big-time golfers, small-time grocers, university lecturers, burlesque strippers, journalists, ranchers, once, I remember, by a parson. He was a Southerner and he said, 'I've had ma fill of savin' souls, I'd just like to hole up in some dogpatch and nurse ma own.'

Englishmen, in my experience, go about it in a far less irascible way. They assume, or maybe they're taught from birth, that any job carries with it daily stretches of boredom. So they jog along for thirty, forty years and patter off sweetly or seedily into an inadequate pension, and then they are galvanized into doing what they've secretly wanted to do: to catch butterflies, collect stamps or book matches, read all of Trollope or grow turnips. An old lady wrote to me a year or so ago from Dorset, a lady plainly engrossed in her singular hobby. 'My retirement,' she wrote, 'which came in my sixty-fifth year, has made it possible for me to pursue my hobby: to catch *The Sound of Music* wherever it is being shown. Sometimes, I sit through all three performances. So far, I've seen it seventy-nine times, and I hope the end is not yet.'

The English live a life of boredom and then switch to mania. With Americans, it's the other way round. They are paranoid for years about the grind and horror of their jobs till they get to the pension, and then they mope and putter and mutter and confront their wives with a new ordeal—the daily nuisance of having to cook a lunch for a hanger-on.

These thoughts came to me when I recalled the pleasure this summer of visiting an old friend, an American newspaperman, who got out of the rat race with a bang one day, no notice given. He had never seemed to complain about the grind, even though he was the always-on-tap head of the Washington bureau of a distinguished Midwestern newspaper, even though he hated the fetid heat of Washington, which was odd in a boy born in the blistering heat of the prairie. It blisters in summer and petrifies in winter.

I imagine we all have a picture in our minds of how and where our friends will retire, the kind of set-up they've been used to and may now be expected to modify, or the kind of retreat they've always yearned for. If anybody had asked me, I could have improvised pretty quickly the ideal haven of my friend in retirement. I had known him best in the Kennedy days. It was a time when the White House press corps was more eager to be at the President's side than at any other time before or since. Not because Kennedy had loads of charm, which he had, but because he chose Palm Beach, Florida, as his winter White House. Let me explain.

Roosevelt's winter White House was the White House. His summer White House was the family home in Hyde Park, New York State, up in the steaming Hudson Valley. After him, Truman slaved away in the White House winter and summer, but he did take quick winter safaris down in Key West, which is frowsier than the travel brochures indicate. Anyway, Truman lived with the Marines at their base, and the accommodation for the press was makeshift at best. Eisenhower simply didn't like the press around anywhere. But then came Kennedy. The moment it was known that he would be hopping off all the time to use his father's mansion in Palm Beach as the winter White House, the rush to become a White House correspondent was indecent. I myself remember writing a fast note to my editor, a cagey Scot with an unpleasant gift for distinguishing between a call to duty and a call to pleasure. I put it to him frankly: my conscience had been riven for some time. We never covered the President except when he was in Washington. Had not the time come for me to attach myself to the White House press corps, however much inconvenience it might entail? I would be the only foreign correspondent so accredited, and think of the opportunities for a scoop: ('President Kennedy today played sixteen holes of Seminole, the famous course named after the local Indian tribe which can be seen, on a clear day, watching things closely from its encampment—on stilts—in the swamp of the Everglades.') The time had come.

Kennedy, you remember, was elected on a promise to settle something called the New Frontier. Well, they had some pretty splendid shacks down there on the New Frontier, which, to all intents and purposes I've ever been able to figure, began and ended at Palm Beach. This was just one of the facts of life we had to face. For the news of the world outside we watched the Miami *Herald*. We were put up in a glittering, medium-size hotel overlooking a lagoon. The palm trees dozed in a blinding sun. The little boats skimmed along. There were some very lively fish, and there was the finest golf course in the South (Ben Hogan once said, 'Play Seminole and die'). The ambulating girls were tanned and nubile. There was nothing we wouldn't do to conquer the New Frontier.

Well, this is where I first met the man I've been talking about: later chief of the Washington bureau, then White House correspondent of the *Chicago Sun Times*. He was tall and languid-dapper, silver-haired, good looking in a wry way. If it hadn't been for his absolutely slack, unhurried manner (a deadline was a daily chore, like washing the dishes, never a seizure) you might have thought of him as a Navy man. I once noted his striking resemblance to a Riviera admiral in an old Jerome Kern musical.

If you'd asked me then what sort of place he'd retire to, I'd have said he'd get himself a very comfortable, split-level, ranch-style house overlooking a golf course, with easy access to a plush bar, and a snappy clothier's and a good book store down the road. One day, in about 1970, I think, years after the New Frontier had been abandoned, or absorbed, he went to his suburban home from his Washington office and announced to his wife that he was quitting. 'To where?' she asked. I see him now, slowly licking his thumb and turning at a turtle's pace the holiday ads in the *Saturday Review*. There was a tiny one, in two lines. It said baldly: 'Cottage for rent, three weeks, Glandore, Ireland.' That's it, he said. They thought they'd begin by using this unseen cottage as a tenting base for roving trips around Europe. They'd look around, in time they'd pick their Shangri-La and have their things shipped there. So they packed up everything—the furniture, clothes, books, records, kitchenware, stereo deck, golf clubs, bird seed, the lot—and put them in a warehouse in Washington. They are still there.

They took the cottage for three weeks, and for the past seven years it has been their only home. It is what they'd call in Scotland a crofter's cottage: one door, one combination living room, kitchen, dining room, study, pantry, with three chairs, a bench, a stove, a lamp, a kettle, some pots and pans. Upstairs, two bedrooms, and a partitioned alleyway with a hole in the ceiling, through which drips a dribble of water known as a shower. From the downstairs room, they look out on a seven-foot-high white-washed wall. They sit and look at that, why I don't know, except it does shut out the thought that over the horizon is another assignment, another deadline. From their bedroom, they look out over dropping headlands and a bay and the sweeping Atlantic, which shores up again at the Antarctic.

At intervals, they read a paperback, bake the gritty, chewy Irish bread and take it—according to my Irish doctor's prescription—with refreshing swigs of the poteen. They breathe in and out. They have an old bone-shaker of an American car, not—so far as I could see—bearing Irish licence plates. If they occasionally infringe the law, like parking near a fire hydrant or picking up a pint ten minutes after closing, they are not apprehended. As my friend says, 'The great thing about this country is—

329

there's always somebody who doesn't care.'

This should be an improving lesson to all of us who fret about retirement and the upkeep of the mortgage payment, and how to stretch the pound or dollar, how to maintain on half-pay our lifestyle, as we now preposterously call any way of life whether it has style or not. The moral is something an old schoolmaster told me. I thought it sententious at the time, as schoolboys think all general reflections on life are bound to be, since they seem meant to deny the particular schoolboy way of life. 'Never', said this middle-aged Welshman, 'let your wants outstrip your needs.' This is no sort of advice to give to a 16-year-old, who's lusting after a new cricket bat, or the latest Venuti-Lang record, not to mention what's left over with which to finance the local bird at the cinema, the tea-dance or wherever.

But it's a good line to say to fretful oldsters on the verge of a pension. And I should have guessed that nobody was more in need of it than my dapper, high-living (on his paper) Jerome Kern admiral. So what happened? Well, with—I suspect—a firm push from his beguiling wife, he became one of the few people I ever knew who got out of the rat race and managed with obvious content to *reduce* his wants to his needs. It is all the more remarkable in that it happened to an American couple, for Americans, as all the world knows, are alternately harried and cushioned from the womb with every brand of material comfort. Not, I hasten to say, like the British who, as we all know, want only to sit by a broken teapot and meditate and grow a flower.

What was at the back of my mind when I began,

what got me off on this high moral theme, was the fact that a couple of years after I first met the admiral, I was invited to dinner in Palm Beach by a new United States Senator who was down there to celebrate his victory at the polls with a holiday. He was an old friend of mine. He'd been Governor of his state twice. And because he'd jumped aboard the Kennedy bandwagon about four years before anybody else, he was rewarded by becoming the first man to be appointed to the Kennedy Cabinet.

This dinner was the first time I'd seen him since his translation from Cabinet officer into Senator. I asked him why he'd made the switch. Why quit the Kennedy administration, in which he might have gone onwards and upwards (he'd actually had an offer of a seat on the Supreme Court)? He was very firm about it. 'You know why?' he said. 'You want to know why?' (He sounded for a moment like Jackie Gleason about to browbeat Alice.) 'Because now, goddamit, I'm my own man.' Go on, I said. 'Well,' he said, 'let me put it this way. When you get to be a Cabinet officer, you think you'll have the President's ear every day. I had great plans for a health and welfare bill, worked on it for months. I drafted it and sent it up to the President. I waited for the phone to ring. Hell, I didn't see him, except casually, in two months. Finally, I got a call from the *real* President of the United States.' Who dat? I drawled. With extraordinary venom for a normally benevolent man, he shouted, 'The Director of the Bureau of the Budget, that's who. He told me they'd looked over the bill. Fine, just fine. Great job. But they thought they'd have to whittle it down, the costs I mean, from—oh, I don't know—

maybe twenty-five millions to two millions! End of bill. Never forget, my friend, the effective President of the United States, when you're in the Cabinet, is the Director of the Budget. What'll you drink?'

Well, it sometimes takes the wheel a long time to come full circle. In this case, fifteen years. The Director of the Budget has changed his title, but not his authority. He's now the Director of the Office of Management and Budget. But he's the same quietly dictatorial figure, unknown to the public, who decides what the President's budget is to be, how much will be spent on what. As I talk, the big man is one Bert Lance, an old, dear friend of the President and, naturally, a Georgian. He is now accused, or suspected, of all sorts of shenanigans with his own bank, and with his securities and investments. Four government agencies and three Congressional committees are looking into these dark matters. The key committee —the one that can save him or break him—is the Senate's Governmental Affairs Committee. Its chairman thought he had enough evidence by mid-week to urge Mr Lance to resign. Either way, this chairman's judgement could be decisive. And his conduct of the Committee hearings was, for him, unusually severe. He is normally gentle, forbearing, wistfully inviting sinners to repentance. In these hearings, he was almost an inquisitor. Very odd. Perhaps it was due to an impulse to get in some final legislative licks before he retires, at the end of his present term.

So who *is* the chairman of that Senate Committee? He is that Senator who discovered to his chagrin, fifteen years ago, who was the 'real' President of the United States. He is the handsome, the able, senior Senator from Connecticut: Abraham Ribicoff.

Two for the Road

23 December 1977

At the risk of seeming to take a short trot through a graveyard (something that only Dickens in one of his familiar morbid moods would do at Christmas time) I should like to say something about two tremendous figures who recently went off—along with Johnny Mercer—into immortality. Or upon what Mercer, the most poetic of jazz lyricists, called 'the long, long road'.

I hope there was no moaning at the bar over the death of Groucho Marx. He was very old, and for several years he had had only short lucid intervals in which he knew much about what was going on.

My first contact with him was about twenty-five years ago, when he wrote to me to say he would very much like to be on a television show that I was running. We were delighted to start negotiations, and at one point we thought everything was sewed up. Then, mysteriously, he backed out. In those days, television was done 'live' (no taping beforehand) and movie stars were petrified by it since they'd have to memorize a whole part instead of thirty-second bits. By the same token, stage actors were eager for exposure over a national network, and you could hire the best of them for a few hundred dollars. Groucho evidently didn't know this. And I soon heard from our business manager why Groucho wouldn't be with us: he had asked an enormous fee. We regretfully declined his services. There was an awkward interval of silence at both ends. Then he wrote to me: 'Like Sam Goldwyn, I believe in art. But my agent, a coarse type, believes in money. And who am I to argue with such a baboon?'

Shortly after that, I was in Hollywood. He invited me to lunch, and ever afterwards, whenever my wife and I were out on the Coast, we saw him and enjoyed him as the slap-happy anarchist he was in life just as much as he was in the movies. The great pleasure in him came from his finicky, and funny, respect for the English language. That, at first hearing, may sound incomprehensible. But whatever his comic style was like when he started out in vaudeville, he had the luck in Hollywood to fall in with the supreme American humorist, S. J. Perelman, who wrote one or two of the early Marx Brothers movies. I dare say nobody alive has a quicker ear for the oddities and absurdities of the language that can spring from taking words— taking the tenses of English—literally. This gift passed over to Groucho and he made it his own. So much so that when I wrote a piece about Groucho's gift to the Library of Congress of his letters, I suggested in it that S. J. Perelman's scripts and letters should be sent along too. Groucho, whose laughable view of human pomp did not extend to his own vanity, kicked up a great fuss and swore our friendship was an unpleasantness from the past. A vow he forgot the next time he embraced me.

The most memorable example I can think of this language game happened when we were lunching with him at the most luxurious of Jewish country clubs in Los Angeles. When the menu was passed around, I raised an eyebrow at what even then were outrageous prices. 'Fear not, my friend,' said Groucho, 'it's only money. The initiation fee at this club is $10,000, and for that you don't even get a dill pickle.' When the main course was over and the waiter came to take the dessert order, he stumbled several times over who was having what. Finally, he said, 'Four éclairs and four—no, four éclairs and two coffees?' Groucho whipped in with, 'Four éclairs and two coffees ago, our forefathers brought forth on this continent a nation dedicated to the proposition—skip the dedication and bring the dessoit.'

On the way out, Groucho lined up to pay his bill behind a fat and fussy lady who was fiddling around in her bag for change. The young cashier gave a patient sigh, and Groucho—his cigar raking the air like an artillery barrage—said, 'Shoot her when you see the whites of her eyes!' The large lady turned around in a huff, which dissolved into a delighted giggle. 'Would you,' she gasped, 'be Groucho Marx?' In a flash, Groucho rasped out, 'Waddya mean, *would* I be Groucho Marx? I *am* Groucho Marx. Who would *you* be if you weren't yourself? Marilyn Monroe, no doubt. Well, pay your bill, lady, you'll never make it.'

The other great man was a world apart from Groucho—in geography, upbringing, temperament and talent. I'm talking about Harry Lillis Crosby who, for reasons as obscure and debatable as the origins of the word 'jazz', was known from boyhood on as Bing. Some years ago, a friend of mine, a publisher, thought of persuading Bing to sit down

335

in several sessions with a tape recorder and put out a book of reminiscences. My friend was very steamed up about this project and came to me one day and said he'd got the main thing, he'd got the title. He narrowed his eyes and said very slowly, *'My Friends Call Me Bing.'* Four words too many, I said. And truly, I don't suppose there are more than half a dozen people in the world who would be instantly recognizable by a single word.

It's been just over fifty years since we were first exposed to the Rhythm Boys and their lead tenor, who provided the first happy breakaway from the ladylike sopranos and resonant baritones of the London and New York stages who were singing Youmans, Gershwin and Rodgers as if they were still commuting between Heidelberg and Ruritania. Then the Rhythm Boys' tenor, never identified on the record label, broke loose on his own, and the word ran through the English underground that a genuine jazz singer—and a white man!—had appeared in the unlikeliest place: breezing along on the ocean of Paul Whiteman's lush 'symphonic' sound. For about six precious months, as I recall, from the fall of 1927 through the spring of 1928, Whiteman, of all people, permitted a small jazz group—Bix Beiderbecke, Frank Trumbauer, Eddie Lang and Crosby—to be given its head. And on the long spring nights, the punts drifting along the Cambridge Backs gave out the easy, vagabond phrases of Bing and the lovely codas of Bill Challis' orchestrations.

For several years after that, the underground went into mourning for the apostasy of Bing Crosby, who turned into a gargling crooner. We abandoned him as a traitor, until after the war

336

years he relaxed again into the unbuttoned troubadour, the mellower jazz singer, known from El Paso to El Alamein as the Groaner, Der Bingle and always Bing. For thirty years or so, there appeared a parade of male singers, from Russ Columbo through Como and Sinatra and beyond, who could never have found their own style if Crosby had never existed.

By then, Bing had done everything he wanted to do in music and movies, and having wisely appreciated the approach of the gentleman with a scythe, he countered him by developing other talents and went off to fire 3-irons in Scotland and repeating rifles in Africa. Never a man to push himself, at twilight or any other time, he crooned only to himself. Then, fifty years after his first record, he cut a final album. Well into his seventies, he was the same Bing, because he had the great good sense to know the right keys, the navigable modulations, where to go and where not to go, unlike some other star-studded egos who like to fancy that the rules of mortality have been suspended for them alone.

I first ran into him on the set of one of the Hope–Crosby 'Road' movies, and I think I picked up a false impression of him right away. Because he was saucy, mischievous, almost gabby when he was working, especially with Hope. They ad-libbed so much and broke down in chuckles so often that at one point Bing turned to a writer who was sitting with the director and said, 'If you hear any of your own lines, shout Bingo!' Of course, Bing was witty, in a droll, tired way (nobody else would have described his face, with its flapping ears, as looking 'like a taxicab with both doors open'), but the movie image of Bing was a very high-pressure version of the man off the set. Once the lights dimmed and the director said, 'It's a take,' Bing visibly drooped into a character so shambling and low key that I got the impression he'd had a sleepless night and would soon be off for a nap. People used to ask me, 'What was Bing like playing golf, I'll bet he was uproarious, right?' In fact, he was relaxed to the point of boredom, good-natured boredom. It's true he always looked you in the eye, but he did it with the grey, tired eyes of a man who had seen everything—a lot of fun but also a lot of grief—and was never going to be surprised by anything said or done.

From his early success days with the Rhythm Boys and on into his movie career, there'd been all sorts of problems in and around his family: sickness, death, the bottle, truancy, spats and sulks with his sons. Until he came into port at last, after some stormy seas, with his second wife and his new family. It is possible that he talked about these things to very close friends, but even his butler couldn't recall any. To everyone, except some missing confidant, he put up the quiet defence of offhand, easygoing small talk.

I can't think of another man of anything like his fame who was so unrattled by it and so genuinely modest. The accursed foible of show business people is prima donnaism: the massive ego, the implication that the whole world is revolving around them and their new picture, their new plans—which they pretend to find delightful but embarrassing. Not Bing. He was in this more mature than any actor or actress, author or musician, statesman or politician I have known in

338

coming to sensible terms with great fame. His mail must have been staggering, with its appeals for favours and money from every charity and every crackpot in the world. He never mentioned it. He was polite to every nice fan, and every child, and every moron who hailed him. All his later concerts, and pro-amateur golf tournaments, passed on the receipts to a raft of favourite charities.

When he died, there was a spate of film clips and replayed old interviews and the like. The most revealing of these was one done shortly before he died by the news interviewer Barbara Walters, who does have a knack for asking the childlike questions we'd all like to ask but don't dare. She asked him to sum himself up, and he allowed that he had an easy temperament, a way with a song, a fair vocabulary, on the whole a contented life. And she said, 'Are you telling us that's all there is—a nice, agreeable shell of a man?' Bing appeared not to be floored. After the slightest pause for deep reflection, he said, 'Sure, that's about it. I have no deep thoughts, no profound philosophy. That's right. I guess that's what I am.'

It was so startling, so honest, and probably so true, that it explained why he'd been able, through hard times, to stay on an even keel. Perhaps he was one of those people who, though not at all selfish, are deeply self-centred: what they call 'a very private person'. Because he couldn't identify with other people's troubles, he was able to appear, and to be, everybody's easygoing buddy, and forget death and disaster in a recording date or a round of golf. He was the least exhibitionist celebrity I have ever known. And because death is so dramatic, so showy, some of us cannot believe he won't show up in the locker room tomorrow and say, 'Well, skipper, how's tricks?'

The Spy That Came Down in the Cold

10 February 1978

We have just followed the first story of general interest to come out of the vast tundra of Canada's Northwest Territories since the Klondike gold rush.

It came at us first as a scare story, like something out of *Dr Strangelove* or *Star Wars*. Then it turned into a technological puzzle as remote from the interests, or competence, of ordinary people as the workings of a breeder reactor. So that, more or less out of boredom, we were ready to sink back into the soap opera or the insurance policy, when the *New York Times* published a long piece that suggested, for the first time in print, appalling possibilities for all of us. The White House promptly denied the gist of the story. And then the whole thing was surprisingly dropped.

What I'm talking about is the Soviet satellite that fell out of its orbit into the earth's atmosphere, burst into flames and disintegrated above North America. For a day or two, the main concern of Canadians and Americans was to know if the accident had happened over any well-populated part of this continent. But once it was run to ground in the empty pinelands surrounding Canada's Great Slave Lake, everybody breathed again, and we all chuckled and quoted the man who said, 'Chicken Little was right.'

340

Yet the Russian satellite was admittedly a spy, whose job was to orbit the earth a hundred and fifty miles above it and keep track of the movements of all the ocean-going American warships—what we now call defence ships— including submarines deeply submerged. The satellite carried a load of radioactive materials, and that was what caused the fright. The debris from the disintegration rained across a two-hundred-and-fifty-mile stretch. But once it was established that none of the sample fragments picked up was radioactive, the scare died down.

It shows how far we've come in eighteen years, how far in stoicism, or a sense of reality, maybe. In May 1960, when an American spy plane was shot down over the Soviet Union, President Eisenhower denied that American reconnaissance planes ever flew over Russia. Then he broke down and said, 'Well, you do it too.' This happened just when the Big Four leaders had assembled in Paris for a summit meeting. But in the uproar over the American U-2 plane, Mr Khrushchev, the Soviet Prime Minister, stomped off home. The other three looked foolish and packed their bags. And the summit never took place.

If we have acquired a new sense of reality, it is no less than a rather fearful admission that we are in a steady *warm* war with the Soviet Union—and at a time when we go on talking about the progress of détente. Whatever it is, it has nothing to do with a change of heart, or with policy, or, indeed, with Mr Carter or Mr Brezhnev. It is due to the inescapable fact that spy planes can now fly too high to be reached. The U-2 reconnaissance planes flew at 65,000 feet, which is roughly twelve and a half miles up. From that height the Americans at least had—so long ago as 1962—cameras that could define with astonishing accuracy objects as small as a woodshed. The Russians must not have known this. Because when they were shown, in the Security Council of the United Nations, the American reconnaissance blow-ups of the Russian missiles being installed in Cuba, they blustered and swore that the pictures were fakes. But the photographs plainly showed missiles mounted and unmounted, all the paraphernalia of bases and launch pads that could not possibly be mistaken for woodsheds. So it was not so much the initiative of President Kennedy that persuaded the Russians to abandon their bluff and dismantle their bases. It was the cameras of the U-2s with their nine- by eighteen-inch negatives and their incredible twenty-six-inch lenses.

Well, by now, photographs of landscape from 65,000 feet are so taken for granted that NASA, the National Aeronautics and Space Administration, puts out infrared prints (you can buy them) of every section of the United States, in reaches of country thirty or forty miles across, on which you can see the sharp divisions of streets in cities of several million population. Obviously, these pictures would not be made public if they represented the known limit of the technical resources of reconnaissance, or spying. Clearly, since 1962, enormous advances have been made in the ways that one nation can scan the land and the industry and the defence establishment of another. We now spy, not from twelve miles up but from a hundred and fifty miles up. Neither the Russians nor the Americans deny it. In fact, since this scanning through radar has passed over into space, we have a situation that could have been imagined a hundred years ago only by W. S. Gilbert and Jules Verne working in tandem. Through several accidents, the two superpowers have become so aware of the lethal consequences of mismanagement in space that they keep each other posted on the movement of their spy ships, the orbiting satellites that are monitoring each other's military movements.

The crash of the Soviet satellite, Cosmos 954, provided the ordinary citizen with, I believe, the first glimpse we've had into this involuntary partnership. I say involuntary, because whether or not the Pentagon or the Soviet Defence Department wants it, the possibilities of accidental devastation from satellites floating *untracked* through space are too awful to be ignored. So it's worth taking a look into how it works. And today it can be done quite openly and the findings published without so much as a squeak of protest from the North American Air Defense Command, whose headquarters are buried deep in the granite of the Colorado Rockies.

Six years ago, I was doing a television programme about the working of the Strategic Air Command's underground headquarters in Omaha, Nebraska. We were given extraordinary freedom to film the whole process that could lead to the President's final cue for a nuclear attack. But there *were* things that were off-limits. We were not allowed to guess at the number of missiles the Americans had at the ready.

The perils of free-floating satellites have changed all that. Today, we know—and the Soviets know—that there are 4,600 machines of various sorts in space and precisely 939 satellites. Perhaps, now, 938. Somewhere in the Urals or wherever, Soviet technicians are tracking them. And, in the bowels of the Rockies, American technicians are doing the same. They marked the launching of Cosmos 954 on 17 September last. They knew its job was to scan the oceans with its radar and tell Soviet ground stations what it saw by way of ships and submarines. The Americans knew that its penetrating radar equipment was powered by a nuclear reactor.

Three months after it was launched, in mid-December, Cosmos 954 began to sag out of its prescribed orbit. The Russians ordered it to break into three parts and dissipate. Evidently it didn't obey. It stayed intact, and every time it went round the earth, it swung a little nearer. In early January, the Americans figured it would fall into the earth's atmosphere over North America. The Soviet ambassador was invited to a secret meeting in the White House, and the Russians were asked for all relevant information. The American anxiety was over the amount of uranium on board the satellite and its chances of disintegrating on or above the earth. Teams of observers and decontamination experts were flown out to likely points of impact. The afternoon before it crumbled, the men of Air Defense Command watched it go across Australia and then the Pacific and then on into northern Canada. When a Canadian Mountie reported a meteorite, they knew it was all over. The fragments were tested, and it seemed certain that the satellite and its nuclear power cell had burned up completely on re-entering the earth's atmosphere.

The Air Defense Command relaxed. The newspapers cooled down. All was well.

Not quite. What came out a few days later was the admission from space scientists that the location of the crash was not contrived by human skill or the magic of computers. It was sheer luck. They calculated that if the satellite had managed to hobble once more around the earth, it would have come down somewhere close to New York City between eight and nine in the morning. This afterthought was not published. The official story was all over, except for a plea from President Carter for a law, an agreement at least, to ban from space any satellite that contains nuclear reactors. The Secretary of Energy said amen, but he couldn't quite see how it was to be done. Mr Brezhnev made the stunning comment, 'There must not be another war.' Ah, so. Apart from that, the Russians said nothing. However, the doubt remains whether any satellite, like Cosmos 954, would be able to spot the movement of submarines unless its radar was powered by a nuclear reactor. In other words, the evidence is undeniable that we are already embarked on the military uses of space. And just how far we've gone was chillingly exposed two days later by a front-page piece in the *New York Times*. It recalled that the United States had become the first nation to put a spy-satellite in orbit, in 1959. That, more recently, Mr Carter became the first President to admit that both countries are developing weapons meant to destroy each other's satellites. And that the Defense Department is well aware of Russian experiments in space with laser weapons.

Then the *Times* dropped its bombshell. It

reported that the Russians have outstripped the Americans, probably by several years, in developing what are known as 'hunter-killer satellites', which 'could knock out the Pentagon's ability to communicate with, and give orders to, ships, planes, submarines, missile silos and ground forces around the world'. Now, this, of course, means that the United States could be paralysed from outer space and rendered impotent even to order an act of retaliation if she were attacked.

The subject was evidently too touchy for security experts in the White House and the Pentagon. They wouldn't talk about it. But the recently retired Chief of Air Force Intelligence would and did. He is General George Keegan. He said that eighteen years ago, a Russian spy working for the allies in the Kremlin warned Washington that the Russians were about to invest on a grand scale in military space research. He says the man was ignored. But two years ago, American experts were startled when the Russians put into orbit a hunter-killer that could destroy a target on earth after making only one pass around it. General Keegan says the threat is 'grim'.

And what does President Carter say? He brushed the story off at a press conference. How could he have said anything of substance? To say, 'Yes, the Russians have them and we don't' would have dealt a crippling blow to the morale of the people.

What we have to face is that whether it's true or not, it is going to be. We are already far gone towards preparing for the kind of war that H. G. Wells conceived as scientific fiction half a century ago, and that Bertrand Russell, twenty-two years

346

ago, foresaw as the almost certain consequence of American and Russian nuclear research. It surely should give an aching urgency to the coming talks on how to limit strategic arms. For, if the wind out of Canada has blown any good, it is the warning that satellites are already beyond absolute human control, that the technology of war is acquiring a momentum independent of national policy or the men who make it. Like that ghoulish computer in an old 1969 movie, the hunter-killer may come to have a mind of its own.

A Letter from Long Island

18 August 1978

As you may have heard, all the New York City newspapers—all three of them—are on strike. How, then, am I going to acquaint you with what is being said, and thought, and speculated about all the great issues of the day? I am not. It may be cold-blooded to say so but this seems to me to offer a golden opportunity to disclaim all responsibility for being well-informed, or informed at all. I could spoil it for you—and for me—by remarking that the television networks are doubling and tripling their coverage from New York and of the local controversies that spring from the strike. So it's possible to sit down at 6 p.m. and emerge four hours later choked and dizzy with facts and fancies.

In the middle of a sweaty August, it seems to me to be a mistake not to make the most of the surcease from the *New York Times*. Far better, I hope you'll agree, if I retreat to where I belong and tell you something about life as it is lived at the end of Long Island. I don't mean to give you the romantic notion that the end of the Island—we are precisely one hundred miles from door to door—is a romantic haven devoid of all involvement with the modern world. On the contrary, it would be possible for a nosey reporter to make it over into a miniature of the nation's plight.

The county politicians voted not to raise the pay of our local sheriffs, so for a day or two the prison guards called in to say they were all feeling very poorly. Rural crime has increased by 3 per cent in the past year—up in our village from ten robberies to—presumably—ten and a third! There is a mild hullabaloo about a proposal to build an atomic plant in the middle of our potato fields. The groundwater supply, our only source of water, is becoming polluted with nitrates from fertilizers used by farmers and golf clubs, and it's going to cost a quarter of a million dollars to keep the water safe for humans. And so on.

Enough. You must picture the island as a fish, a very long fish with its snout on the left and its tail on the right. Its mouth is hooked to Manhattan and its body reaches into the Atlantic in a direction more easterly than anything, for about one hundred and twenty miles. Its tail is divided into two flukes, which enclose a bay about thirty miles long, five to six miles wide. This is called Peconic Bay (the Peconics were a tribe of Indians, fishermen, whom the refugees from Suffolk came on in the seventeenth century).

There are certain places of the earth I would rather be than anywhere else, at certain times of

348

the year. In the fall, there is nowhere I would rather be than Vermont, for the beauty of its scarlet and gold landscape—except Long Island, for its shining days and its miraculous draught of fishes. In fact, there is nowhere I know—not the Mediterranean, or the Crimea, most certainly not California—where, between May and November, there is such a succulent haul of so many kinds of splendid eating fish. We are just at the point where the northern cold-water fish nibble at our shores and where the warm-water fish abound. First, for the gourmet, are the noble striped bass, and the bluefish. Then the swordfish, and the flounder, and the lemon sole. But there are also other very tasty species, which city people either don't know about or despise out of genteel ignorance. In the summer months, the fat flat porgy is always mooching along the bed of the bay. It is very easy to catch by bouncing a sinker on the bottom and stirring up enough sand and mud to blind it. It is a paranoid species that feels it's being chased by submarines and so comes to the surface along a zigzag course, as if in convoy during wartime. Baked porgy is delicious, and I simply have no idea why it never appears on restaurant menus.

Then there is the blowfish, known to the local tots as the swell-belly, for the exact reason that when it's grounded it blows itself up like a balloon in the hope of disposing of the hook. It is regarded by weekenders as a pest fish, but it has down its backbone a slim triangular fillet of firm flesh, the closest thing we have to the delicious rubbery texture—I'm afraid there is no other word—of a Dover sole. More remarkable still is the city's non-acceptance of the weakfish. I have caught it and

349

savoured it for forty years. It is so called because it has a weak, papery mouth, which it cheerfully—I presume—rips in order to dislodge the hook. It then swims off and grows its mouth together again. Maybe its name is the snag. Some years ago, droll Italians who owned fish markets on the South Shore took to laying out weakfish and marking them with a sign saying, 'Sea Trout'. They were out of stock within an hour of piling up the weaks.

The island, like all other bits of geography, has its own local lingo for its different districts that will not be found on maps or in atlases. Thus, the northern fluke—where I live—is known as the North Fork. But the southern fluke is known as the South *Shore* (never mind that some old families over there try to retain the South Fork). The natives of the North Fork say they are going 'South Side' whenever they are disposed to do so, which is not often, for reasons I hasten to explain.

The South Shore used to be the exclusive monopoly of early Dutch and English landowners. One of the latter, William Floyd, was a signer of the Declaration of Independence and achieved a very late badge of immortality by having a motorway named after him. The early settlers were a little miffed, at the end of the nineteenth century, when some of the robber barons and their heirs moved in. One of them, name of Vanderbilt, visited Scotland and saw the natives playing the peculiar game known locally as 'the gowf'. He accordingly imported some clubs, hired a landscape man, or golf architect, and commissioned him to lay out the first twelve-hole links course in the United States.

Until the Second World War, the fashionable resorts of the South Shore—Southampton,

Bridgehampton, Easthampton—were pretty choosy places. But following the immemorial custom of all Western societies, the latest batch of the new rich moved as close to the old rich as possible in the hope of having some of their effortless poise brush off on them. In the past twenty or thirty years, these once fussy compounds have been invaded by brokers, interior decorators, bankers, chic painters, actors and actresses, television producers, and infested by ten-percenters of all kinds.

If you detect a note of inverted snobbery in this account, your instinct is correct. I have summered and autumned (fallen?) on the North Fork for forty-two years. We stand out on our hundred-foot high cliff or bluff and look across the five or six miles of the quarantine waters that separate us from the chic, the bad and the beautiful. The North Fork is not chic. It is not rich. I doubt there are more than half a dozen residents whose combined securities could match the portfolio of any one of several hundreds of the denizens of Easthampton and Southampton. The North Fork was for two and a half centuries the province of English settlers from Suffolk, and you can follow the family lines through platoons of tombstones, the victims of seventeenth-century epidemics, and all the wars since the Revolution, in the local graveyards or what—in my village—is known as 'the burying ground'. I know old people, and not so old, who only once in their lifetime have made the hundred-mile trip to New York. They didn't like what they saw, and went no more.

Shortly after the robber barons invaded the South Shore the North Fork was invaded by immigrant Poles: Catholic farmers. Like all immigrants, they had a nostril tuned to the smell of their native soil. And the North Fork, planted as far as the eye can see with potatoes and cauliflower and corn, is interrupted only by a few old colonial churches but more conspicuously by squat wooden churches with blunt spires. The Fork could be used today with great accuracy as the location for a film about central Poland.

The Poles were industrious and very thrifty and in no time took over the big duck farms, which had been run in a comfortable way by the Anglos. So now, our Fork is populated mostly by the descendants of the original English and by third-generation Poles. And in the manner of long-settled rural communities, the North Forkers tend to take a dim view of the South Shore. But then, the South Shore takes no view at all of the North Fork. In fact, friends of ours on the South Side have lived and died there without having the faintest idea where the North Fork was or how to find our point, though it's clearly visible from the Peconic shore of their side. I still have friends who ask us every summer, 'How are things at your place in Southampton?' Which is like asking a proud Lancastrian, 'How are things in Bradford and Leeds?'

Our point is called Nassau Point. After the English occupation it was rechristened Hog's Neck, but it reverted later on to Nassau since, under the Dutch, it had been designated as a sliver of crown property by King William (Prince, you'll recall, of Orange and Nassau). Since then the Point has managed to remain unmentioned in the history books or even in the newspapers. In fact, we are so obscure that when Nassau Point achieved the fame of a new comet, nobody noticed it. It needed no newspaper strike to leave us unhonoured and unsung. But that is another story. Another letter.

The Presidential Ear

8 December 1978

The newspapers and the television commentators have just paid their annual respects—or regrets—to the Japanese attack on Pearl Harbor on 7 December 1941, a day, President Roosevelt said when he went before Congress, 'that will live in infamy'.

However, two days before that was 5 December 1978, a night which will surely live in American history. For there occurred an event that has never before taken place in the history of the Republic: an incumbent President of the United States took his seat at the opera. The doors of New York's Metropolitan Opera House—either the old or the new—have never been darkened, or lit up, by the presence of a President.

Nothing ought to be made of the fact that the opera was *Aida*, an opera on an Egyptian subject commissioned by Ismail Pasha and first performed in Cairo, though it's possible something may be made of it by ill-meaning journalists in and out of Israel. In which case, the President could make amends by commissioning a performance of Handel's *Israel in Egypt*.

The fact is that President Carter is something of a freak among the long line of American

Presidents. He is a music lover. I don't mean that he has his favourite tunes (as haven't we all). President Eisenhower, I believe, let it be known that he had an album of favourites, which he liked to have piped in so that he could hum to them, as George V on a memorable occasion—his fifth visit to *his* favourite opera, *Rose Marie*—sat in the royal box and, having conquered his favourite song in the whole of music, accompanied the chorus singing 'Totem tom tom, Totem tom tom.'

I mean that President Carter is the phenomenon of a very hard-working President who yet makes time every morning—every dawning, I ought to say—to listen to a half-hour or so of Mozart or Beethoven. It is hard to think of a better prescription for rinsing out the mind before the growing cacophonies of the day. It is fascinating, though perhaps not very instructive, to wonder why politicians, who regularly acquire some strange bedmates, should so rarely relax with the muse of music, with classical music, that is. Franklin Roosevelt and John F. Kennedy would have paid any price to avoid a symphony concert. Disciples of the late Harry Truman will be bound to protest that he actually played the piano, chopped his way through bits of Chopin, and at all times was ready to give a soulful performance of 'The Missouri Waltz'.

But, having heard him and followed his tastes, I must say that his range was that of the excerpts we staggered through on the piano when I was a boy: a series of what was called 'The Three Star Folio', which incorporated the more swinging bits from the *Poet and Peasant* overture, 'Zampa', Handel's 'Largo' and the 'Four Indian Love Lyrics' of the

354

immortal Amy Woodforde-Finden. They were conveniently known as middle-brow classics.

And I'm sure that out of Texas will storm the reminder that whenever at a barbecue or other local festival Lyndon Johnson heard 'The Eyes of Texas', the tears flowed down the clefts of his endless cheeks. President Nixon, too, was almost as eager to get to any piano in sight as was George Gershwin, about whom a close but clear-eyed friend said, 'No question about it, an evening with Gershwin is a Gershwin evening.' Nobody thumped away with more zest and pleasure than President Nixon, and I imagine he treasures as one of the precious mementoes of his Presidency the evening when, in full view of a delirious audience, Duke Ellington kissed him on both cheeks—the last time, I believe, Mr Nixon was ever kissed in public, except by next of kin.

In case any overseas listener is beginning to preen himself on the superior cultivation of his own politicians, as distinct from the rude American kind, I beg him or her to take thought. Name offhand, or even after much boning up, any politician of the first chop who is or was a known lover of classical music. Apart, that is, from the blinding exception of Mr Edward Heath. Mr Gladstone, my father told me, was properly reverent when called to Buckingham Palace to listen to performances of sacred music commissioned by Queen Victoria. He would have been a brave Prime Minister who dared to refuse *that* royal command to listen to any music, however sacred, however stupefyingly dull. But I don't remember from the memoirs that Balfour, Lloyd George, Asquith, Bonar Law or any of their generation had the slightest interest in music. In the many volumes of the works of Winston Churchill, I can't recall a reference to any of the top-flight or even third-flight composers, though Mr Churchill was also known to weep whenever the 'Battle Hymn of the Republic' was played. As for the succeeding generations of British politicians—and I hope I do them no insult—I cannot find either that Anthony Eden was an accomplished bassoonist or that Mr Callaghan devotes his spare hours to reading the scores of the Bach fugues. I do recall, and was actually present once, when the astonishing thing happened: the first Lord Birkenhead was tone deaf and had to be nudged whenever the band went into the national anthem.

Going back for a minute or two to the startling event that provoked all this meditation, I must say it seems very unlikely that some President, at some time or other, did not find it expedient, let alone pleasurable, to attend the opera. A friend of mine, who knows not only all the obscure operas of the great composers but all the mediocre operas of the obscure composers, did a little digging and came up with the nugget that in 1918 President Wilson did appear at the Metropolitan Opera House. But it turned out that he was there, as usual, not to listen but to perform. Not, so help us, to sing, but to make a speech before a rally called to stir up popular support for the League of Nations. There is also an unauthenticated rumour that at another time, President Wilson dropped a hint to the authorities that he might come up to New York to attend the opera, but when he discovered that it was to be performed on a Sunday, he was shocked into withdrawing his request.

Further painstaking research at last reveals that there is one other President who not only had the wild impulse to go to the Met but yielded to it. Not, however, in New York. The Metropolitan company was on tour in the winter of 1905–6, and when it appeared in Philadelphia President Theodore Roosevelt—in the full flush of what had been till then the biggest popular majority any President had ever had from the voters—took himself off to see and hear Enrico Caruso. Roosevelt must have slipped into the house—if a mountain can ever be said to have slipped in anywhere—or he had not tipped off the company. Because when the performance was over and he went backstage to greet the great man, the other great man, Caruso, we are told, believed for an awkward time that he was meeting an impostor. But when he realized that he was indeed being visited by the one and only T.R. or Teddy, he threw his arms around the President and—anticipating Duke Ellington—smacked a kiss on each cheek. There was a photographer present—a small fact I mention because the following April Caruso was performing in San Francisco, and early in the morning of the 18th he was asleep in his regal suite in the Palace Hotel. Just before dawn, the bed started to shake and the chandelier to swing and, in a word, the hell of the famous earthquake was let loose all around him. He dashed out, like all the other guests, in a nightgown into the courtyard of the hotel and begged for any form of transport that would take him to the ferry, which in turn would take him to the railroad and save him from disaster. In what must have been an agony of conflict, between egotism and self-preservation, he tried to think of some single possession he could not bear to lose. My opera historian records—and who is to question him?—that what Caruso rescued was the photograph of himself with Teddy Roosevelt.

I was pondering on this unexplained mystery— why politics apparently works through the nervous system to produce an allergy to first-rate music— when one of the television networks ended its nightly news roundup with a five-minute visual essay on two minority peoples, most of whom live outside China but some of whom spill over the northern and southern borders: namely, Mongols and Thais. This piece was put on, I imagine, partly to tell us more about our now Communist friend, and partly to offset the chill of the twenty-year treaty of friendship that the Soviet Union has just signed with Afghanistan.

These two ancient peoples are, of course, resident aliens, or what the Bible calls 'strangers within the gates'. They have their own strong cultures, and we were assured that the Chinese in no wise want to reform them. To keep them friendly, on both sides of the borders, we were told that the Chinese allow them to live—I quote— 'independent lives according to their own customs, within the framework of Chinese Communism'. I must say this sounded to me like saying that the Jews were 'allowed to live independent lives, according to their own customs, within the framework of the Third Reich'. Anyway, what we saw mostly was young children dancing to charming music, and I was told later that this was not any Oriental equivalent of rock or pop but classical folk music. It was very pleasing. And because these were the only films we'd ever seen of these people, we got the impression that they did nothing else but dance to classical music. It was as if American propaganda films sent to China showed the American people as one mammoth Mormon choir singing the *St Matthew Passion*.

The shock was in what the delightful children were doing to the music. The Mongol tots danced with rifles, the Thais with rifles and fixed bayonets. Evidently, there are some nations whose rulers have learned how to soothe the savagery of their system by marrying music to politics. For export only.